BARNETT JANNER
A personal portrait

*For Barney's Children
and
Grandchildren*

BARNETT JANNER

A personal portrait by ELSIE JANNER

Edited by Gershon Levi

Robson Books

All royalties from this book will go to the Barnett Janner Charitable Trust.

FIRST PUBLISHED IN GREAT BRITAIN IN 1984 BY
ROBSON BOOKS LTD., BOLSOVER HOUSE, 5–6
CLIPSTONE STREET, LONDON W1P 7EB.
COPYRIGHT © 1984 ELSIE JANNER

British Library Cataloguing in Publication Data

Janner, Elsie
  Barnett, Janner.
  1. Janner, Barnett 2. Zionists—Great Britain—Biography
  3. Politicians—Great Britain—Biography
  I. Title
  956.94'001'0924 DS151.J/

  ISBN 0-86051-271-1

Printed and bound in Great Britain by
The Garden City Press Limited
Letchworth, Hertfordshire SG6 1JS

CONTENTS

FOREWORD

I have been greatly helped by many people, and I want to thank them all. In particular I am grateful to the Trustees of the Sherman Foundation for their generosity which has enabled this book to be published.

My appreciation goes out to the Rt Hon. Lord Wilson of Rievaulx, to Councillor George Billington, the Lord Mayor of Leicester; Councillor Janet Setchfield, the Chairman of the Leicestershire County Council; Councillor Colin Grundy; to past Israel diplomats to the Court of St. James's; to Gwyneth Jones; and to other busy friends here and in Israel who have given their valuable time to allow me to record their memories of Barney; to the Rev. Dr. Isaac Levy who translated documents from Hebrew; to Mrs. Johanna Sherring for translating the ones in German; to David Masel for the trouble he took to open the archives of the Board of Deputies; to the Editor of the Leicester Mercury; the Editor of the *Jewish Chronicle*; the Librarians in the House of Lords and the House of Commons; to the Zionist Archives in Jerusalem; to Stanley Smith, the Lord Mayor's Secretary in Leicester for supplying me with the information I needed.

E.J.

INTRODUCTION BY THE RT HON. LORD HAILSHAM OF ST MARYLEBONE

Spoken at the Service of Thanksgiving for the life of Barnett, Lord Janner, of the City of Leicester, Knight Bachelor, held at the St John's Wood Synagogue, London on 20 June 1982 and conducted by the Chief Rabbi, Sir Immanuel Jakobovits.

This is a service of thanksgiving. So let us be thankful.

A long life full of honour and devoted to the service of his fellow men is an appropriate occasion for thanksgiving to the author of all good, in whom we all believe or we should not be here. But, since this is also a memorial service, it is a thanksgiving tinged with melancholy, for pain at parting is the price which, in this world, we pay for the gifts of love and friendship. The price is a high one as each one of us knows to his cost, but, since love and friendship are two such precious gifts from heaven, it is a price we willingly pay, for without pain at parting there would be no love in companionship.

Therefore, before I recount Barney Janner's achievements and praise his virtues, my first words must be of condolence to his family, and particularly to his widow. I have learned from experience that sorrow shared is sorrow more easily borne.

That said, however, I must turn to my task. The bald facts of Barney Janner's life give food for reflection. He was born on the 20th June 1892. Today would have been his ninetieth birthday, had he lived but a few more weeks. 'With long life shalt Thou satisfy him'; the words of scripture rise easily and appropriately in our thoughts.

His parents were Lithuanian immigrants. I suppose, though I have not verified the fact, that they left from dissatisfaction with the condition of the Jews in Tsarist Russia. Let those who are disposed to decry all immigration ponder the immense enrichment of our life by Anglo Jewry ponder this fact. Ninety years later — all but a few weeks — this child of poor immigrants departed this life with a knighthood and a life peerage after nearly 40 years in one House of Parliament or another. His son is an MP and a Queen's Counsel. His widow, Lady Janner, from the same religious community, is a Justice of the Peace, and a CBE.

Barney fought for his country in the First World War, and sustained the painful injuries of poison gas. His country for which he fought and suffered injury was Britain. In the Second World War, Barney was an air raid warden. In peace, he belonged to one of the most honoured, and honourable professions in the land, that of a solicitor. In religion, he rose to high honour in his own community, perhaps, as President of the Board of Deputies, the highest honour that British Jewry can bestow, and he held this position for nine years between 1955 and 1964. His reputation extended beyond these shores. He was decorated by the King of the Belgians and the Queen of the Netherlands for his services to the Inter Parliamentary Union of which I think he was chairman. I do not speak of his services to World Zionism; others are more qualified than I to do so. I mention these bald facts less out of tribute to the man than as an example of the enrichment to the life of the nation to our tradition of public service by a distinguished member of the cultural minority to which Barney pre-eminently belonged. I refer to them specifically because there has been too much talk lately of our society no longer being homogeneous. What do we mean by homogeneous? Does homogeneousness demand uniformity? My answer is an unqualified 'no'. I would cite Barney as an example particularly distinguished, certainly, but happily not at all unique. Public service, obedience to law, positive and moral, an exemplary family life, a living honourably earned, yes, of course. These are demanded of all of us whatever our religion or community. But uniformity, I think not. A common loyalty to a common citizenship is required of us all in a pluralistic state. Barney showed these qualities to a superlative degree and so enriched our conception both of Jewishness and British nationality.

In the end, however, it is the man for whom we give thanks, whom we honour, and of whom, here, we take sorrowful farewell. At the age of nearly 75 myself, I find it odd to be saying, as I must, that he belonged to a generation older than mine, and, in that sense, he was not an intimate friend. He was one of the last survivors of the generation which grew to maturity before the First World War, of whom I am constantly saying, quoting from Talleyrand: 'Qui n'a pas vécu avant la Révolution n'a jamais connu la douceur de la vie.' There was, about that generation which knew young manhood before that terrible Bank Holiday of 1914 which drew the curtains on our hundred years of relative peace, and ushered in all the blood-stained horrors of this terrible twentieth century, something of quiet reasonableness and civilization which none of the rest of us have ever been able to attain again. Barney was in his ninth year before the old Queen Victoria died, and, as I saw him in the House of Lords rising to speak or ask a question of one of his many causes or on behalf of his own distinguished profession I said to myself more than once: 'there is one of the last of the Victorians', honourable, dignified, persistent, patient. He lived to see the era of Hitler and the holocaust, an utterly unthinkable event in the Europe in which he and I were both brought up, the creation of Israel as a separate and independent nation, the eclipse of the British Empire, and many other things bad and good through which we have all lived. He was, of course, an occupant of a different part of the political spectrum from myself. But his voice was always one of sanity and civilization in a world which in some ways has become rough, uncouth, and raucous with hatred. May his calm spirit rest in peace, and may the example which he has set never wholly pass out of our minds. I am reminded at the end of the words of the scripture which, year by year, is read in my College at Oxford on the occasion of the remembrance of the departed in November. It is at the end of the passage which begins with the immortal words: 'Let us now praise famous men, and our fathers that begat us.' It ends peacefully. 'These were merciful men whose righteousness hath not been forgotten. With their seed shall continually remain a good inheritance, and their children are within the Covenant. . . . Their bodies are buried in peace, but their name liveth for ever more.'

1 · GROWING UP IN WALES 1892–1926

Barney's most vivid early memory was the sight of beacons glowing on the hills around Barry in South Wales to celebrate the relief of Mafeking in 1900. On nearby Barry Island, 10,000 people watched a grand display of fireworks, and the roasting of an ox which was cut up and distributed to the town's poor.

Barney was then a happy little boy of eight — his mother was still alive.

His own lifetime was to span almost a century. Born on 20 June 1892, he grew up in an age when Britain's place in the world seemed pre-eminent and secure. The Edwardian era was the Indian summer of the British Empire when the certainties of the old order seemed destined to last forever. But not so far beneath the surface, even in the decade of Barney's birth, there were signs of deep unease and uncertainty. These were the last years of a century in which an overriding sense of confidence masked the growing insecurities below.

Barney died towards the end of another century which has seen the collapse of that confidence, and the spread of an all too acute awareness of universal uncertainty. While the world lurched from crisis to crisis, and Britain underwent rapid and sometimes turbulent change, Barney fought for the values of reason and human rights.

By the early 1890s, when his father, Joseph Vitum-Janner, settled in South Wales, there were signs that Britain was facing a threat to her industrial supremacy from countries like Germany and the United States of America. Not that anyone in Barry would have known, for the little Glamorgan town was experiencing a spectacular expansion. In 1881, only 50 people lived there. In 1886 Barry, Merthyr Dyfan and Cadoxton — all of them secluded villages full of rural charm — were joined together to form the civil parish of Barry. By 1921 it had a population of 38,945.

1

Joseph Janner (born Ofse Vitum-Janner) found his way from Lithuania to Barry by a circuitous route. He came from Lucknick in the province of Kovno. Anyone familiar with East European Jewry will recognize that as the heart of Litvak country.

Joseph went from Lucknick to South Africa, where apparently he made some money in the gold rush. From there he moved to the United States of America, where he must have done well, for he brought over the rest of his family from Lithuania and settled them in Chicago. The family was a large one and Joseph was the oldest child. His mother, who lived to be a hundred years old, is buried in Chicago. There seems to have been a streak of longevity in the family; a sister of Joseph's died in Chicago at the age of 101.

At this point there is some uncertainty about Joseph's travels, because the next we hear of him he is landing at Barry Dock in South Wales. What seems likely is that he had left the United States and gone back to Lithuania, where he married Gertrude (Gittel) Zwick. She came from Telzh, a centre of Jewish learning. Barney was always very proud that his mother's brother, Shmuel Zwick, had studied at the famous Yeshiva of Telzh.

Gittel was a young woman from a very religious family, tall, beautiful and cultured, who spoke several languages. She was the idol of Barney's life; he was absolutely devoted to her during the short time that they were together. There were three children, of whom Barney was the second. His sister, Ray, was two years older than he, while Sarah (Sally) was eight years younger.

Why the Janners landed at Barry must remain a matter for speculation — perhaps they happened to get passage on a vessel with a cargo bound for the Welsh coast. Several millions of Jews left the Czar's domains between the pogroms and anti-Jewish 'May Laws' of the 1880s, and the outbreak of the First World War. They went principally to the Americas, North and South, to the United Kingdom, to South Africa and to Turkish Palestine. Sometimes they were more concerned about getting out than about their destination. In any event, the Janners became the first Jews in Barry, a dozen or so miles from Cardiff.

Among the few notes towards an autobiography which Barney left, is one that says: 'We were the only Jews in the town in which we lived, Barry, for many years, and as I went to school from childhood upwards I was pretty well known in the town, as indeed was my father who had a business. Being of an unusual religion the family was known as a kind of mascot. But I had never heard an antisemitic word or seen any unfriendly gesture until one day a Conservative candidate for Parliament came into the town to address a meeting.' I will quote the rest of his words a little later.

Although Barry had no Jewish families until the Janners arrived, there were quite a number of Jewish communities in South Wales in the second half of the nineteenth century — Swansea, Tredegar, Merthyr Tydfil, Ebbw Vale, Llanelli and more. They based themselves on the growth of the coal, iron and tinplate industries of the region. The Jews in South Wales had arrived after the influx of migrants from England and from North Wales, who were attracted to the area because of the expanding industries and the services which had developed around them.

The reason for Barry's transformation from village to town was its dock. Ideally placed for shipping the great quantities of coal being mined in the valleys to the north and the west, Barry was given a totally new dock in 1889 under the inspiration of David Davies of Llandinam, and John Cory. (Davies was also known as 'Dafys yr Ocean' because he was the founder of the great Ocean Coal Company.) An Act of Parliament had to be passed to authorize the building of Barry Dock, and the Royal Assent was given on 14th August 1884. By the time the docks were opened they were linked by rail to the mines of the Rhondda, fifteen miles to the north. New docks were added in the following years and Barry proved a formidable competitor to Cardiff, its more established rival. Coal exports from Barry rose from three million tons a year in 1890 to eleven million tons by 1913, outstripping Cardiff and setting a world record for the export of coal.

When the Janners arrived in Barry it was well-used to immigration, as were all the coastal towns of South Wales. They had absorbed many English and Irish immigrants long before 1850. In Barry, because of the labour required to build the massive new docks, immigration was rapid. When work started in 1884 on an additional dock there was an influx of five thousand men who were housed in the characteristic navvies' huts.

3

At that time Barry was almost like an American frontier town. Many of the navvies indulged in night poaching, and it was not uncommon for people to carry a revolver for protection. Immigrants from the rest of Wales, the West Country, Ireland, Scotland and elsewhere flooded into the area to find work. There was a great demand for houses, and prices were high. Some were sold and occupied even before the doors and windows were fitted. The rows of terraced houses, which make up most of the late Victorian and Edwardian parts of the town, are made of Lias limestone and yellow brick. By 1914 Barry had grown into a town of nearly two hundred streets, well paved and well lighted, with a good supply of gas and clean water but no electricity.

So once again Joseph Janner was in what might be called a gold rush. He set up shop as a house-furnisher at 29 and 31 Holton Road, one of Barry's main thoroughfares and shopping centres. The family lived above the shop. Hanging just below the first floor window was a sign: 'J. Janner. Complete Furnisher'. Later, sometime after 1911, Joseph moved to High Street in Barry Town proper and opened a shop there.

Joseph saw himself as a businessman, but he was never really able to make a living. He had good ideas but no business sense. Barney used to recall that his father would sell furniture to sailors on credit and then they would sail away without paying. Occasionally Barney went out to collect from debtors only to be drenched with water thrown from the upper windows of their houses. As the furniture business was not successful, Joseph opened a penny and sixpence-halfpenny bazaar which did comparatively well until a branch of Woolworths opened nearby. They charged one half-penny less than he did for every item, and he was forced to close.

Until 1902 Barney's home life was happy and uneventful. Home was strictly kosher. Joseph was a learned man and knew his Judaism well, and like most Lithuanian Jews, instilled in Barney a strong sense of the importance of Jewish tradition. His father gave him Hebrew lessons every day and he could always recite his prayers quickly and well. But he never learned to speak modern Hebrew. It is not easy to change from the one pronunciation to the other late in life, and he had no time to take lessons.

4

He attended Holton Road School at the corner of Holton Road and Court Road — the local 'Board' school, a red brick building with tall windows, which first opened its doors to pupils in 1892. Although Welsh country families had a passion for education, schooling in the town up to the 1870s was generally poor. Educational standards were low and illiteracy was prevalent throughout the Principality.

Improvements began to make an impact in the 1900s following the passage of Forster's Education Act. Nonconformity was dominant in these new schools and Holton Road must have been no different, since Barry had a very strong nonconformist community.

In 1902, five days after giving birth to twin sons, Barney's mother died, and the babies did not survive for long. People who knew his mother say she was a gentle soul. They remember her walking with Joseph hand in hand along the streets of Barry. To her family her passing was a terrible blow. For Barney, life was never the same again. He was, even at that time, a boy in whom everyone took an interest, and who was able to establish good relationships. He had dark wavy hair and rather fair skin and large grey eyes. He was not a beautiful child but he had an interesting face. His head was shaped rather like an egg — with a high forehead which gave an impression of even greater height than he had. In addition his hands were always very beautiful, his pointed fingers more artistic than workmanlike.

Not long after the death of their mother, Barney and his sisters had to undergo another difficult emotional experience. The youngest, Sarah, was then only two years old, so that Joseph had to take in a house-keeper; subsequently he married her. Unfortunately she was exceptionally plain with dark greasy hair, and she thoroughly disliked the children. She treated them in an appalling manner. What hurt Barney most of all was that she sneered at him and called him 'Lord Muck'. Little did she think the day would come when he really would be a Lord. I never saw her until Barney's father was dying; to this day I don't know her first name. She was always referred to in the family, and still is, by a very uncomplimentary name.

This woman really made the childrens' lives a misery, and cast a dark shadow over the sensitive boy's existence. His father, an easy-going man, was of no help, or chose to blind himself to what was going on. It is interesting that in later life Barney drew a veil over this part of his existence. He seemed to remember almost nothing about his early years. I understand that this is known as a 'denial mechanism'.

It was Barney's luck that he later had a wonderful headmaster, and a very happy time at school. He also had fond memories of a year spent in Cardiff with the family of Israel Cohen, while studying for his Barmitzvah. Mrs Cohen and Barney's mother had been very good friends and he got on well with the children. The friendship persisted throughout his life. While in Cardiff he continued his education at Howells School. As for his Barmitzvah, he did not remember where it took place, nor what happened, an indication that it was not a happy event and that his mind had blotted it out.

I blame this period of his life for the fact that whereas he was at ease and very popular in public life, he never found family relationships easy. Not having had a proper family life at home, when he married he entered into an environment new to him. (There were many little things which delighted him, chiefly having a fuss made of him on his birthday. We would all gather together, with the cake and secret presents on the table, and then the 'Birthday Boy' would come in, to the singing of 'Happy Birthday'. He took nearly as much pleasure preparing the same ceremony for me.)

After the year in Cardiff he returned to Barry where the Jewish community had grown to four families. As a result they were able to organize services for the High Holydays.

At the age of thirteen Barney won a scholarship to the Barry County School, situated on a two-acre site at the top of the hill near the Buttrills. The award was at that time worth sixpence a week, and took care of the costs of his education. Barry County School, which opened on 10 October 1896 with 111 pupils of both sexes, was an outstanding example of the best in Welsh education. Its reputation was the work of one man who had a tremendous influence on Barney's life, as he had on the lives of hundreds of his pupils. Major Edgar Jones, headmaster from 1899–1933, was one of the most illustrious names in Welsh educational history.

The Major, or as Barney affectionately called him, 'Edgar',

6

was a tall handsome man with penetrating blue eyes. A kindly and authoritative figure, he was an important personality in the life of Barry and of Wales as a whole. For many years he was Chairman of the Art and Archaeology Committee of the National Museum of Wales. Professor Glyn Daniel, an old pupil of the school after it split in 1913 into separate boys' and girls' schools, says: 'The brilliance of the Major was his skill and ability to run a large school with complete authority but no apparent rigid discipline: to allow his boys the maximum latitude and yet never have to question their loyalty, devotion and good sense. There were no compulsory games.'

Barney remembered vividly how Edgar would bring the pupils together on Tuesday and Friday mornings and recite verse to them. He read very well — Houseman, Tennyson, Kipling, Walter de la Mare, Masefield — and would talk to the sixth form about his art and archaeological holidays, showing them lantern slides of Florence, Siena and Venice, and the painted and engraved caves of the Dordogne. Barney said he made them feel that they had been travelling with him, so good was he at bringing his travels to life.

During his early days at Barry County School, Barney started to take an interest in politics, no doubt due to Edgar Jones who was a very keen and prominent Liberal. In the half a dozen pages which he dictated for a draft autobiography just before his last illness, Barney writes:

One day a Conservative candidate for Parliament came to the town to address a meeting. Barry had a very strong non-conformist community with a much smaller Church of England community, and an attempt was being made to establish a Church of Wales, which was part of the Liberal programme. Once a Mr Gaskell (of the A1 Brewery) spoke at a meeting which was held in the church hall. In those days meetings were very exciting and quite different from today. People came to oppose the speaker, to interrupt him, and to create a fuss and bother, and the speaker was subjected to a lot of heckling. At the end of his speech he always invited questions. This was also an exciting time for the speaker because he was in a position to pit his own wit against those who asked the questions and those who had

7

heckled. I thoroughly enjoyed these meetings, both at my own local candidature and at the Parliamentary ones.

At this particular meeting, church people were sitting on chairs (these were chiefly Conservatives), whereas those who had come to disturb the speaker stood at the back of the chairs. In the course of his speech Mr Gaskell said, 'It has been said that there is a horrible unclean bond between the Church of England and the Conservative Party, but it is between the cosmopolitan Jew of Swansea and the Liberal Party.' He was referring to Sir Alfred Mond who was a strong Liberal, and associate of Lloyd George, and Liberal Parliamentary candidate for Swansea. Never having heard this before, the lads turned to me and said, 'You can't allow this, Janner,' and pushed me to the front of the crowd. I was very disturbed. The speaker then said that he was quoting from the most eminent person to ever grace Parliament. I knew what was coming because this was the manner in which Disraeli was regarded, particularly by Conservatives. He then mentioned the name Disraeli.

I shouted out, 'A cosmopolitan Jew, Mr Chairman.' He replied, 'It's a lie,' and added 'What is your authority?' 'Moneypenny,' I replied, referring to the famous biography. He retorted, 'Moneypenny is bosh.' He mentioned Lloyd George who was the idol, particularly of the Liberals, and one of the big boys shouted 'Three cheers for Lloyd George.' The Liberals gave three hearty cheers. The speaker then said, 'Three cheers for Sir Rufus Isaacs.' Unfortunately at that time there was some scandal regarding a transaction in the Marconi set-up. The meeting cheered reluctantly. Someone then said, 'Three cheers for Mr Godfrey Isaacs.' My hair was standing on end and I asked the speaker, 'Is this a political meeting or mere vituperation?' and added, 'Three cheers for the cosmopolitan Jew of Swansea,' which the crowd did with great acclaim.

One of the Conservative women came and said to me, 'Go back to school.' I replied 'Madam, it sounds as if you did not go to school at all.'

Barney was a little boy whom the townsfolk had taken to their hearts. He already had the sort of personality that drew people to him; a warmth and friendliness which grew in his public relationships as the years went by. He was a brilliant student, but despite the scholarships his father intended to remove him from school. Fortunately Edgar Jones and his wife regarded him practically as a son, and the Major went to see Joseph and persuaded him it would be a terrible mistake to take Barney away from school.

Barney was good at all subjects, particularly English and maths, and he loved debating and amateur dramatics. He was always fond of reciting poetry; Wordsworth was a great favourite. (I remember him quoting from 'Daffodils', and we spent part of our honeymoon in the Lake District.)

He never had any potential as an athlete. Anyway, most games were on Saturdays when he was not allowed to play, because the family observed the Sabbath. His appointments as Senior Prefect and House Captain were thus all the more an achievement because these honours were traditionally given to those who were also leading athletes. Again this was a tribute to his personality, and to his exceptional powers and ability to work hard. Perhaps also his inner anxiety played a role; he worried about every little detail. Thus the many old boys of the school whom I have met all say the same thing about Barney: 'He was always in a state.' In truth, he was usually agitated about some issue or problem.

He remained close to the Jones family all his life, and when their only son Gareth, a brilliant young journalist, was killed by bandits in Manchuria in 1936, Mrs Jones said to me 'Now Barney is our only son.' Throughout his life Barney kept a photograph of Edgar on his desk.

Barney wrote about his school days for the 1946 Golden Jubilee issue of the school magazine. The Major was still alive and his daughter Gwyneth Jones was Headmistress of the girls' school.

> I know none of my contempories as students at the school who does not experience a thrill of pleasure whenever he or she meets Major Edgar Jones. . . . Was it not he in the school, and his family in the soirées and other functions, who were responsible for creating the atmosphere of ease

and happiness which prevailed? I remember how we put on our best oratorical efforts when he visited us at Lit. and Deb. (Literature and Debating Society). Even the rapier thrusts of Melville and Iowerth Rees against each other, which were so frequently exercised on Friday evenings, were then restrained . . . I recall the unhappy occasion on which, at a school concert in the Gym, having chosen to recite 'Horatius' because of its striking length, I found myself stuck half way, when the Head (whom I had not provided with a copy of the poem) suggested in his kindly manner that I should have another try later on, with the result that I failed to 'stay the course' even as far as I had done on my previous attempt. I remember the sensational win of the mile race at the sports by the 'dark horse', Frank Dixey, after having covertly trained for some considerable time; the first appearance of Mr E. P. Evans (E.P.) in the classroom when he rattled out the question, which set us all thinking about and liking maths, 'What is a number?'. He made the subject so interesting that every boy in the class took maths in his higher examinations.

E. P. Evans was the typical 'mad professor'. Barney used to relate two stories about him. One was that going to school one windy day he turned round to light his pipe. He then continued walking until he reached home — much to his wife's surprise. Another was that he was stepping on to the pavement and left one foot in the gutter. He went on walking with one foot in the gutter and one on the pavement, and on reaching school enquired why he was lame. He was another of Barney's life-long heroes.

Barney's writing continues:

The unorthodox experiments in the chemistry lab, when only a merciful Providence saved the school from being blown up or being choked by noxious gasses; the excitement caused when Tom Whelan fell between two ships in the dock; the gloom cast over the school by the untimely death of our hero Pia (P.E.) Amor; the strutting on the stage of 'Gotty' (G.O.) Thomas in *The Taming of the Shrew*;

the clinging melodies of the school orchestra conducted by Mr E. H. Davies (Long Tom); the disputations in the sixth form room with Jenkin Edward Jones and Billy Miles; the running uphill to school in order to keep pace with long-legged Guest Habbakuk; the panting attempts (rarely successful) to negotiate the Buttrills Hill on a bicycle; the reckless rushes downhill from the school on a 'bone-shaker' with only the pressure of one's foot on the tyre available as a brake; and the breathless excitement of taking the daring turn into Gladstone Road which would have caused many a circus artist to quail.

Life was indeed very full for me from the moment when, filled with awe, Reggie Lloyd, Ernie Davies, Cyril Lakin and I walked over the threshold of the school and saw for the first time the begowned staff, until the last day at school which was to be succeeded by violent rushing along Dock View Road, racing the train to the station and hurling myself into a compartment at the twelfth hour so as to be in time for 'Niner' at Coll.

The intensity of Barney's schooldays comes over very vividly from this description. It is remarkable that from a small county school quite a number of his contemporaries went on to become well-known figures in politics, business, the professions and academia. Politically, Edgar Jones also played a big part in moulding Barney's early views. The Major was an active member of the Liberal Party at a time when the Liberals were in the ascendancy throughout almost the whole of Wales.

By the time Barney was in his teens the Labour Party, officially founded in 1906, was only beginning to make inroads into Liberal areas in South Wales. The General Election of 1906 was the year of the great Liberal landslide. That was the Parliament which saw the start of social welfare legislation, that cushioned Britain's working population during the terrible years of recession, slump and depression which followed the First World War. If you were progressively inclined, it was still natural to choose the Liberal Party. David Lloyd George, speaking in Cardiff in 1906, laid great stress on the Liberals' 'zeal for temperance, education, and land reform' which, he said, showed that they were truly the party of the working man.

By the time Barney came to the end of his happy school days, he had grown into a tall, rather solid young man, slim and interesting-looking. He was keen to teach, and he would undoubtedly have become a teacher but for an early experience which cured him of this ambition. While still at Barry County School he went as a pupil teacher for a day to another school in the town. Working there was a Mr Morgan who had taught him while he was at Holton Road School. 'Oh, so you want to be a teacher,' said Mr Morgan. 'All right, draw a map of Scotland on the board and give the boys a lesson in the geography of Scotland.' Barney recalled that he 'sweated blood' as he could not draw at all, let alone draw a map of Scotland from memory. By the end of the lesson he was in a 'terrible state'. Mr Morgan approached him and said, 'That will show you what it is like to be a teacher. Go back to school, continue your studies and choose a different career.'

Thus the influence of two schoolmasters led him to the law and to public life.

Barney's success as a student was reflected in examinations taken and passed. He won a scholarship to the University College of South Wales and Monmouthshire in Cardiff (now Cardiff University) of which he was a governor at the time of his death. His college registration form — 'No. 4804' — shows that in October 1911 he was still officially living at 31 Holton Road, Barry, but actually in term-time he had lodgings at Gloucester Terrace, Cardiff.

In 1913 his older sister Ray married Charles Davis. They lived in Glyn Rhondda Street, Cardiff. Sally had become so unhappy at home that soon after her sister married she ran away from Barry, and lived with Charles and Ray Davis. When Barney returned from the war in 1919 he never went home again, and he too lived with the Davis family. Later they all moved to Richmond Road.

To revert to Barney's college days; he passed his Central Welsh Board examinations in the year 1911 with honours and applied for Matriculation in the University of Wales. The range of subjects he studied before qualifying in 1914 for the degree of BA was wide: History, English, Latin, Maths, Economics and Political Science. His special qualification courses were in English, Applied Maths and Pure Maths. He remained attached to the university after getting his BA (honours) Degree, for the purpose of preparing for his law examinations. He was active in student life until 1917.

It was at university that Barney began to gain experience of public life. He was clearly a central figure in the student body, for his name appears frequently in *Cap and Gown*, the college magazine, in the years 1913–17. He was President of the Students' Representative Council in 1916–17. In 1914–15 he was President of the Literary and Debating Society and from his second or third year Barney was on the committee which helped produce *Cap and Gown* and was editor of the magazine in the 1916–17 session.

Little teasing snippets about him and articles by him appear in this college magazine. Most are written in the kind of private language common to student life then, but are almost unintelligible to a modern reader. Still, some of Barney's characteristics and expressions are recognisable.

One of the issues Barney edited contains a long editorial by him and verses for two songs in the style of W. S. Gilbert: 'A Fool's Paradise' and 'A Professor's Lot is not a Happy One'. (Barney liked composing songs. Once on a cruise he wrote a parody of 'D'ye Ken John Peel?' which he sang at the ship's concert. He also won the fancy dress prize with a wonderful topical idea.) Though debating was clearly a passion, he loved acting and was a leading performer in the Dramatic Society. He never tired of relating how he acted in *Arms and the Man* by George Bernard Shaw and sang in *The Pirates of Penzance*. He also appeared in *Box and Cox* (as Cox on a number of occasions) and as Spigott in *My Lord in Livery*. I have always maintained that politics and the stage are akin.

From that time on he had a great liking for Gilbert and Sullivan, although he had little understanding of classical music. At one time Barney tried to learn the violin, but the music teacher discovered that he had no joint in the fourth finger of his left hand — a trait that our son Greville and grandson Daniel share with him — in fact Greville has no joint in either of his fourth fingers.

Barney supplemented his small income at university by teaching at the Cardiff School of Commerce, essentially a secretarial college, known as Bloggs School, in Grey Friars Road,

Park Place. He coached boys for examinations. Here his desire to teach was satisfied while he earned a little much-needed money.

He had decided on a career in law, and as he could not afford to be a barrister, which he would have loved, he became articled in 1914 to a very reputable firm of Cardiff solicitors, Messrs Sidney Jenkins and Howell. He then began to acquire his professional skills, while remaining on the roster of university students for his law examinations. For relaxation he would take a girl rowing on Roath Park Lake — praying nobody would see him.

By 1917 the First World War had intruded into most people's lives in one form or another. The war was expected to be over by Christmas of 1914, but soon developed into the first 'total war' of the twentieth century. Eventually all the resources of British society were mobilised. There was heavy enlistment in the Welsh university colleges, and Officer Training Corps flourished. College students saw their friends volunteer, go off to the war, and not always return. The edition of *Cap and Gown* which Barney edited in 1917 carries a list of former students killed or wounded in action.

He himself enlisted early in the war, but was not called up until he had qualified as a solicitor. By mid 1917 he had joined the Royal Garrison Artillery as a private. With his education he could quite easily have applied for a commission, but even then he was so much a man of the people that he wanted to go into the ranks and get to know his fellow men, to mix with them, eat with them and fight with them.

As a practising Jew he was bound to face some problems. Unable to obtain kosher meat in the army he had to eat non-kosher meat rations — the only time in his life that he did so — but he never ate pig. He used to tell the story that at breakfast one day the Mess Sergeant discovered that he was giving his bacon to his neighbours. The Sergeant was furious that no food was supplied that he could eat. After a bout of swearing, he ordered that Barney was to have steak instead of bacon. This lasted for two days until the other soldiers became annoyed that Barney was receiving better food. He then insisted on eating only his porridge and bread for breakfast.

According to the Ministry of Defence records he enlisted in

the Royal Garrison Artillery on 2 March 1916, but was not called up until 7 August 1917 when he was posted to 490 Siege Battery. As Gunner No.172092, Janner, Barnett, he left for France and the front with No.1 Reinforcement Depot on 24 November 1917, together with men drawn from all over the country. In France he was posted to 355 Siege Battery.

The Battery consisted mostly of men enlisted under the Derby scheme introduced by Lloyd George, with a sprinkling of regulars and Territorials. After training at Aldershot and Lydd the Battery had been mobilized at Abbey Wood, near Woolwich, equipped as a four-gun tractor-drawn unit, armed with six-inch Howitzers.

When Barney reached the front the disastrous Third Battle of Ypres — popularly known as Passchendaele — was still going on. The British had advanced a precarious four miles. The men struggled in mud up to their waists, and the guns sank. The sacrifice in human lives was immense. British losses were put at over 250,000.

At home, life for civilians was getting worse. There were food and fuel shortages, and economic and political discontent. After the October Revolution, the Russians sued for peace at Brest–Litovsk and withdrew from the war. There were widespread mutinies in the French Army, with parallel civilian unrest on the home front.

On 27 September 1917, 355 Siege Battery with its six officers and 128 other ranks was thrown into a great battle raging on Flanders field. Following a devastating bombardment on 15 November every gun was put out of action and the Battery withdrew.

The guns were repaired, and on 5 December the Battery moved into a position recently held by a French Battery at Pont Pétain, close to Noordschoote in the Belgian Army area. As the Battery Record puts it:

> Here, for some weeks, in almost undisturbed surroundings, the Battery enjoyed complete immunity from shell fire, whilst to the south the roar of battle died fitfully away. A spell of severe cold set in, and Christmas, ushered in by a heavy fall of snow, found us correctly garbed, though not exactly in the environment we could have wished.

Barney said his main job as a gunner was lying in the dug-out using his mathematical knowledge to work out the shoots for the guns. There were, of course, no automatic sights, and Barney had to tell them the range and angle to shoot. He was promoted — as he always said with a chuckle — to acting Lance-Bombadier, unpaid.

In the early part of 1918, 355 saw much action in the Amiens sector, fighting off the desperate efforts of the Germans to win the war before American troops arrived on the Western Front. In July, after a somewhat uneventful three months, the Battery was involved in the attack which followed Marshal Foch's counterstroke that changed the face of the war.

On 16 August 1918 Barney was returned to base on his way to 504 Siege Battery.

After fitful progress that August, the advance began on the 23rd when 504 went into action at Derancourt. On the 26th they were at Fricourt, and reached Carnoi village on the evening of the 27th, where Barney joined them on the 29th.

The next day the Battery at Carnoi village was bombarded with mustard gas shells. One man died immediately, another later in the day. Eighteen other men, Barney among them, were badly gassed. Barney was already semi-conscious when an unknown soldier seized his gas mask and put it over Barney's face, so saving his life. He never discovered the identity of the stranger who did him so great a service.

The gassed men were evacuated to hospital in Le Havre. For a couple of days Barney could not see, and it was feared he might be permanently blind. However, within a few days he regained his sight, to his intense relief.

The Battery continued to see action until the beginning of November 1918. On 16 October Barney was discharged from hospital and returned to the Brigade, but saw no more action himself. He was recategorized as Class 'A' on 12 November 1918, the day after the Armistice was signed, and on 4 December 1918 he returned to the UK. On 5 February 1919 he was demobilized.

The Battery, reduced to 'cadre' strength, returned to England in June 1919 and was disbanded at Ripon.

Like all old squaddies Barney had many stories he loved to recall. He told of one incident during the advance when, arriving at a small village, they found a big barrel. They opened it and found it contained salt herrings. Barney's non-Jewish comrades had no idea what they were. Of course Barney knew but, suspecting the Germans might have poisoned them, he threw one of the herrings to a dog. When nothing happened to the dog they all tucked in to a good meal of salt herrings and thick black bread.

Another time he was sent out on a motorbike to deliver a message. Soon he met one of the officers who said 'Where the hell do you think you're going?' Barney explained he had to deliver a message. 'You're heading straight for the enemy lines, you bloody fool!' the officer said. 'Turn round and go back to your base.' Barney said he did not have to be told twice.

Despite his experiences in the trenches, Barney said he quite enjoyed the war. He got to know and understand men he would not otherwise have met, and appreciated their friendship. He had no fear, and was immensely brave. However, due to the poison gas, his chest condition got progressively worse, and had to be given much care throughout his long life.

When Barney returned to Cardiff to resume civilian life he had no capital at all. But Charles Davis guaranteed a bank loan for him. With this Barney rented two rooms in 1919, at 6 Working Street, Cardiff, bought a typewriter, a table, a desk and a couple of chairs, and with one secretary started out in practice as a solicitor. Blessed with a beautiful speaking voice, he soon built a reputation for himself as an advocate in the courts.

As far as possible he avoided prosecuting people, for he had a great desire to help, and this influenced the way in which he ran his practice. If people could not pay he would still defend them. Not surprisingly he had an extremely busy practice but not a very lucrative one. The waiting room in his office was always packed with people. Most of his time was taken up with court work and he used to handle nearly all the cases for the Jewish Board of Guardians. He had to support his sister and in part, his father as well. He started to save up for Sally's future, and put money away every week not to be touched until she married. By the time we married in 1927 he had saved enough to buy her a house and a trousseau, and to give her a very delightful wedding. He was happy to be able to do this, for he thought the world of his brother-in-law, Isie Goldman (later Graham) of Leeds, whom she married in 1929.

An interesting relic of his early days as a practising solicitor survives — his first 'Letter Book', dated 20 April to 10 June 1919. It contains copies of typed letters, a method used before carbon paper became common. The letter was placed under one of the practically transparent damp tissue-like sheets in the book and pressed down, leaving an image of the original in blue. His first letter was to Messrs Gibson & Weldon of Chancery Lane, London, thanking them for sending his 'Practice Certificate'. Gibson & Weldon were authorized to issue such certificates to those who had passed the Law Society exams.

Most of the letters relate to routine work concerned with property, debts, and the like. But his interests and concerns can be seen in some of them. In one he accepts an invitation of the Committee of the Cardiff Jewish Institute to act as their honorary Solicitor. In others he takes up the question of naturalization for Russian subjects who served in His Majesty's Forces during the First World War. He was also involved in defending people with rent and lease problems, an interest which persisted throughout his life and became one of his special concerns when he entered Parliament.

Barney began his career in politics in the municipal elections of 1921 as a candidate for the Comrades of the Great War. The main issue was the supply of dustbins. But when in the municipal election of November 1924 he fought the Central Ward as a Liberal, both local and national issues were at stake. His introductory pamphlet for the election that year showed his concerns to be re-adjustment of rates, education, ex-servicemen, unemployment, 'hygenic conditions' (a more efficient system of removing refuse — those dustbins again), 'tramway and omnibus services', allotments, public rights of way and common land, and economy in the city's government.

His background and education, especially the influence of Edgar Jones, led him not unnaturally to the Liberal Party. Lloyd George was still in the ascendant after the war and the Liberal MPs were a central force in Parliament after the 'khaki coupon' election of 1918. Nevertheless, Lloyd George governed only with Conservative support, and by 1922 the Coalition government fell. The Liberals had certainly dominated Welsh politics for nearly three decades but post-war Wales was markedly different. The Liberal Party which had been the party of the Left had been squeezed into the centre by the increasing popularity of the Labour Party. In both of Barney's municipal election attempts he was beaten by a Labour candidate.

In Jewish public life and politics, circumstances were very different. He began in a very modest way. The *Jewish Year Book* of 1911 records him as Honorary Treasurer of the Barry Dock Jewish community of '9 families'. At university in Cardiff he founded the first Zionist society in South Wales with three other students. Back from the war he continued to pursue the cause of a Jewish National Home in Palestine with an intensity known to very few in those days. Zionism inspired him at a time when not many found it interesting, or had the courage to come forward to express their views; but he never wavered then or thereafter.

Once he established himself in Cardiff he began to participate in the various activities of the Jewish community. He joined and became a leading member of Cardiff's main synagogue in Cathedral Road, which had been opened in 1897 by the Chief Rabbi, Dr Herman Adler. Later he was elected Chairman of the South Wales Zionist Council.

Shortly after he left Cardiff Barney was presented with a volume paying tribute to his devotion to the Jewish community. It is a beautiful work of calligraphy and contains the names of all the organizations he was associated with in Cardiff — some twenty-one altogether. He had been Chairman, President, Treasurer or Honorary Solicitor of practically all of them at one time or another. Apart from the Cardiff Hebrew Congregation, the Jewish Institute (where, incidentally, he met Tessie O'Shea when she was a child actress; she adored him all her life) and the Board of Guardians, he had been Chairman of the Elsie Fine Achei Brith Lodge — a women's lodge — and, more esoterically, Chairman of the Cardiff Bread Distribution Society.

At that time Jewish communal and organizational life in Cardiff was known to be the rowdiest and most unruly in the country. Barney was ever in the thick of it and revelled in it. There was always some row or argument going on — mostly minor problems blown up out of all proportion, but insoluble without hours and hours of discussion, often of a heated and acrimonious nature. But the community loved this bright and energetic young man, and many of them wanted him as a son-in-law. With his family responsibilities and fourteen hours' work a day, he had other things on his mind — and none of them got him.

After our marriage Barney always came home from synagogue meetings with the edge of his right hand red from banging it on the table to keep order.

The minister of the Cathedral Road Synagogue, a man of excitable temperament, often used to attack Barney in his *Shabbos* sermons, only he would employ a euphemism. Instead of mentioning Barney by name he would refer to the faults of Moses — but everyone knew who the target was. This constant criticism annoyed me intensely. But one Saturday before our marriage when my father came to the synagogue he found the minister's sermon highly amusing!

Seven years after being 'demobbed' from the army in 1919, Barney had built up a large solicitor's practice from nothing, with no financial resources of his own. He had become the leading figure in the Jewish community, and he was still only thirty-four years old.

2 IN THE ARENA
1926–1931

I met Barney one Sunday afternoon in London at the wedding of my best friend. It was on 12 December 1926, that Ray Rubinstein was married to Ben Harris of Newport, Monmouthshire. Ben's late brother, who was killed in action in the Great War, had been a good friend of Barney's. As Barney was in London that Sunday for the monthly meeting of the Board of Deputies of British Jews, he took the opportunity of coming to the wedding celebration. We had an instant feeling for each other, or it may have been that Barney talked so easily to people that I immediately felt I had known him for years. He was a very good dancer and that day we danced a lot together. Later that evening four of us went out to a night club.

We had been courting for not quite two months when, on 6 February 1927, we became engaged. It was a long-distance engagement. Barney would come up to London at the weekend, usually travelling back to Cardiff on the Sunday overnight train. But all that came to an end on 12 July 1927 when we were married at the Hampstead Synagogue in London by the Reverend A. A. Green and the Reverend E. Drukker of Jesmond, Newcastle-upon-Tyne, my Minister and Hebrew teacher from the age of nine. We honeymooned in Scotland and in the Lake District, where Barney insisted on taking me to see the grave of William Wordsworth.

Although we were brought up in very different circumstances, our parents came from the same area of Russian-controlled Lithuania. My grandfather told my father that Barney's maternal grandfather, Boruch Aron der Meler, was a remote relative of ours.

Under the Czars, Jews were allowed to live only in an area of Western Russia which came to be known as the Pale of Settlement. They were restricted in other ways, too. For example, it was impossible for a Jew in the Pale to qualify formally as a medical doctor. However, a diploma was available which entitled Jews to practise as paramedics. My maternal grandfather, Idl Noson (Yehuda Nathan — from which came my mother's family name) received such a diploma, and was the doctor in the small town of Plungyan. He was known as 'Idl der Felcher' (Idl the Doctor) and he rode around making his calls in a horse and trap. My mother, who was born in Plungyan, boasted that they possessed a bath in their home.

My father, the youngest in a very large family, was born in the tiny village of Medinyan and brought up in Riteve near the Baltic Sea. He came from an environment very different from my mother's. Learning and scholarship were always part of his life, and he attended a *Yeshiva* (a religious seminary). At the age of seventeen he left Lithuania, escaped over the border into East Prussia in a hay cart, and joined his eldest brother who was then living in Königsberg.

After two years he left Germany for Dublin where some of his friends were then living. With two pounds in his pocket he bought a tray of needles and cottons and began knocking on doors. He worked hard, like most new immigrants, and soon opened a wholesale business with the father of Max Nurock (Max later became the Israeli Ambassador to Australia).

In 1897 he saw a photograph of Yetta Nathansohn, who was very beautiful, and fell in love. He travelled back to Plungyan in Lithuania to woo her, and after ten days they were married. He brought her back to Dublin, where my two eldest brothers were born. Later on, the family moved to Newcastle-upon-Tyne where I was born at 35 Osborn Road in Jesmond, the first English member of the family.

Barney and I both came from orthodox homes. Our fathers were both learned Jews, and both our mothers were beautiful women and accomplished linguists as well. But there the parallel ends. His adolescence was loveless and unhappy; I grew up in security and comfort.

In my family, where we were eventually six children, we lived in beautiful homes in Newcastle and then in London, and we never had to worry about money. Not that my father believed in indulging his children. He was strict in the Victorian manner, and he kept us on a tight rein. Pocket money was never plentiful, but we never knew what it meant to be deprived.

Here was the real difference in our backgrounds. Barney's

father only thought himself a businessman; Joseph Cohen really was, and a highly successful one at that. By the time the First World War began, my father had built up a considerable retail furniture business in the north of England. After the war the head office was moved to London, to Curtain Road, EC.

At that time the East End was the centre of cabinet making. Young men would learn the trade, some of them at the Jewish Board of Guardians, and would then make a suite of furniture and try to sell it. Word got around that Joseph Cohen was a man who would always give a young fellow a chance by buying his product immediately even though he himself could get all he needed on credit from the big manufacturers. My brothers remember Curtain Road on Friday afternoons, when there would be a line of young cabinet makers outside, each pushing his barrow of furniture. Most of these fellows made good, and are full of praise for my father to this very day. One of them, our good friend Morris Leigh, has told me many times of his love and respect for father, who helped him get his start in life.

On the other hand, where his daughters were concerned my father remained firmly Victorian in his convictions. He believed strongly that the business should belong to the boys, and he would not allow me to go into it, much as I wanted to. In addition, he gave the shares to his sons; my sister Edith and I got rather modest marriage settlements. As a consequence, Barney and I and our family have had to work hard all our lives to make a decent living. I once asked my husband how he felt at charity functions when he heard young men giving away in seconds more than he would ever be worth. His answer was: 'I don't mind. We have other things to give.'

All this aside, I must admit that I had a privileged upbringing. I went to Central High School in Newcastle, to South Hampstead High School in London, and then to finishing school at Lausanne, Switzerland. I knew very little of what went on in the real world. Nevertheless, when I left finishing school I rebelled against my father's injunction to 'Stay at home, help your mother and practise the piano!' To be sure, I had very little idea how to direct my energies and interests. None of my friends worked. We all had plenty of free time, much of it spent at the Chandos Lawn Tennis Club. A vague desire to help the poor (how patronizing that sounds now) led me eventually to the East

End of London, where I worked as a volunteer at the Jewish Welfare Centre in Mulberry Street, and also began a lifelong involvement with the Brady Clubs in Whitechapel.

By 1926, when I met Barney, I was a plump, carefree young girl with lots of friends and a very happy family life. With his devotion to public service, Barney brought a completely new dimension into my life.

We spent the first day of our engagement in the East End. On Sunday 7 February I had to attend the Brady Play Centre prize-giving at Camperdown House, where Sir Robert Waley Cohen and his wife were to be the guests of honour. I picked Barney up in father's car after lunch, and we went careering through the East End. That evening there was to be a concert party given by the Brady Club managers, the first of its kind for the club, and I was to be the pianist. But first we headed for Abrahamson's Restaurant in Whitechapel Road for dinner, with Barney unsuccessfully giving me directions. When we eventually arrived, everyone cheered madly. From there we went to the Brady concert, and then back to my home for a party. One of the managers in the concert troupe was a superb comic actor and together they all put on, quite impromptu, a mock wedding ceremony, using a blanket as a chuppah. Barney, who had lived an altogether more serious life since his socially active student days, looked at them as if they were all completely mad . . .

I remember one night during our engagement when we were at a charity garden party and Barney spoke to me seriously about how much there was to do for people in the world and how we had to work together to achieve things. He felt very deeply about social injustice and saw his life as being dedicated to mankind. He used to say: 'There is so much to be done. We must try to help everyone we can.' My work in the East End was obviously important to him. He had not intended getting married and my being active in social work made a great deal of difference to him.

His idealism inspired me. After all, my horizons were pretty limited in 1927, and Barney was much older and more experienced. He was thirty-five, the leading Jewish public figure in South Wales, and also very involved in local Liberal politics. I had a great deal to learn.

My father bought us a nice house in Cardiff at 50 Tydraw Road, Roath Park. I was completely starry-eyed and thought that the future held only the pleasure of living with Barney in our own home. Cardiff was bound to be a little strange, since every provincial community has its own special characteristics (though Cardiff was in a class of its own). And of course it was my first encounter with the full scope and pace of Barney's public activity. I saw little of him, since he was in his office all day and had meetings practically every evening and all day on Sundays. He was well used to a bachelor's life and the freedom of living on his own, so it took him a little while to conform to the demands of married life.

After three months I became pregnant with Greville. It was a bad pregnancy and a difficult labour. That both of us were alive after Greville was born on 11 July 1928 was a miracle due to the skill of my obstetrician, Sir Ewen Maclean, a brother of Donald Maclean, later Minister of Education in the 1931 National Government and uncle of Donald Maclean the Communist spy.

Barney had limitless energy, and was blessed with the marvellous ability to be completely rejuvenated and refreshed by long or short periods of sleep. When he had any free time he went to bed. Sometimes he would sleep his way right through a weekend, only surfacing now and again for food. On Monday morning he would look fresh as a daisy. Throughout our life, whenever I was reluctant to attend a meeting in the evening, Barney would always say: 'Come on — pull yourself together! We must go.' And go we did.

Less than a year after Greville was born Barney had his first real chance to gain experience of national politics. He had been active in the Cardiff Central Liberal Association since its formation and stood twice, unsuccessfully, as a Liberal in municipal elections in 1924 and 1925. On 8 April 1929 he was unanimously adopted, on the recommendation of the Executive Committee, as prospective Parliamentary candidate for Cardiff Central. The General Election, which was dominated by the question of how to tackle unemployment, was to be held on Thursday 30 May.

South Wales, so industrially vigorous before the First World

War, was being laid waste by the intensifying recession. The short-lived post-war boom soon collapsed and gave way to a sharp slump in 1920–21. Unemployment began to bite, and a creeping paralysis of the industrial and commercial life of the region set in. Of the insured working population in Wales, 23·3 per cent were unemployed in December 1927 and the figure continued to rise. In the two towns Barney knew so well — Barry and Cardiff — the slump virtually killed off trade altogether. These two ports, so dependent on the export of Welsh steam coal from the Rhondda and elsewhere, were in a state of near collapse, with the main docks practically closed down for long periods.

The human cost was shattering. Between 1921 and 1940, 430,000 Welsh people left their country, forced out by the absence of prospects and the sub-standard social conditions. Barney was well aware of this migration, which was in part encouraged by the Tory Government, and he referred to it in his campaign election addresses. In Cardiff the percentage of houses containing more than one family increased from 28·3 per cent in 1925 to 57·8 per cent in 1927. Medical Officers of Health reported that 2,025 houses in Cardiff were unfit for human habitation. Cardiff City Council, which was relatively public-spirited by the standards of the day, was simply unable to cope with the immense problems.

Barney was always a left-wing Liberal. If Edgar Jones had been a Labour man Barney would almost certainly have gone into the Labour Party. When he joined the Liberals, they were still the main radical party, though Labour was rapidly ousting them from this position, especially in Wales. The collapse of the Lloyd George coalition government in 1922, preceded by growing criticism of Lloyd George himself, took this process a stage further, and in the General Election of that year Wales returned eighteen Labour Members of Parliament, six Tories and eleven Liberals. In 1924 the same number of Liberals was returned, but it was already clear that Liberalism had become the party of a past era, confined principally to rural constituencies where the old traditions still held.

Nevertheless, during the years 1925–29 Liberalism mounted a new challenge. The two wings of the party, which had split when Lloyd George replaced Herbert Asquith as Prime Minister during the First World War, were reunited in November 1923 and Lloyd George came to dominate the party in Wales more completely than ever before. A new programme devised by such brilliant economists as John Maynard Keynes and Hubert Henderson was described in the 'yellow book' on industrial recovery in 1928 and the 'orange book', *We Can Conquer Unemployment*, in 1929. This last was the centrepiece of the Liberals' 1929 election programme.

Barney had studied them thoroughly, and wholeheartedly endorsed Lloyd George's ideas on conquering unemployment — not surprisingly, since they were more radical and far-reaching than anything proposed by the Labour Party at the time. The Liberal plan was to finance public works schemes which would not only provide work and reconstruct the country, but would generate further income and employment. These were ideas which came to be generally accepted during and after the Second World War, but in 1929 were still considered impractical. The prevailing view, held to unflinchingly by the Treasury, was that if the Government created jobs, other jobs would disappear.

Barney used to show just how radical the Liberal Party was in some respects by recalling a song sung by Liberals in that 1929 election, to the tune of 'Marching Through Georgia'.

> *The land, the land,*
> *T'was God who gave the land,*
> *The land, the land,*
> *The ground on which we stand,*
> *Why should we be beggars*
> *With the ballot in our hand?*
> *God gave the land to the people.*

The Cardiff Central seat had been won for the Conservatives in 1924 by Sir Lewis Lougher with 14,537 votes. The Labour Party had been second with 9,684 and the Liberals a poor third with 4,085. Sir Lewis's majority was 4,673. In 1929 Barney had little chance of winning, but he threw himself with vigour into the campaign. Again it was a three-cornered fight with Captain Ernest N. Bennett standing for Labour.

Barney's main concerns, apart from the Liberals' industrial

policy, were free trade, education and housing, and leasehold reform. The constituency was very mixed. It included one ward which consisted almost entirely of railwaymen; part of Cardiff docks; part of the centre of Cardiff; some lower middle class housing; and some bad slum areas — this was the first time I had seen 'meths' drinkers.

From the very beginning Barney concentrated on personal canvassing, and on addressing as many meetings as he could arrange. Lloyd George and Sir Herbert Samuel came to support the various Liberal candidates in the South Wales area.

Before the election campaign got underway Barney was invited, together with some other provincial Liberal candidates, to dine at Lloyd George's home in Addison Road, London. Barney enjoyed it thoroughly. Lloyd George had arranged a special fish course for him. Barney said he was a sparkling host.

Going back to the time before Barney was selected as candidate, I remember one amusing evening in 1928 when he addressed a meeting in Maerdy in the Rhondda. A man called Jack Jones, who came from a small village in South Wales, had defected from the Labour Party and joined the Liberals. He was to have addressed the Maerdy meeting, but at the last moment he could not come and Barney was asked to deputize for him. On the way down there in the train we were joined by Dr R. D. Chalke, the prospective Liberal candidate for Rhondda East, who told us that Maerdy was known as 'Little Russia', and that they were waiting to give Jack Jones hell . . .

We arrived at a packed school hall — it was so full, people were sitting on the windowsills and hanging from the rafters. I sat down, very pregnant. Without wasting any time Dr Chalke immediately called on Barney who put down his briefcase, which he always carried, and amidst jeers and catcalls began his speech. 'They tell me you eat people like me down here,' he said. 'I advise you not to do so or you will get violent indigestion.' They all laughed, and after that he had them eating out of his hand. By the end of the evening they even cheered him and some called out: 'Come again soon, and bring your little bag!'

Welsh politics was a good school for aspiring young politicians, and such meetings sharpened Barney's skills as a speaker. Once the election campaign began in all earnestness in 1929, it

28

was Barney's ability and spontaneity as a speaker, his open and direct manner when addressing an audience, which made him such a popular candidate from the very start. He would always devote much, and sometimes all, of the time available at meetings to questions from the audience — a practice often commented on by the press then and later when we moved to London and Barney three times contested the Whitechapel seat. The *Daily Chronicle*, a Liberal paper naturally overoptimistic about Liberal fortunes in Cardiff, said:

> Mr Barnett Janner . . . has impressed the electorate with the vigour and thoroughness of his campaign, his ability to answer questions on every phase of politics and his clear exposition of every feature of the Liberal programme. At his street corner meetings Labour men have again and again thanked him for his lucid explanation of the Liberal unemployment policy, and promised to vote for him.

Since both Labour and Liberal parties were presenting schemes for getting rid of unemployment, Barney obviously saw Captain Bennett as his main opponent. Sir Lewis Lougher was defending the record of a Government which intended to continue the same orthodox monetary and fiscal policies it had followed for the previous five years. The electorate in Cardiff Central had grown from 38,026 to 47,282, and most of the new voters were potential Labour supporters. Barney, well aware of the importance of trade to Cardiff with its docks and shipbuilding, attacked his Labour opponent on the question of free trade, claiming that there was a split in the Labour ranks on the issue. Captain Bennett, equally aware that free trade was a life or death issue for Cardiff, vigorously rejected Barney's assertions. But Barney was able to come back with quotations from a Labour candidate, and from the Financial Secretary to the Treasury in the 1924 Labour Government.

I concentrated my efforts on canvassing and helping produce a 'popular' weekly bulletin in the style of a wireless broadcast. We were very up-to-date and even ahead of our time — the fourth issue of the bulletin, 9 May 1929, was intended as a television broadcast with Barney's photograph on the front page! Many friends and supporters assisted Barney in his campaign and by the time of the election there was a considerable amount of optimism that the Liberals would make a strong showing.

The result was announced on Friday 31 May. Captain Bennett topped the poll for Labour with 12,903 and Barney was third with 9,623. It was, in the circumstances, a very good performance. Barney had doubled the Liberal vote at a time when there was a strong national swing to Labour. The Tories were squeezed badly in Cardiff, losing all three seats to Labour. The overall outcome for the Liberals was bitterly disappointing. Expecting to make substantial gains, they won only fifty-nine seats.

In Cardiff, a crowd of about two thousand heard the Lord Mayor announce the result from the balcony of the City Hall. The three candidates followed him, and each made a speech. Barney congratulated the winner and spoke so sportingly that the crowd cheered him to the echo.

Afterwards Sir Lewis Lougher came up to Barney and, very annoyed, said: 'You lost me this seat.' Barney replied, 'What about me? You stopped me from being elected.'

Years later Barney loved to repeat certain anecdotes about his election campaign in Wales. Once at a meeting in Cardiff a heckler shouted out, 'Didn't Lloyd George promise us a land flowing with milk and honey?' Barney answered, 'I have a great respect for Lloyd George, but I cannot put him in the same category with my great ancestor Moses.' Another time when a heckler challenged him with 'Are you a Rechabite?' he replied 'No, I am an Israelite!'

We had already made plans to move to London before Barney was selected as Liberal candidate in Cardiff, and the local party knew this. Barney thought he stood a much better chance of winning a seat in Parliament if he was at the centre of national political life.

The Cardiff Jewish community gave him a farewell banquet at the Park Hotel, with 450 guests attending, including the Lord Mayor. Barney was presented with a beautiful illuminated album signed by the principal officers of all the local Jewish societies with which he had been associated, and a Jewish

National Fund Certificate marking the inscription of his name in the Golden Book.

The opportunity to move had come when Barney was offered the position of solicitor and secretary to two new companies being run by my father's firm, Cavendish Furniture Company and James Woodhouse and Son. We bought a house in Brampton Grove, Hendon, the only made-up street in the area at that time. When we moved in that November, Hendon was still like the countryside, and I would take Greville in his pram to watch the cows grazing.

I was used to London, but for Barney, it was an unfriendly place where he felt a complete stranger. He was desperately unhappy. He missed the close-knit provincial life which he had known since childhood. In Cardiff, he was a leading public figure — in London, nobody knew him.

His one real pleasure was the Zionist movement. When he lived in Wales had had been a provincial member of the Zionist Federation Executive, and now he was co-opted as a London member. London was very much the centre of world Zionist activity at that time, because Britain held the Palestine Mandate. The Zionist meetings invariably went on until late into the night, and Barney was in his element there. When he attended his first London meeting I expected him to be home in time for his dinner. Eight o'clock passed, then nine, then ten. By midnight I was so terribly worried that I phoned the number of Percy Baker, the only other Executive member whose name I knew. Mrs Baker answered. I asked, 'Is your husband at home?' Obviously shocked she said 'No — who are you?' I then explained the reason for my anxiety. 'Oh, you don't have to worry,' she reassured me, 'they never come back from the Zionist Executive before one in the morning.' Barney roared with laughter when I told him. For years afterwards he used to tell people how I had asked for Percy Baker in the middle of the night. Poor Percy and his wife and son were killed during the Second World War by a direct hit on their garden air-raid shelter.

One day in September 1930 a Mr Manus telephoned and told Barney that Lloyd George wanted to see him. Wondering what it was all about, Barney made an appointment to see Lloyd George at Liberal headquarters. The Liberal leader told him

that the Labour Member of Parliament for the London constituency of Whitechapel and St. George's, Harry Gosling, President of the Transport and General Workers Union, was dying,
and that when the by-election was called, he wanted Barney to
fight the seat for the Liberals.

At the 1929 election Gosling had won easily for Labour with
13,701 votes. The Liberal had been second with 4,521, and the
Tory third with 3,478. Gosling had had a big majority of 9,180.

Barney looked at the figures and said that since he had
already fought a seat with a four thousand Liberal poll, he felt
he was entitled to something better at his second attempt. Lloyd
George, whose patronage was vital at this time, since he controlled a private fund (the famous 'Chest', acquired by selling
peerages to wealthy individuals when he had been Prime Minister) told Barney:

> We don't expect you to win the seat but we want the
> Liberal vote to be increased. I have looked at all the
> election results in the country and yours was by far the
> best. We want you to do well in Whitechapel and hearten
> the Liberals in the country before the next General Elec-
> tion. The way I see things at the moment, it cannot be far
> off.'

He also promised Barney that the Liberal Party would pay all
the expenses for the fight, would provide him with the very best
agent in the country, and that after it was over Barney could
have the choice of any seat where there was not already an
adopted candidate. Barney said he would think it over. We
discussed it at home and decided he had nothing to lose. I was
delighted to think that he would be involved again in the hurly
burly of political life. So Barney accepted the offer. A few weeks
later Harry Gosling died.

Meanwhile, the Passfield White Paper was published by the
Labour Government in October 1930. It departed from the
British policy followed since the 1917 Balfour Declaration and
introduced severe restrictions on Jewish immigration into
Palestine. This was to become an important issue in the by-
election.

The Whitechapel and St George's Liberal Association still

had to choose the candidate, and despite Lloyd George's backing there were others who were very anxious to fight the seat. Miss Miriam Moses, a very prominent local social worker and councillor, was keen to be the candidate. She had considerable support, and when Barney went down to the meeting on 3 November 1930 he had no hope of being adopted. I went round to the Brady Boys Club while he went to the meeting.

Afterwards he told me that once Miriam had spoken and been questioned somebody called out: 'What about this fellow that headquarters want? Let's hear him.' Barney was very astute, and started his speech by saying that if Miriam was adopted he would work for her, fight hard and do his best to help them in the campaign. Then he launched into his beautiful and compelling oratory. The local association was completely overwhelmed. They had never heard a Liberal speak like him and were very excited. When it came to the vote he won easily.

I expected him to call for me at the club. Imagine my surprise when he arrived with a smart-looking gentleman sporting a buttonhole, whom he smilingly introduced to me as Mr W. C. Johnson JP, the President of the Whitechapel Liberal Association, adding: 'I have been adopted as Liberal candidate.' I was astounded, and at the same time delighted.

Barney began work immediately at the Liberal Committee Rooms on Osborn Street, EC1 (now demolished) a few yards from Blooms, the kosher restaurant. He used to go in there to eat when he had time, and crowds would gather outside the windows watching him. Eventually, the date of the by-election was fixed for 3 December 1930.

This parliamentary seat in the heart of working-class London was regarded by the Transport and General Workers Union as their very own, and they were anxious not to lose it. In a constituency which was one-third Jewish, the fact that the Passfield White Paper had just been issued gave them reason to be apprehensive. Ernest Bevin, Secretary of the Union, held long consultations with a delegation of the Jewish Labour movement in Palestine, the Poale Zion, who were in London at that time. They were Haim Arlosoroff, Joseph Sprinzak, Dov Hoz and S. Kaplansky.

Bevin argued that not everyone in the Labour Movement was in favour of the White Paper, and that if the Jews supported the

Labour candidate it would greatly help them in their future negotiations with the government. He persuaded them, and they agreed to throw their support behind Labour. But there was a good deal of heart-searching on the Jewish side, and many members of the British Poale Zion were not convinced.

It was an exceptionally rough campaign, especially at the meetings of the Labour candidate. I can remember one such rally where the police had to be called in, and at which Dov Hoz was howled down. The only speaker who got a hearing that night was Ernest Bevin.

During the campaign Hoz accused Barney of exploiting the White Paper for his own political ends, and this was echoed by others. Barney resented the implication very much.

Apart from the Liberal and Labour candidates, there were two others. One was Loel Guinness, who had stood before for the Tories. The other was Harry Pollitt, the leader of the Communist Party.

Barney was a fantastic candidate. He addressed enormous meetings on the street corners of Whitechapel throughout the campaign.

It was lucky that he had very powerful lungs and a voice which carried far. The enthusiasm in Whitechapel was intense and supporters of the Liberals and of the Jews came from all over London to help him.

The people of Whitechapel and St George's found a young man in their midst who never seemed to tire; who addressed meetings on street corners until late at night surrounded by massive crowds. He was a great propagandist for the Jews and for the Jewish National Home, and also a great believer in the Liberal programme. Very quickly he became a sort of folk hero. All the little boys and girls in Whitechapel used to sing:

> *Vote, vote, vote for Barney Janner,*
> *Kick old Hall in the eye,*
> *When he comes to the door,*
> *We will punch him in the jaw,*
> *And he won't come voting any more.*

Men who have done well all over the world met Barney later in life and told him how, as little boys, they used to sing this song.

Hundreds still say they had canvassed for him.

There were issues of great importance to the Jewish people, but it has to be remembered that the Whitechapel end of the constituency was only one-third of it. There were also St George's, Shadwell and Wapping. Shadwell was a very broken-down neighbourhood. In Cable Street, St George's, there lived many sailors from all over the world, while down at Wapping, near the docks, they used to say it was not safe for a Jew to walk alone. Whitechapel itself was very different from the present day. It was practically entirely Jewish, and most of its inhabitants were immigrants from abroad who had fled from the pogroms of Eastern Europe. Unfortunately, many of them had not bothered to become naturalized, so they could not vote.

It was a real community. Despite the poverty and the grinding hard work, the people had brought their love of education with them from 'the old country', and wanted their children to go to school, attend the Talmud Torah, and grow up to be fine British men and women.

The constituency as a whole was a varied and exciting place, with the open-air markets on Wentworth Street and Watney Street and Hessel Street, and the shouting of the hawkers in Petticoat Lane, a great tourist attraction on Sundays with its 'Mock Auctions'. They used to say you could lose your watch at the beginning of the Lane and buy it back at the end.

It is interesting how it got its name, or nickname, for actually it was called Middlesex Street. In the olden days the Mile End Road was a fashionable area; it was wide and lined with trees. After church, the ladies used to parade down the streets showing off their smart petticoats. Hence the name, Petticoat Lane.

The Tower of London was in the division and all the Beefeaters had votes. Unfortunately for Barney, they nearly all voted Tory. The Royal Mint was there in Royal Mint Street. Spitalfields fruit and vegetable market was a landmark — originally it was the silk market founded by the Huguenots.

Above all, this was the throbbing centre of Jewish cultural life, with the Yiddish theatre, the Jewish hospital and the headquarters of the Friendly Societies and many other organizations. Every prominent Jew visiting London went to Whitechapel to speak at meetings. With its alleyways and narrow streets it was of constant interest. In Black Lion Yard, off the Whitechapel Road, the local milkman was a Welshman called Jones who advertised outside his yard 'Milk straight from the cow!' which indeed it was in those days.

The Labour Party was really worried about holding the seat and brought down all their big guns: Bevin, Hoz and others. When polling day came, after great excitement and huge crowds at open-air meetings, Barney was defeated by only 1,099 votes. Jimmy Hall received 8,544 votes, Barney 7,445, Loel Guinness 3,735 and Harry Pollitt 2,106. Hall was returned but the Labour Party lost its overall majority.

Barney had made a name among the country's Liberals. Immediately the election was over Lloyd George asked to see him again. When Barney reminded him about the good seat, Lloyd George said: 'Janner, you have done extremely well in Whitechapel and St George's. When you have made a mark in a constituency it is far better to stay there and try to pull over the extra votes than to go and start again in another constituency. Take my advice and fight the same constituency at the next General Election.'

Barney agreed to fight the seat again.

The next election came in October 1931, after Macdonald formed the National Government to cope with the country's financial crisis. A few Labour MPs joined him, but the bulk of the party stayed in opposition. He appointed Sir Herbert Samuel (Liberal) Home Secretary, and the Marquis of Reading, also a Liberal, Foreign Secretary. This caretaker government remained in power for some three months, until Macdonald called a general election for October 1931.

The Liberals were split. In June 1931 Sir John Simon had resigned the Liberal whip. In July Lloyd George had become seriously ill. His followers were led by Sir Herbert Samuel, while Sir John Simon headed a group known as National Liberals. The latter were in complete sympathy with the government, while the Samuelites remained independent Liberals, giving the government only qualified support. They called themselves Liberal and National candidates. Lloyd George faded into the background.

Barney had been adopted as the Liberal candidate early in

October, at the local party rooms, 80 Commercial Road. In his acceptance speech he had urged 'the necessity for national unity in this time of crisis.' I became his election agent.

Barney worked day and night. Conditions in the area were appalling, but he had the gift of being able to lift people out of their misery. That was a very strenuous contest in Whitechapel, described by a local newspaper as 'by far the most entertaining election in East London'. Jimmy Hall, the Labour candidate, was a very decent fellow and at that time Morgan Phillips (later, Secretary of the Labour Party) was his agent.

Barney had been nursing the constituency since the by-election. A local paper said 'the arrival of Mr Barnett Janner in Whitechapel and St George's is of immense importance. He has been nursing the constituency in company with Mrs Janner, and they have undoubtedly made themselves respected and popular, taking part frequently in social gatherings and charitable efforts.'

The Communists said that Barney would not debate with Harry Pollitt; Barney said he would. But he was no fool, and when the Communist agent came to our committee rooms Barney said: 'I'll be chairman for Harry Pollitt and he will be chairman for me.' That way he knew he would get a fair hearing. The meeting took place in the open air on the corner of Cannon Street Road and there must have been two thousand people present.

During the campaign all Ted (Kid) Lewis, the Mosley candidate, could say for the most part was 'Rome wasn't built in a day'. In a rare moment of eloquence he told a *News Chronicle* man: 'I would give the National Government or any other Government a fair chance, but it must always be understood that I shall press upon it the necessity for a policy of real vigour and real action.' The reporter continued: 'When I asked Mr Janner what he thought of it, he took a throat pastille from his pocket, sucked it thoughtfully and counted ten.'

The *Jewish Chronicle*, though it supported Barney's candidacy, as it had done during the 1930 by-election, principally because of Barney's opposition to the Passfield White Paper, did not expect him to win — it wrote: 'Labour is expected to retain the seat without much difficulty.' They were wrong. Barney won the seat with a majority over Jimmy Hall of 1,149 votes. Ted (Kid) Lewis polled 154 votes.

During the count when everyone was shaking hands with everyone else, Ted (Kid) Lewis went up to Harry Pollitt and put out his hand, but Pollitt refused it and turned aside. Lewis said: 'Why, I haven't done anything to you! I haven't harmed you at all!' Harry Pollitt replied: 'Nothing personal, it's just that I never shake hands with a capitalist.' Actually, Lewis did not have two farthings to rub together.

Although they won more seats than in 1929 the Liberals were split three ways. The National Liberals under Sir John Simon had 35 seats; the Samuelite Liberals, of whom Barney was one, had 33 seats; and Lloyd George led a personal group of four Independent Liberals. The Labour Party with 52 seats, was decimated. The Tories won 473 seats and 55·2 per cent of the total vote.

After the declaration of the poll at Limehouse Town Hall, big tough fellows carried Barney shoulder high right through the Whitechapel area shouting at the tops of their voices: 'Janner, the new MP!' Men and women workers were at all the workroom windows waving to him and cheering. It was a thrilling sight.

3 THE MEMBER FOR WHITECHAPEL AND ST GEORGE'S
1931–1935

Barney became a Member of Parliament in 1931. He was thirty-nine years old, which in those days was considered a young age. The 'Londoner's Diary' in the *Evening Standard* said that he made the best maiden speech among the new intake of MPs. 'Both in his beliefs and in his personal appearance he is a Jew of the Jews . . . Yet in Cardiff, where he practised as a solicitor, he was invariably employed by the numerous Arab litigants.'

This was a momentous Parliament. It saw the rise of Hitler, the emergence of Oswald Mosley and his Fascist Party in Britain, and the continuing economic depression. The Labour Party was demoralized, the Liberals were divided, and the Tories dominated Parliament. There was little effective opposition. Ramsay MacDonald had asked for a 'Doctor's Mandate' and the new Government introduced heavy cuts in public spending. Even MPs took a ten per cent cut in salary, leaving them with only £360 a year. It was lucky that Barney had a regular job and that we did not have to rely on his MP's salary. Many of the Labour MPs were literally starving.

Barney made his maiden speech in the Commons on 23 November 1931, in a debate on leasehold reform. The Labour Party was proposing an amendment intended to help the tenant. Barney already had years of experience dealing with housing problems and tenants' rights in his solicitor's practice in Cardiff, and he saw a flaw in the amendment that would have negated the very thing it was trying to achieve. The issue was complicated, but Barney made his point confidently. In the middle of his speech Jimmy Maxton, a fiery Scottish left-winger, rose to intervene: 'The speech which the honourable Member is making is one which we usually expect from the Front Bench.'

Barney came back immediately: 'I am doing my best to help

my honourable Friend and to keep him from ruining the very matter he is trying to bring to the notice of the committee . . . I assure my honourable Friend that, knowing as I do the terrible conditions under which people live, and that these conditions are responsible in many instances for the major portion of the distress, and for a very large proportion of the crime that exists in the country, I am anxious that something should be done in that direction.'

It was contrary to Parliamentary etiquette to interrupt a maiden speech, and Jimmy Maxton, realizing his mistake, said 'I wish to apologize to the honourable Member for interrupting. I had forgotten that he was delivering a maiden speech. My intervention, I am sure, was a compliment to him, because he was doing it with all the assurance of a very old Member.'

One of the first things Barney did when he entered Parliament was to found the Parliamentary Palestine Committee. He knew how important it was to interest MPs in the Jewish National Home and the Zionist Movement, since they could help convince the Government to fulfil its commitments under the terms of the Mandate. As soon as Parliament had assembled after the election, he began talking individually to a large number of MPs. Few of the new Members in the 1931 Parliament were acquainted with Palestine affairs, but he found a considerable number who were prepared to interest themselves in the subject.

Barney later published his own account of the origins and work of the Parliamentary Palestine Committee, which he called a 'striking example of the parliamentarian's desire to act in accordance with his conscience.' The Committee was 'unofficial', different from the Standing Committees of the House, and fuctioned irrespective of the politics of the Government of the day, or of party affiliation. No member of the existing Government could belong to it, so that when the Joint Honorary Secretary, Lord Hartington, was appointed Parliamentary Secretary for the Dominions, he had to resign.

The Jewish National Home was under threat because of differences in interpreting the 1917 Balfour Declaration, and also because of the Shaw and Hope Simpson reports, and the

Passfield White Paper. It was a time when Zionism badly needed support in the House.

But as Barney wrote, 'this group by no means constituted the only friends of Zionism in Parliament'. What distinguished it from the individual supporters was the fact that its members 'made Zionism one of their Parliamentary duties. Some of them acted out of deep Christian conviction; others were moved by the sheer dimensions of the tragedy of Jewish homelessness and persecution; while there were some, like Josiah Wedgwood, Lloyd George and his daughter Megan, who were romantic nationalists unable to regard in apathy the possibility of reviving the Jewish nation on a revitalized Jewish soil.'

What united them all was the conviction that 'Zionism was good for Britain', good for British interests in the Middle East, and good for the Commonwealth. It was this attitude that Jos Wedgwood had expressed in his advocacy of making Palestine the 'Seventh Dominion' of the Commonwealth. When Barney made his first speech on Palestine, Jos passed him a pencilled note which Barney kept ever after: 'If you ever want a pro-Zionist speaker and I am free you can rely on me. I have always backed Zionism and I have spoken on the same platform with Weizmann.'

'The Committee did not restrict its activities to Parliamentary advocacy alone,' Barney wrote. 'It sent deputations to the Government, spoke at public demonstrations with members of the Jewish Agency, and grew to know leaders like Weizmann, [Moshe] Sharett, [Selig] Brodetsky, and [Berl] Locker intimately.'

To get the Committee going in the new Parliament of 1931 a letter was sent in December of that year to Members of the House inviting them to a special meeting to form the Committee. It was signed by John Buchan (Conservative), Josiah Wedgwood (Labour), Leopold S. Amery (Conservative), the Duchess of Atholl (Conservative), Sir Austen Chamberlain (Conservative), Winston Churchill (Conservative), R. D. Denman (Conservative), Megan Lloyd George (Liberal), the Marquess of Hartington (Conservative), George Lansbury (Labour), Major Harry Nathan (Labour) and James A. de Rothschild (Liberal), as well as by Barney. The meeting was well attended. Professor Selig Brodetsky gave an account of the position in Palestine, and explained the difficulties and problems.

John Buchan (later Lord Tweedsmuir) and Jos Wedgwood were elected joint Chairmen of the Committee. Barney and the Marquess of Hartington were elected joint Honorary Secretaries, and Victor Cazalet, Honorary Treasurer.

When Lord Hartington, father of the present Duke of Devonshire, was later given a Government ministry, he wrote to Barney saying that his one regret was that he would have to give up his office in the Parliamentary Palestine Committee. Among other members of the Committee were Herbert Morrison and Walter Elliot, whose widow, Lady Elliot, is a keen supporter of Israel.

Barney continued to run the Committee during the time he was in Parliament and even during the years that he was out of the House. He carried on with it when he returned to Parliament in 1945. It is now known as the British–Israel Parliamentary Group, affiliated to the Inter-Parliamentary Union.

In 1934, with the rise of Hitler and the growth of antisemitism, Barney conceived the idea that if Members of Parliament could see Jews at work in their own land they would have living proof that the accusations made by the Nazis were false. He did not want MPs to feel in any way beholden to an organization, so he collected money privately from a few individuals. Thus on 17 May 1934 the first ever group of Parliamentarians left for Palestine, consisting of Captain William F. Strickland (Tory), Major H. A. Proctor (Tory), Charles H. Summersby (Liberal), Barney and me. I did the organization for the trip, saw to it that everyone was on time and generally looked after the health and problems of the party, and the luggage.

After a stopover in Alexandria and Cairo, we sailed for Palestine. At six o'clock the following morning as the ship neared Haifa, we all went up on deck. What a thrill! Barney and I were speechless when we saw Mount Carmel looming in the distance. As we passed the white stone breakwater enclosing the harbour we could see Haifa in all her beauty nestling against the mountainside, a scene neither of us ever forgot.

It was some time later that Barney told me how apprehensive

he had been as that moment approached. Here was the land of which he had dreamed so long, and for which he had worked so hard. Would it come up to his expectations? He was delighted to discover that not only did it not let him down, but that the National Home and its people were even better than he had dared to hope.

We were greeted in Tel Aviv by Mayor Dizengoff and the members of the Tel Aviv municipality at the then Municipal Buildings. Dizengoff was a marvellous character, one of those who had founded Tel Aviv on the sand dunes. In Tel Aviv we attended the Levant Fair, a British trade exhibition run on a large scale and opened by the High Commissioner, Sir Arthur Wauchope, who also entertained us all to dinner at Government House. Barney and Will Strickland broadcast on the radio.

The party also went to the Dome of the Rock and had a long talk over coffee with the Mufti of Jerusalem, who expressed his strong opposition to the immigration of Jews into Palestine. (At the outbreak of the Second World War he went to Hitler's Germany.)

We visited nearly every part of the country, including what was then Transjordan. In Amman we had a session with the British Resident, who was very anti-Zionist and pro-Arab. His home was filled with all kinds of rugs and other things which the Arabs had given to him.

On returning home, these MPs became great protagonists of the Jewish National Home. They made continuous representations to the Colonial Secretaries Sir Philip Cunliffe Lister, Ormsby-Gore (later Lord Harlech), Arthur Creech Jones and others.

The following year, in March 1935, Barney took another party to Palestine under the same conditions, this time arriving at Jaffa. In the group were Sir Murdoch McKenzie Wood OBE (Liberal), and his wife Lady McKenzie Wood, Sir Wilfred Sugden (Tory), R. H. Morgan (Tory), who represented the National Union of Teachers in Parliament, and Tom Williams (Labour), later Minister of Agriculture.

On our way to Palestine we stayed in Alexandria and Cairo for a couple of days, as we had done in 1934. In those days there was little flying. We travelled to and from Haifa on French ships of the Messageries Maritimes which always stopped over in

Egypt. There we spent an evening with the leaders of the Jewish community. My diary of that visit says:

In April 1935 visited the Grand Mufti. Good-looking man but with wicked eyes. One of the MPs asked a question which drew a flood of explanation from His Eminence translated by his secretary. He said, among other things, that the Jews were the poison in the bloodstream and must be eradicated before one could consider what could be done. Then, 'The Government favoured the Jews and had forgotten the Arabs fought in the war on their side' (what a lie) 'and forgotten pledges to the Arabs.'

12 April left for Transjordan motoring over the Allenby Bridge. Stopped and talked to various workers in the field. They all said the land was poor as nobody had money to buy seeds. We later heard that many people had died of 'malnutrition'. Arrived at Amman the capital, a straggling village with a splendid amphitheatre. We wondered when the population had been large enough to fill such a place.

13 April. We had an interview with the Emir Abdullah in his palace. We were introduced by his physician, and in the palace during the audience were Colonel Cox, the British Resident, and the Emir's Secretary. The Emir said that everything in Transjordan was good — people contented, land greatly improved compared with fifteen years ago; the new method of taxation generally satisfactory to the people. He denied that the country needed money. In answer to a question whether there was a move by the Transjordanians towards Palestine he said, 'No, very little.' (We had seen dozens of them crossing into Palestine with their families and baggage.) He refused to answer a question as to whether any people died of starvation last year. When asked if he would like to question the MPs he said, 'I will not speak as the Emir Abdullah but as an individual.' Later when asked, 'Would you welcome any form of immigration?' he answered, 'Never Jewish immigration.' Then he qualified this by saying 'I do not speak as the Emir Abdullah. I give the opinion of the Palestine Arabs which I have

got from the press.' A very remarkable statement.

Another note of interest to this biography is:

> 18 April. Jerusalem — Went for a walk round Talbiah.
> Barney knew every Tom, Dick and Harry — he might
> have been on Hampstead Heath. He is amazingly well
> known over here.

With this party, apart from visiting the whole country, we also attended the Second Maccabiah, the Jewish international Games. They were opened by the High Commissioner, Sir Arthur Wauchope. Henry Mond (later the second Lord Melchett) was the President.

The first Maccabiah had been held in 1932. At that time Barney had successfully intervened with Mr Parkinson, who was in charge of Palestine affairs in the Middle East Department of the Colonial Office, to arrange group passports and a group visa for the athletes. Now, in 1935, the British Government did not want to allow the German–Jewish athletes to enter Palestine because they feared that they would not go back to Germany. Barney made constant representation behind the scenes and eventually the Government gave in, on condition that Henry Mond and Barney sign that they would personally see to it that all the Germans went back to Germany. Did they? Who counted? Barney was also instrumental in getting the headquarters of the whole Maccabi Movement taken out of Germany and settled in London.

The 1935 visit coincided with Passover and we all attended *Seder* at the home of Dr Nahum Sokolow's daughter. Dr Sokolow, a great Zionist leader and a very impressive figure, presided, dressed in robes and a multi-coloured embroidered cap.

This visit, too, had highly successful results. The members of the delegation subsequently worked hard in Parliament and in the parliamentary committee to keep other MPs informed of the true position. Later, during the war when Tom was Minister of Agriculture and urging everyone to 'dig for victory', he used to say that he had learnt a lot from seeing what was being done on the land in Palestine.

During his years as an MP in the 1931–35 Parliament, Barney made a real name for himself. He was tremendously active, not only within his constituency, but also on the broader scene, concerning himself with matters of national importance, with international affairs and with everything touching Jewish life and Zionism. In December 1931 the *Jewish Chronicle* wrote:

> Mr Barnett Janner is winning his spurs early, and in a House of Commons composed of so many young men of promise it is gratifying to see that he has succeeded in getting over the first fence with no little credit. He has already shown his strong Jewish allegiance . . .

But it was not only as a Jewish MP that Barney was known and would want to be remembered. He had time for everybody, whatever their origins or beliefs, and his interests ranged very wide. Barney's help for Stepney Catholics is a good example.

At the end of 1931 he was approached by Canon Ring, who was head of the Catholic community in Stepney. Canon Ring was a remarkable character — forceful, powerful, political, and very friendly and kind. He usually got what he wanted but in doing so he made friends and not enemies. St Mary's and St Michael's Catholic Schools were overflowing and many hundreds of Catholic children could not receive a Catholic education. Canon Ring wanted Barney's help in approaching the Board of Education to obtain permission to enlarge the school.

Barney went down to the school, thoroughly investigated the position, and became convinced that Canon Ring was right. He then arranged to see Donald Maclean, the Chairman of the Board of Education, who had previously refused permission for the enlargement of the school. Canon Ring accompanied Barney and together they succeeded in changing the Minister's mind.

The Catholic community in Stepney was jubilant. At St Patrick's Day celebrations in 1932 at Limehouse Town Hall, Canon Ring paid a grateful tribute to Barney. In the following year Barney and I went to the opening ceremony of the New Johnson Street School, where Barney was greeted as the Guest of Honour. As we walked down Johnson Street people cheered and clapped him, and he was given an ovation in the school hall.

46

When we visited Palestine in 1934 we went into the Ecce Homo Convent on the Via Dolorosa in Jerusalem, where Barney conveyed greetings from Canon Ring. He also paid for a stone to be inserted in the convent wall in Canon Ring's name.

It was while he was MP for Whitechapel that he started the practice of taking groups of children round Parliament and then giving them tea across the road at Lyons Tea Shop, which was next door to Westminster Tube Station. He used to pay 1s 6d and the children ate a full three-course tea. They always had a marvellous time. Each child went away with an autographed picture of Barney, inscribed: 'Souvenir of a visit to Parliament'.

A vivid illustration of the impact these visits had is contained in a letter Barney received on 29 January 1976 from the well-known actor Alfred Marks, who wrote:

> At that time (in the 30's) I was a pupil of the Jews' Free School in Bell Lane. As such I have fond memories of your association with the school. A visit from Barnett Janner MP was an occasion to look forward to. In fact, my first visit to the Houses of Parliament was made on a tour which you organized and escorted. The impressed and excited schoolboy whose trembling hand you held was mine.

Barney continued this practice when he became MP for Leicester West in the 1945 election, until Lyons closed down. After that we used to give the children tea at the House of Commons, which was very much more expensive, until the cafeteria could not cope with the large parties that he brought. However, all the children got the souvenir photograph.

There was an amusing sideline: thousands of children in London and in Leicester had these photographs, of which they were very proud, and many of Barney's opponents used to say goodhumouredly: 'I have to have your photograph stuck up in my child's room although I don't belong to your Party!'

Barney became an integral part of the teeming Jewish life of Whitechapel and his tour of East End synagogues on Yom Kippur became an East End tradition. He would meet people, talk, give sermons, his indefatigable energy taking him on from one synagogue to the next. All the time he was fasting, observing the traditions of the holiest day in the Jewish year. It was a practice he kept up throughout his life, long after he was no longer MP for the area. When Dr Maurice Heller, remembering his days as a Canadian Officer, wrote to me from Florida after Barney died, he recalled sharing a hotel room with Barney one Yom Kippur eve and the next day, experiencing 'a most memorable time walking miles and miles with him to four or five different synagogues. At each place he was the main speaker of the day and they welcomed him with open arms as if he were the Messiah — every congregant treated him with such reverence.'

Although we lived out in the suburbs, Barney spent much of his time among his constituents. In *East End Story* A. B. Levy writes: 'You saw here in the early 1930s the then Member for Whitechapel, Mr Barnett Janner, exchanging pennies for beigels.'

Joseph Leftwich also recalls that time:

I remember Brodetsky and Janner speaking Yiddish publicly at Jewish functions. I have, for instance, a memory of Janner speaking a good homely natural Yiddish at the opening of the YIVO Exhibition in London, which was opened in Yiddish, of course, by Sholem Asch.

During those years a number of interesting things happened to us, the most important of which was the birth of our lovely daughter Ruth. In 1931 Barney was presented at a Royal levée, dressed in full regalia, including the ceremonial sword which gave him a lot of trouble. The following year I was presented at Court by the Duchess of Devonshire (grandmother of the present Duke) who was Mistress of the Robes. It was, of course, all part of being the wife of an MP.

Lady Astor, the first woman elected to Parliament, was very fond of Barney. Once she invited us to a party at her magnificent home in St James's Square to meet the Prince of Wales (later Edward VIII). Beforehand we had to attend a function with the Tory MP for Mile End, Dr O'Donovan. His wife asked me if I had brought gloves, and I replied innocently, 'No, why?' She said: 'You can't shake hands with royalty without gloves.'

As things turned out, the Prince did not receive the guests

with Lord and Lady Astor, so all was well. Suddenly, however, Lady Astor grabbed Barney's arm and said: 'Come along, Janner, I want to introduce you to the Prince.' We went to the other end of the ballroom, and there I had to shake hands without gloves. I felt like a Bateman cartoon, caught with large bare arms for all to see.

The Prince was very friendly, and said to Barney, 'Your face looks very familiar,' to which Barney replied: 'When you opened the new wing at Cardiff College I was the fellow in the fourth row, three seats from the right.' They both laughed heartily.

That summer we went to a beautiful garden party at the Astor country house at Cliveden. I scarcely think that qualified us as members of the subsequently famous 'Cliveden set.'

Barney was one of the first to realize the danger inherent in Hitler's rise to power. A group of German Jews was sent over to England to reassure British Jews that what was being said about Hitler's actions against the Jews was false. They went to see Barney in his office and begged him to lock the doors. Their families were still in Germany so they had to be very careful, but they desperately wanted to unburden themselves to someone and to tell the truth about how bad things really were.

So when Barney raised the matter in a Foreign Affairs debate in the House of Commons, he knew what he was talking about. A Jewish Tory MP came up to him and said 'You can't talk about the Jews here, Janner. They don't like it, so don't say anything.' Barney literally felt sick and went out into the lobby to get some water. There he met Rufus Isaacs (Lord Reading) and told him what had happened. Lord Reading said, 'Don't take the slightest notice, go in and speak, and say what you have to say.'

This was probably the first time that a Jew had had the courage to stand up in the Commons and speak on behalf of the Jews. When Lord Reading died in 1935 his widow wrote to Barney: 'My husband believed in you so much and was so profoundly grieved when the election went against you. He told me at the time how much he felt you had been an influence for good in the last Parliament and how much he looked forward to your return.'

Within the Jewish community, concern at the position of the

Jews in Germany had been expressed for some time. But there were always people who refused to believe that anything really terrible could happen. After all, they argued, Jews had been living in Germany for so long, and were so much part of German life, that it was inconceivable Hitler's antisemitism could do very much harm. There were also those who said that if Hitler ever came to power he would tone down his anti-Jewish rhetoric because the business of government would civilize him. So when Hitler did seize power in March 1933, and there seemed no sign of his antisemitism abating, there was shock and consternation among Jews everywhere. The problem was, what to do about it?

Naturally, Barney joined other Jews and non-Jews in the various organizations and committees set up to help German Jewry. But as an MP he clearly saw it as his duty to try to influence the Government of the day to bring pressure to bear on Germany.

It was on 31 March 1933 that he first raised the question of the treatment of Jews in Germany in the House. Sir John Simon, Foreign Secretary in the National Government, had been asked by Commander Locker Lampson whether he would raise the issue of the position of German Jews at the next meeting of the Council of the League of Nations. In a supplementary question Barney asked whether Germany's anti-Jewish policy was not a matter affecting international relations within the sense of Article II of the Covenant of the League. Sir John seemed to think that the situation was not covered by the Covenant, but he was sympathetic to the concern being expressed in the Commons.

Barney came back to the issue again on 6 April when he asked whether a report from the British Ambassador in Berlin on the treatment of Jews had been received. The reply was unsatisfactory, so he asked Sir John again on 10 April. But there was still no definite response.

Concern within the Jewish community was increasing, particularly in the East End. In Whitechapel posters and placards appeared, calling for a boycott of German goods. The police took objection to the posters and ordered them to be taken down. Questioned by Clement Attlee in the House of Commons on 10 March, the Home Secretary, Sir John Gilmour, said that the police feared a breach of the peace would occur because of the strong feelings the posters would arouse. But Barney pointed out to him that the placards had been exhibited for about two weeks without any trouble. Sir John did not know this, and after repeated questioning said that the posters could be put up again, to the applause of the House.

In fact, the night before, Barney had been in Whitechapel talking to police officers who explained to him their reasons for ordering the posters to be removed. As Barney told the *Evening Standard*: 'This was done, I am sure, not out of any opposition to the boycott which has been instituted, but more in the nature of friendly advice to avoid possible trouble.' After Barney spoke to the police and things were smoothed over, permission was given for the posters to be replaced.

In a telling speech in the House of Commons on 13 April in a Foreign Affairs debate, Barney dealt with the plight of German Jewry. He spoke as a member of the Jewish community representing a constituency 'where the heartbeat of the Jewish community is so strong'. He urged the Government to act, saying:

> The fact which is most disturbing to the civilized people of the world is the cruelly deliberate policy of suppression which is now in process of active realization. It is this fact which is filling the world with the gravest anxiety and moving it to protest. There is no question of any exaggeration here. The policy is openly avowed; it is part and parcel — if not the whole — of the Nazi programme, which seeks to extirpate all non-Aryan influence from the national life. Its operation in practice is manifested in the columns of the Nazi press, which daily publishes long lists of Jewish doctors driven from hospitals, Jewish lawyers and judges expelled from the courts and Jewish nurses prevented from carrying on their merciful work . . . In fact night after night Nazi spokesmen proclaim on the wireless that Jewry will be destroyed. Jews believe that appeals made by this House, and from the British people — ever the guardians of religious liberty — will not go unheeded.

Early in May a Special Emergency Committee dealing with the German situation called a protest meeting at the Whitechapel

Art Gallery. Lord Mount Temple presided and the speakers included the Rev. S. C. Carpenter, Sir George Jones MP, Mr Holford Knight KC, MP, Mr Charles Dymond (Editor of the *Catholic Herald*) and Barney. When Barney spoke he received a great ovation. He felt that no differences of religious opinion could be allowed to stand in the way of their united protest, which was being raised from everywhere. The Nazis had instilled poison into the minds of decent German people for many years. They had to be made to realize that human beings in a civilized age could not carry on in that manner.

He was tireless in his efforts to bring the situation to public attention, and thereby encourage the Government to do something about it. In May he was at the new Town Hall in Pontypridd at a meeting organized by the League of Christian Churches to protest against the treatment of Jews in Germany. George Lansbury MP, the Labour Party leader, also spoke to the three thousand people who came to the meeting.

At the same time Barney was raising in the Commons the specific problem of the Jews in Upper Silesia who were ostensibly covered by a special international agreement.

A speech he made on this subject incurred the anger of Herr Silex, the London correspondent of the *Deutsche Allgemeine Zeitung*, so Barney was denounced in the Nazi press.

For Barney the problem of German Jewry was directly linked to the fate of Jews in Palestine and the future of the Jewish National Home. He was anxious for immigration certificates to be released for German Jews, and put this to the Colonial Secretary, Sir Philip Cunliffe-Lister. Back in March he had attended a meeting in Aldgate, presided over by the Rev. J. K. Goldbloom, at which he angrily attacked certain German Jews who had expressed their loyalty to Germany, and their desire to co-operate with German nationalists. He called them 'irresponsible'. He had few illusions about the way in which they should be saved. For them Zionism was the answer.

Since arriving in London Barney was increasingly active in the Zionist Movement, mainly through his involvement with the Zionist Federation, but he was also becoming active internationally. He first attended a Zionist Congress as an elected delegate at the seventeenth Congress in Basle, from June to July 1931. It was an eventful occasion. Nahum Sokolow was elected leader of the World Zionist Organization, replacing Chaim Weizmann.

There was an uproar when Vladimir Jabotinsky, head of the Revisionists, tore up his credentials as a delegate and stormed out of the hall. Barney witnessed it all and with the other delegates from Britain reported on the proceedings to the Executive Council of the Zionist Federation on 27 July. In January 1932 he was elected a London Vice-President of the Zionist Federation.

From the very beginning Barney's Zionism was non-party. He joined the General Zionists because he felt that all Zionists outside Palestine should work together to achieve the National Home. He had admiration and respect for all constructive work being done in and for Palestine. In Parliament during this time he was constantly pressing the Government to encourage investment there and always pointed to that country as an example of a successful economy, made so by the blood and sweat of Jewish pioneers.

He also concerned himself with problems of world peace and disarmament. Addressing a Jewish peace meeting against the use of the hydrogen bomb and the atomic bomb, he said there were certain types of lethal instruments today which could wipe out complete populations; and he urged those who had any voice at all in the control of affairs to make it their business to see that the disarmament conference in Geneva should remove those 'vast and vastly increasing methods of eliminating mankind'.

For the Jews of Germany in 1933 disarmament was a distant thought. In Parliament Barney quoted examples of continued discrimination.

> In Germany today even children of immature age who go to German schools and who happen to be Jewish are asked to rise and sing Nazi songs which are anti-Jewish and invite violence against their own fathers and mothers. If that is the spirit which prevails I can hardly believe that the nation can be thoroughly genuine in asking for peace with its fellow nations.

It was in this speech that he treated the House of Commons to a new version of an old epigram: 'When Adam delved and Eve span, who was then Aryan?' In a later speech he quoted from Hitler's *Mein Kampf* to illustrate what the Jews could expect. Barney thought that the spirit of hate and racial discrimination was a menace to the peace of the world and particularly to people living in Germany. He asked the Foreign Secretary to take the issue to the League of Nations.

One major issue of constant Jewish interest which Barney watched very carefully as an MP was that of *shechita*, the Jewish ritual slaughter of animals for kosher meat. In 1933 the Slaughter of Animals Bill was being piloted through the Commons, and he was vigilant against attempts to have *shechita* banned, put forward by well-meaning people who believed the method to be inhumane. Roy Wise and a number of other MPs had tabled an amendment to the Bill to reject Clause 6, which exempted *Shechita* from the legislation. Barney approached Mr Wise and told him that if the amendment were carried he, Barney, would never be able to eat meat again. The MP was shattered and said 'What do you want me to do?' Barney replied: 'Come and see the animals slaughtered in the Jewish method and then judge for yourself.' In the early hours of a June morning Barney, Roy Wise and Mr Elsley Zeitlyn, Chairman of the Shechita Committee of the Board of Deputies, visited the Islington Abbatoir and saw *shechita* in practice. When Mr Wise returned to the Committee he said that he wished to withdraw the amendment because, having seen the Jewish method of slaughter, he had found it to be 'extremely humane'.

In August 1933 Barney went as a delegate to the eighteenth Zionist Congress in Prague and explained to the gathering what British Zionists had been doing to combat the Passfield White Paper. He stressed the need for unity at a 'time of unprecedented crisis for Judaism'. He spoke about his work with the Parliamentary Palestine Committee; but the main point of his remarks was to protest against the party politics at the Congress, which he saw as a complete waste of time. Referring to England he said:

Our greatest problem is the occasional speeches of Zionist

political party members before authorities and representatives, without any knowledge or experience of the functions and directives of Congress. We do not question the bona fides or the intentions of these people but we do complain of the lack of discipline which is too often an unnecessary hindrance placed in our way. This has to stop in the interest of the Movement!

Congress applauded.

On 28 September 1933, with Parliament in recess, we set sail on the *Majestic* for a tour of the USA and Canada. Barney's main purpose in going was to help enlist support for German Jewry. We travelled to New York, Chicago and Montreal, where Barney spoke to a large gathering of men in the Young Men's Hebrew Association auditorium on Mount Royal Avenue.

In the USA we found American public opinion seriously perturbed by the Nazi attacks on the Jewish people in Germany. Prominent American newspapers gave detailed accounts of the atrocities and the discrimination. American anger was also expressed in public denunciations made by organized Christian communities. American Jewry supported the boycott of Nazi goods, but they were aware of vigorous Nazi propaganda which stirred up anti-Jewish prejudices in the USA, although not too successfully.

Barney was very impressed by the evidence of Jewish activity in the United States and Canada. As he told a *Jewish Chronicle* reporter when we returned:

> One of the most touching sights within my experience was the enthusiasm of the huge audience of some 25,000 people which filled to overflowing the New York Armoury, where a Jewish pageant, 'The Romance of a People', was being performed at the time of my visit.

We returned from Canada in time for the opening of the Parliamentary session, and there was no slowing down for Barney. He was constantly addressing meetings. The local community in Whitechapel knew they had a valuable and approachable MP working for them. One local paper said: 'Mr Barnett Janner is something of a discovery. When he came to Whitechapel and St George's he was taken on trust, and very admirably has he satisfied the confidence of the electors. As a speaker [in the House of Commons] he comes 22nd in a list of 615 members.' He was a wonderful constituency MP; it was through helping people that Barney felt he was achieving most. And he was loyal to his friends and to his past.

He found the time to help in the formation of a London Society of Old Barrians. The first meeting was held at the Polytechnic Institute in the West End with fifty people who came from Barry. Barney was elected President.

Throughout the rest of the life of the 1931–35 National Government Barney denounced Nazism and fought for the German Jews. Early in 1934 he was concerned about the position of Jews in the Saar, which was to be handed back to Germany under the terms of a League of Nations plebiscite. In 1935, not long before the General Election of that year, he again pressed the House of Commons to use its voice to influence Hitler. 'When is this lunacy going to be stopped?' he asked.

> The Jewish people, who after all have their good and bad among them equally with every other people, claim very little, but at least they claim to be loyal to the countries in which they happen to be resident and of which they happen to be citizens. For 1,000 years some of these Jewish families have been living in Germany. Today Germany is asking, as she is rightly entitled to ask, and I do not suggest that she is not entitled to make the claim, that she should be given proper treatment; but when she is asking for that, when she is seeking equity, she must do equity and come with clean hands.

His fellow MPs had by now heard him many times on this subject, but the speaker who followed him in that debate called Barney's speech a 'most eloquent and moving appeal'.

Barney also found it necessary to impress upon his fellow Jews the need to find out exactly what was happening in Germany. More than once he was critical of the Board of Deputies of British Jews for not doing enough to make people aware of what was going on. In July 1935 he told the Board they were making only inadequate efforts to counteract German propaganda — they should 'stop footling and walking round the problem'; the anti-German boycott had to be strengthened.

Besides showing how Palestine offered a solution to the problems of German Jewry, Barney used Zionism and the achievements of the Jewish pioneers as a way of discrediting the despicable ideas of the Nazis. From his very first major speech on Palestine in the Commons he expressed his idea that the Jewish National Home would be an example and a credit to the whole world. The development of the country would only be successful with 'a considerable amount of idealism' and the 'interest of visionaries who believe that that is the only spot in the world where they can find some common centre for their common ideals . . .' Barney was always determined to draw attention to the economic success Palestine was experiencing, and used this as an argument to persuade the Colonial Secretary, Cunliffe-Lister, to grant more Palestine immigration certificates, particularly for use by German Jews. At a time when the rest of the world was undergoing a recession, in Palestine there was a shortage of labour and fruit was rotting on the trees. After our trip to Palestine with a party of MPs in 1934 Barney often asked the President of the Board of Trade about the results of the Levant Fair which we had attended in Tel Aviv — the Federation of British Industries had given a 'very favourable report' on the Fair. For Barney, it was important that Palestine be seen as a successful enterprise, and not as a mad scheme which depended only on charity for survival.

He demonstrated his concern for the Zionist Movement in a variety of ways. Apart from asking questions in Parliament and speaking in debates which dealt with the subject (or ensuring that some other MP supporter of the Zionist Movement was ready to speak), he shared the platform at many public meetings with Dr Weizmann, Dr David Eder, Selig Brodetsky, Sir Osmond d'Avigdor Goldsmid and others. One main theme of these meetings was protesting against the British Government's restrictive immigration policy.

He was a delgate to the 19th Congress in Lucerne in August and September 1935, where he emphasized the practical successes in Palestine and contrasted this with German Nazi propaganda. From Lucerne he travelled to Vienna and Warsaw to get first hand information about Jewish conditions in Europe.

The Parliamentary Palestine Committee remained perhaps his outstanding contribution to the Zionist Movement at this time. Before the 1935 General Election the *Palestine Post* (forerunner to the *Jerusalem Post*) wrote about Barney and the Committee:

> We hope [the Committee] will be strengthened in the new House . . . [it] owed much to the energy and resourcefulness of Mr Barnett Janner who twice visited Palestine with a group of fellow MPs. There was hardly a phase of activity in this country with which he did not concern himself, whether it was of economic, political or cultural weight. The questions he put to the Government were the fruit of careful inquiry and his remarks in a debate gave it a practical flavour. Moreover, he was ever ready to befriend the representatives of Palestine in London, and to lend his influence in favour of every constructive undertaking. Quite irrespective of Party affiliations, we trust that the new Parliament will include him and his friends . . .

The whole time Barney was in Parliament as a Liberal he said that the weakness of the Liberal Party was its freedom — every MP could vote as he wished — there was no party policy. For example, when the question of Ribbon Development came up and a Bill was introduced to restrict the spoiling of the countryside, Barney led for the party and decided its policy. He was in favour of the Bill, and urged that it be placed on the Statute Book as soon as possible.

He used to say to me that he would like to join the Labour Party because he found himself in the lobby with them on every vote. Then, in February 1933, Major Harry Nathan, the Liberal Member for Bethnal Green crossed the floor of the House and joined the Labour Party. That day, Barney returned home and said to me: 'That finishes me for this Parliament. I cannot let the Liberals say that two Jews left them in the course of one Parliament.'

In some ways his concerns were traditionally Liberal. He spoke out against import duties — one of the important pieces of legislation introduced by the National Government — because of the effect taxes on food would have on poorer people. Freedom of the individual was important to him. This extended to trade and commerce, because he was concerned that restrictions would only lead to suffering for the poor. But he also knew that without encouragement from the Government industry would never get back on its feet and unemployment would remain at intolerable levels. In December 1934 he supported the Special Areas Act which recognized the problems of distressed areas, and he urged the Government to give as much help to such areas as they possibly could within the framework of the Act. Having seen the decline of Barry and Cardiff after the First World War, Barney was acutely aware of how the desperate difficulties of areas like Wales could become self-perpetuating, unless there was outside help.

He could talk about the wider issues of economic policy, but it was the economics of ordinary human lives that bothered him most — whether people had adequate houses to live in; what protection they had from unscrupulous landlords; how much rent they had to pay; and when they faced difficulties that required legal assistance, whether they were able to consult a solicitor. And so, whenever housing, rents, or law reform were discussed, Barney had a contribution to make, because he had a wide knowledge that came directly from his own experience as a solicitor dealing with these problems.

To be effective in Parliament on these issues meant mastering intricate and complicated details. One can make impressive speeches about how things should be in an ideal world, but it is far harder trying to improve things within existing legislation, or by calling for new legislation. Barney was an idealist when it came to describing visions of the future but, as a member of a minority party in the House, he knew he had to make the best of what was available and fight against those measures which he was convinced would make the lot of the poor even more unbearable. He had wide interests, including the lot of young people, unemployment assistance, workmen's compensation, rates, insurance, transport, infant and maternal mortality, pensions and the police. These kept him very busy. One local paper wrote:

Police and officials, who are quick and never failing in their judgements of members, regard him as one of the busiest in the House . . . His work in the House, both in debate and in Committee, has brought him shoals of congratulations, particularly for his fight against food taxes and his leadership of the opposition to the Fancy Jewellery Bill. . . . Many of the improvements in the Children's Bill were due to his indefatigable work during the Committee stage.

In August 1933 the *Bulletin* of the Leasehold Reform and Leaseholders' Protection Association called him 'one of the most fearless champions of leasehold reform in public life', and he was unanimously elected Vice-President of the Association.

These were also the interests of his constituents, and Barney always made sure that he knew what mattered to the people he represented in Parliament. If he could pull something off for one of his constituents it gave him the greatest pleasure. He was always going off to some local meeting in Stepney. It might be the Stepney Rotary Club, where he spoke about the persecution of Jews in Germany, or the annual dinner and dance of the Stepney employment exchange, where Barney praised its work and spoke about the Unemployment Bill going through Parliament in 1934. In the same year he opened the Jewish Communal Restaurant and Centre for East London at 214 Whitechapel Road. Together with Isaac Foot MP (former Minister of Mines and father of Michael Foot), he was shouted down by Communists at a meeting of Liberals in St George's Town Hall. Sometimes emergencies took him off in the middle of the night. In January 1935, when the Wapping Gas Works exploded and a big fire raged, Barney went down to see what he could do to help. There was no such thing as a quiet life for the Whitechapel MP.

Life in the East End was colourful; but there was one colour which began to appear in Whitechapel that the Jewish community and everyone else could easily have done without — the black of Mosley's Fascists. Disillusioned with the Labour Party, Mosley left to form his own party — the New Party, in February 1931. After failing to win a single seat in the 1931 election, he went to Italy in 1932 to 'study' Mussolini's Fascist state.

When he got back, it became clear that he had learned his lessons well. He renamed his party the British Union of Fascists (BUF) and adopted a programme of virulent antisemitism. He had brought along the whole bag of Fascist tricks — black shirts, straight arm salute, marches and deliberately provoked street clashes. The BUF never became a mass movement, but it attracted enough recruits and made enough disturbance to become a nasty menace. Its natural field of battle was the East End with its large Jewish population.

Barney had been denouncing Fascism for several years — and here it was at his doorstep. Now he redoubled his efforts against the menace on the home front, addressing meeting after meeting. When the British Anti-Nazi Council jointly with the Non-Sectarian Ex-Servicemen's Committee held a mass demonstration at the Grand Palais, Commercial Road, in September 1935, Barney was there. He lashed out at Nazi brutality, adding hopefully: 'When Germany realizes what the world thinks of her she will not only hang her head in shame, but will rise against the oppressor in her midst.'

The following month there was a massive anti-Nazi demonstration in Hyde Park, attended by a hundred thousand people. Barney's fearless denunciation of the Fuehrer and all his works rang out across the park. He may have known that he was already high on Hitler's hit list, but it did not deter him.

The life of the Parliament in which he sat was drawing to a close, and a new election was called for 14 November 1935. In 1931 it had been a four-cornered contest in Whitechapel. This time there was neither a Communist nor a Tory candidate, so it became a straight fight between Labour and Liberal. Jimmy Hall was again the Labour candidate. Barney stood as the 'Liberal and Anti-Fascist' candidate. This angered Walter Citrine, the Trade Union Congress General Secretary, who claimed in the *Daily Herald* that this was a ploy to gain credit among Jewish voters.

Barney was at home in the House of Commons, had mastered its ways and believed deeply in the democratic system of which Parliament was the guardian and practical expression. He was deeply disturbed by events in Europe, and by the presence of Fascism in Britain. In a debate on the Unemployment Assistance Bill in February 1935, when he spoke out against the

Means Test, he called on the Minister to consider defects in the system and said:

> Will he understand that, if we do not deal with these things in the House, we shall find ourselves in a position that will enable dictators . . . to rear their heads here as they are doing in other places?

In similar vein, speaking at the annual banquet of the East London Licensed Victuallers he said that Parliament and all it stood for were being put to the severest test that any institution had been called upon to face, but he hoped we would emerge with the present system victorious. If not, there was not the slightest doubt that the whole future of the world would be adversely affected.

At this time an evening newspaper, *The Star*, wrote: 'Mr Janner has won golden opinions in Whitechapel since he went to the House of Commons. It would be a calamity if his services were lost to the House of Commons and the nation.' But we knew it was going to be an uphill struggle.

I was election agent once again. We operated out of the Central Committee Rooms at 94 Commercial Road. It was my birthday during the campaign, and all our helpers presented me with a birthday cake — but I could give none of them a piece, because by distributing it I might have been prosecuted for bribery under the Corrupt Practices Act!

Morgan Phillips was Jimmy Hall's agent. He said that he had read every word Barney ever uttered in Parliament, in order to try to use something against him, but he could find nothing at all. He always maintained that Barney was the best candidate in the country from any party, and the Labour Party worked extremely hard to dislodge him.

Barney decided to campaign on his record. He would appear at election meetings accompanied by several friends carrying bound volumes of Hansard containing his speeches in the House. Each time he and the books arrived the audience would call out 'Here come the prizes.' When someone questioned his record on a certain issue, he would look up exactly what he had said and refute the accusation. For example, his Labour opponents tried to suggest that he had opposed children's allowances. But Barney was able to show that he was a vigorous member of the Committee which secured milk for schoolchildren and that he had also, for months, urged on the Minister the need for higher unemployment allowances.

The Liberals were only a shadow of their former selves, putting up 161 candidates but returning only 21 MPs. The Tories had 432 seats and a massive majority (though the title of 'National Government' was retained). Labour recovered from the disastrous defeat of 1931, and won 154 seats. This time Barney lost to Jimmy Hall, 13,374 to 11,093. It was a rough and noisy election, with the Communist withdrawal giving Labour the edge. Barney polled more votes than he had in the previous election, but his total was not enough to give him victory. In his speech at the Limehouse Town Hall when the result was announced, he reminded his opponent that he had a responsibility to the Communists whose vote of over two thousand had given him the election victory. He also drew attention to the incessant interruptions at his election meetings, which he said did no good to anyone.

Barney never expressed disappointment after his defeat. Naturally, he was upset, but he did not show it. He looked ahead, prepared to meet whatever was to come next.

4 THE YEARS IN THE WILDERNESS
   1935–1945

' **M**r Barnett Janner goes out of Parliament to the regret of a host of friends and the whole of Jewry whose interests he so stoutly defended', wrote the *Western Mail*, the leading South Wales daily paper. I had written to Sir Wilfred Sugden, the Tory MP and member of the Parliamentary Palestine Committee (he was in the 1935 party to Palestine), commiserating with him on the loss of his seat in the election. He replied: 'What a kindly thing to do: altho' Barney and yourself had the fight of your lives, you had a thought also for a defeated Tory!' And he added: 'Please tell Barney we must continue our small efforts on behalf of the Jews though we are now *out* of Parliament.'

Some months later Barney decided that he must join the Labour Party, but before doing so he went to see the President of the Whitechapel Liberals, W. C. Johnson, Chairman of the local magistrates' bench, a keen worker at Toynbee Hall, an extremely good Christian and a very helpful friend and supporter. Barney said he saw him in Toynbee Hall while he was preparing a collection of tennis balls for children, and told him he was very embarrassed but that he had something to say to him. Mr Johnson said: 'You need not be embarrassed at all, I know exactly what you have come about.'

Barney said: 'Well, how could you possibly?'

'It's been obvious right along that you are on the left wing of the Liberal Party so I assume you have come to tell me that you want to join the Labour Party.'

'Yes,' said Barney.

'Have they offered you a good seat? They should do.'

'No. I haven't even approached them yet. I will just join as an ordinary member. I wanted to talk it over with you first.'

Mr Johnson said 'Of course we shall all be sorry, but if you want to join Labour by all means do.' He then wished Barney the best of luck.

Later, a very singular thing happened. After Barney had

joined the Labour Party, the Liberal Association in Whitechapel passed a vote of thanks to him for what he had done in Parliament. This was tremendously generous, and I doubt that it will ever happen again.

His decision was announced finally in September 1936. According to some press reports at the time Barney's decision 'to desert Liberalism and join the Socialist Party has come as a considerable surprise and something of a shock to his political associates at Westminster, Whitechapel, Cardiff and Barry.' Barney had told one reporter that the Labour Party's policy was the only effective way of securing 'a strong progressive Government that would safeguard democratic institutions at home and ensure international peace and goodwill, the reorganization of a strong League of Nations and the maintenance of collective security.' Everybody knew that he had frequently voted with the Labour Party, especially on such fundamental issues as unemployment, housing and international peace. In fact, most people had expected him to cross the floor.

Not being an MP did not mean that he had less to do. He was still joint Honorary Secretary of the Parliamentary Palestine Committee. In May 1936 he arranged for another group of MPs to visit the Levant Fair. The group included Wing-Commander A. W. H. James (Tory), Sir Joseph Lamb (Tory), Mr H. Holdsworth (Liberal), Mr Morgan Jones (Labour) and Captain Will Strickland (Tory). However, the Foreign Office made us cancel the trip at the last minute because of the disturbances which had broken out in Palestine, and which were to last, off and on, until the outbreak of the Second World War.

In March of that year Barney was elected President of the Association of Jewish Friendly Societies, succeeding Lt Col C. Waley Cohen CMG. The Association, with a membership of 50,000, was the largest organized Jewish body in the country. Its societies had been founded by immigrant Jews to provide social welfare and mutual aid. Barney conceived the idea that they should counter the Nazi propaganda which the Fascists were spouting nightly at street-corner meetings. He proposed that, wherever such meetings took place, the Jews should appear at the same spot the following evening and answer the Nazi smears. The Association took up the idea, and organized a cadre of trained volunteer speakers, teaching them how to deal

65

with the Fascists. A special team acted as co-ordinators of the project.

This was the start of the community's defence work. The Friendly Societies carried on with it for several years. However, their original purpose was taken over by the state in 1945, when social legislation came into effect, and the need for volunteer welfare ceased to exist. At that time Barney arranged for the Board of Deputies to do the work of defence. The Defence Committee of the Board, which now takes care of this important activity on behalf of the Jewish community, has its origins, therefore, in those street meetings organized by the Jewish Friendly Societies.

The first open-air meeting was held at Duckett Street, Stepney, late in August 1936, with a large crowd in attendance. One of the speakers was Barney, who stressed the fact that under English law it was unfortunately impossible to prosecute anyone who slandered a whole community. (He was ahead of his time. Postwar legislation made it an offence to incite to racial hatred.)

This was barely six weeks before the famous attempt of the blackshirts to march through the East End of London, only to find their way blocked by masses of people, Jews and non-Jews, who had come out in protest. It was the time of the 'United Front', and the Communists undoubtedly had a part in organizing the demonstrations. The *Jewish Chronicle*, in its issue of 9 October 1936, wrote:

> The attempted march of some two or three thousand Fascists into the heart of East London, headed by their Führer in a brand new uniform . . . ended in a complete fiasco. The East End turned out in its hundreds of thousands and barred the way. . . .

To the events of that volatile time must be added our change of address. On the day after the 1935 election we moved from our house in Brampton Grove; first to temporary accommodation off the Finchley Road and then to 3 Lancaster Gate Terrace, W2, on the north side of Hyde Park.

In October 1936 we went to the Labour Party Conference in Bournemouth. Barney was impressed by the quality of the debates and spoke of the 'capacity, the frankness, the virility of the discussions and the knowledge revealed by the speakers.' Hannen Swaffer wrote in the Labour *Daily Herald*:

> I sat one night with him and Wedgwood Benn (the father of Tony Benn), who met for the first time, although they had both sat, as Liberals, for the same locality. Both spoke of their affection for the great human qualities of the East Enders.

Towards the end of the week Barney met some delegates from the West Leicester consituency, and had lunch with them. Suddenly Fred Jackson, the President of the local party, said, 'We are looking for a candidate for West Leicester. Do you think you would be interested?' Barney said, 'Well, I might be.' Fred Jackson then asked: 'Would you be prepared to come to Leicester and meet our honorary officers?', and Barney agreed. Returning to the Conference together we passed on the steps Jimmy Hall, Labour MP for Whitechapel, whom Barney had fought in three elections. We stopped and chatted and Barney introduced Hall to the West Leicester people. Out of the blue Jimmy Hall said to them, 'If you are looking for a candidate, you can't do better than take Janner. He's a marvellous candidate.' This was a wonderful recommendation. In fact Barney was always on excellent terms with his opponents and maintained friendly relations with some of them to the end of his life. There was never any bitterness in his political career from any party. Writing to me after Barney died, the Tory MP Sir Nigel Fisher said: 'Political views never impaired our friendship, indeed, I was unconscious of any difference. We never had a cross word or a disagreement and he had many friends — as you know — across the party barriers.'

The West Leicester seat had been won in 1935 by Harold Nicolson, the author, critic and diplomat, who stood for the National Labour Party which had supported Ramsay Macdonald when the National Government was formed in 1931. In 1935, eight of their candidates were elected to Parliament — Harold Nicolson by a mere eighty-seven votes in a three-cornered fight. Ramsay Macdonald himself had held the seat from 1906 to 1922, when he was defeated in the Coupon Election of that year. In 1923, Mr Pethwick-Lawrence, leader of the Suffragist Movement, had won the seat again for Labour, defeating Winston Churchill. Then he had lost it in 1931 in a straight fight with Mr Pickering, who defeated him by 14,000 votes.

Barney did not expect to hear from the West Leicester Labour Party again, but a week after the Conference he received a letter asking him to go to Leicester to meet the honorary officers. He went and they were so impressed with him that they asked him to come back the following week to meet their executive.

The executive liked Barney immensely and was unanimous in recommending him to the Selection Conference. When that body met on 9 November there were three names on the short list: Barney, Councillor J. D. Mack of Liverpool (nominated by the National Association of Life Assurance Workers) and Mr W. H. Hynd (a clerk on the headquarters staff of the National Union of Railwaymen). Mack thought he would win, since Hynd's name was only put forward at the last minute. Before that time, Barney had not known a soul in Leicester except for Ben and Ray Harris, at whose wedding he and I had met. All three nominees addressed the meeting, which lasted for over two hours, and Barney was chosen on the second vote. It was the beginning of a long and happy association.

Barney immediately set about getting to know his prospective new consituency, and on 18 December 1937 met West Leicester Labour Party's Councillors and officials at a social at the Memorial Hall, New Walk.

Unfortunately he had a long time to wait before having a chance to fight the seat, because the next election didn't take place for another eight years. During the war there was a party truce, and if a seat became vacant it was automatically handed to the party which had held it before. The Labour Party did not nominate for its vacancies anyone who had already been adopted elsewhere. So Barney was out of Parliament for ten years.

In 1937 he and his employers in the furniture trade decided to part company. He did not like being an employee, and was probably not a very good one as he spent much time first in Parliament and then in Jewish communal work outside the office. So, at the age of forty-five he put up a plate at 200 High Holborn and started to practice again alone as a solicitor. It was an uphill fight. He was fortunate enough to take a young solicitor into his practice, his nephew Gerald Davis, the son of his eldest sister who had died many years before, also to have as his secretary Mabel Vickers, a wonderful woman who stayed with him for forty years.

The rise of Hitler, and then the *Anschluss* in Austria brought to England many Austrian Jews who wanted to stay in this country. Barney saved the lives of many of them by taking their passports and locking them in his safe. He would say, 'Don't go back. You will never be able to get out. Stay here and I will help you get your wives and families over.' This he usually managed to do. There are many people in this country today who admit to having had their lives saved by Barney in this fashion.

In one such case, a man called Halpern came over from Vienna for a short visit to see if he could arrange to settle in this country. He had left his pregnant wife behind, and was desperate to get back to her. But Barney warned him not to go. Instead, and by means known only to himself, Barney got someone on the continent to enter Austria, accompany Mrs Halpern out of the country into Switzerland, and put her on a train to London. Her baby, born here, is Ralph Halpern, today Chairman of the Burton Group, one of the great public corporations in Britain.

Word seems to have got around among some of the people anxious to get out of Central Europe that there was a man in London who might be able to help. Mrs Trude Dub, now of Leicester, wrote in the *Jewish Chronicle* after Barney died:

When Hitler invaded Czechoslovakia in 1939, my husband and I ran for our lives and managed to get on the last train from Prague, hoping to reach London. Just before we boarded the train, a friend arrived breathless on the platform, thrust a piece of paper in my husband's hand and whispered: 'He will help you if the going gets rough.' The paper bore the name of Barnett Janner.

We kept it as a talisman throughout the most difficult years of our life but never made use of it until my sister, my family's only survivor of the Holocaust, was refused a month's visa to Britain to recuperate from her terrible experiences in a concentration camp. We then wrote to Barnett Janner and in no time at all my sister and I were reunited.

Today I cherish the memory of what Lord Janner did for me and countless others with such simplicity and ease and compassion.

After the *Anschluss*, when Hitler gobbled up Austria, the Jewish Refugee Committee asked us to take into our home for three weeks a refugee lady and her fifteen-year-old son, until permanent accommodation could be found for them. We readily agreed — and never forgot the sight of two tall, thin, frightened people edging their way through our front door. They were Irma Ehrlich and her son Paul.

Jacob Ehrlich had been the representative of the Jewish Community on the Vienna City Council. When the Nazis marched in he was arrested and immediately murdered. After much effort she and her only child were allowed to leave the country, taking with them nothing but a few clothes. They were without a penny, and could not even buy a cup of coffee.

These two lovely and refined people became members of our family. They continued to live with us for fifteen months. After the outbreak of war, we managed with the help of friends to get Paul taken as a pupil at Brighton College, where he was a brilliant student, and also played the violin in the student orchestra.

When their visas arrived for immigration to the United States, Irma and Paul left us. He has since become a well-known scientist in America. I still hear from Irma, who is well over ninety. She never fails to express her thanks and appreciation.

There was much to do, and even though Barney was not an MP he still knew many Members, and was able to use his contacts for good causes. In 1936, for example, the Peel Commission Enquiry was under way and Eliahu Elath, who was later to be Israel's Ambassador to the Court of St James's from 1950–59, was brought over from Palestine by Leonard Stein to give evidence before the Commission. Almost immediately on arrival he met Barney who was very kind to him.

It was Eliahu Elath's first visit to London and Barney invited him to the Anglo–Palestine Club, and to lunch at the House of Commons. The following year Elath accompanied Yitzhak Ben Zvi (later the second President of the State of Israel) to the Coronation of George VI. Ben Zvi and his wife were official guests of the British Government, since he was Chairman of the Va'ad Leumi (the Jewish National Council), and the Jewish Agency had attached Elath to him as his adviser. The latter immediately renewed his contact with Barney who introduced him to a number of friends in the House and arranged for him to speak to them. By that time the Peel Commission Report had already appeared but the attitude of the British Government was not yet known, and the Zionists wanted Members of Parliament to be fully informed about Palestine. In Eliahu Elath's words, 'Our relationship became much closer than on the first occasion when I was there only for a fortnight or so, and it was renewed from time to time either when I would come to London . . . or when he would come to Palestine.'

During these prewar years Barney travelled regularly to Leicester, nursing the constituency and speaking at meetings on the European and world situation. After the *Anschluss* in March 1938, he addressed a meeting together with Herbert Morrison at de Montfort Hall in Leicester saying: 'We can literally hear the tramp of the gangsters and the thugs marching into Austria. We have to realize that the reason these things have become possible is that the League of Nations has been trampled underfoot by our own National Government.' At another Leicester meeting two weeks later he returned to the theme: 'The law of the jungle will prevail if the Fascist powers succeed. It is not too late. On the contrary, if the powers of brute force were to realize that the democratic peoples intend to take a course of this description they would be checked in their advance.'

Much of Barney's energy was devoted to building up his legal practice. It was at this time that he first began to represent Jack Solomons, the well-known boxing promoter. He appeared for street traders, foreign seamen who were accused of unlawfully leaving their ship at Wapping, many refugees, and a colourful variety of other clients. One client recommended him to another, and so his practice grew.

Those years between his departure from Parliament in 1935

and the outbreak of war in 1939 were tense and dramatic years for the Jewish National Home. From the 1935 proposal for a Legislative Council with a built-in Arab majority, through the Arab riots beginning in 1936, the Peel Report in 1937 recommending partition, the Woodhead Commission reversing that proposal in 1938, and the Macdonald–Halifax White Paper of 1939, which foreclosed the future growth of the Jewish population in Palestine — there was plenty for the Parliamentary Palestine Committee to do. Barney continued to be very active in the Committee, although he was no longer a sitting Member. He was in the thick of the discussions when these events and proposals were debated in the House, especially the White Paper, which was vigorously condemned by such figures as Tom Williams, Sir Archibald Sinclair, Winston Churchill and Leopold Amery, and by Herbert Morrison who called the paper 'a cynical breach of pledges given to the Jews of the world.' The Chamberlain government, which had a majority in the House of some two hundred, squeaked through on this one by a bare majority of twenty votes.

In August 1939 Barney went to Geneva for the Twenty-first Zionist Congress. I was at the seaside at Birchington on holiday with the children, when I heard on the wireless that Stalin and Hitler had made an alliance. I immediately packed, took the children back to London, and phoned Barney urging him to come home. He was reluctant to leave the Congress at that tragic moment, but he deferred to my wishes and left for England. When I went to pick him up at Victoria Station, I saw trains arriving every minute, bringing back from the continent thousands of British families who felt that war was imminent.

For us, as for many parents in London, the war began a few days ahead of schedule, with the evacuation of the children from the capital. During the year after Munich, schools had arranged places in the countryside to which they would remove if war broke out. When the time came the organization and evacuation of hundreds of thousands of children was an epic. Each child had to be at school with a label pinned on him, giving his name and school, carrying one piece of luggage and food for one day. The trains bearing them fanned out from London without crossing the city, regardless of their ultimate destinations. The schools which our children attended, The Hall, and

South Hampstead High School, left for Northampton from a little station in Finchley Road. On arrival the children were met by kindly hostesses who took them temporarily into their homes. Greville and Ruth had no idea they were so close to each other.

Three days later, when all the children had been evacuated, they proceeded to their destinations. Greville was with his school at Claydon, Buckinghamshire, and Ruth with an elderly lady and her daughter at Berkhamsted, where South Hampstead High School shared Berkhamsted School. It was a strange London, completely empty of children.

At that stage we thought, perhaps naïvely, that there was a difference between military and civilian targets. Our own flat was dangerously near Paddington Station, and as my parents were staying in Bournemouth, we decided to move into their house in The Bishop's Avenue, Hampstead. Once there, Barney went round to the ARP post nearby and joined up. During the whole of the Blitz and after, he served as an ARP Warden and was on duty all night twice a week. I remember him riding off to the post on his bicycle. I joined the Mechanized Transport Corps, a uniformed body of volunteers which tied me in with the war effort, but still enabled me to live at home. I was also a fire-watcher, which kept me up all night once a week.

One night a cluster of fire bombs landed near us, setting our garage roof ablaze and starting five other fires in the neighbourhood. Barney and I worked with other neighbours, and managed to put out the smaller fires. The house opposite burned to the ground.

During this time Roy Jenkins lived with us for three months. His father, Arthur, Member of Parliament for Pontypool, and later Parliamentary Private Secretary to Clement Attlee, was an old friend of ours. Roy was working temporarily at the American Embassy, while waiting for his commission to come through.

My father's house was roomy, so we made it available to friends and members of the family who were in town overnight, or who were blitzed out, as one of my brothers was. All those in England made a point of staying with us when my brother, Radio Officer Sidney Cohen, had shore leave. These were rare and happy occasions. In addition to the pleasure of seeing him, he brought goodies not available here. But we were horrified when on one such leave he gave us a terrifying description of what it was like to be afloat in the cold, dark Atlantic after his ship had been torpedoed while escorting a convoy. Occasionally Barney would bring home some stranger who had been caught by the blackout. These were nearly always good experiences, but one of them left an unpleasant taste.

Barney had been in Leicester, and arrived back in London about ten o'clock at night. On the train was a woman who was dismayed at having missed her connection for Plymouth. Barney phoned from the station and asked if we could offer the woman and her child a bed for the night. Of course I said 'yes'. After the child had been put to bed, she and Barney and I sat up chatting. Her husband was a naval officer, and she had to travel about a good deal. I sympathized: 'The same thing happens to my sister-in-law. Her husband, my brother, Edwin, is an anti-aircraft officer, and keeps moving about.' She said 'But I thought you said you were Jews. I didn't know there were any Jews in the forces.' With that she went to bed. In the morning she was up and gone before breakfast, and I never received a word of thanks from her.

We had relatives and friends in Montreal, and when France fell in 1940, my parents left for Canada, along with my sister Edith Tarsh and half a dozen grandchildren, including our Greville and Ruth. It was a very traumatic moment when Barney and I saw them off from Liverpool docks. There were hundreds of children going on board, afraid to give up the gas-masks they had carried with them for the past year. With pain in our hearts we watched the ship sail. But at the same time there was a sense of relief, knowing that whatever happened in England, our children would be safe.

Our connections with Canada and the United States brought it about that many visitors from abroad looked us up. Canadian and American servicemen on leave, whether related or just referred to us, would bring greetings, and often stay over. We set aside a room, barricaded and sand-bagged, and prepared with iron rations and a first aid kit. 'Just like living in the jungle,' said one Canadian friend of the family, 'you never know who you're going to bump into.' He promptly dubbed it 'Janner's Jewish Jungle', and the name stuck.

Some of these fellows now lie under the Star of David in France or Belgium. Others survived to become lifelong dear friends of ours. One of the latter was Col. Morton M. Mendels of the Canadian Army, who was later to become Secretary of the World Bank in Washington. Another was Major Gershon Levi, Senior Jewish Chaplain to the Canadian Forces, who made our home his base whenever he was not in the field. After the war he brought his wife, Shonie, to meet us, and we have visited them often in America and in Jerusalem.

Barney continued his various activities. He still travelled to Leicester regularly, keeping in touch with Labour Party workers and with the people of the constituency. He would hold regular 'surgeries', where people could come to discuss their problems. Train service during the war was very erratic, so that these visits took much longer than they do nowadays.

He also continued his work for the Jewish National Home. In 1940 he was elected Chairman of the English Zionist Federation, meanwhile carrying on his activities with the Parliamentary Palestine Committee. In 1943 that Committee was reconstructed, with two Joint Chairmen, Lord Winster and Mr S. S. Hammersley, MP, and two Honorary Secretaries: William Strickland MP and Barnett Janner.

Another activity to which Barney devoted a good deal of time and attention was the formation of a Committee for a Jewish Fighting Force. Shortly after the outbreak of hostilities Chaim Weizmann had proposed to the British Government that the Jewish people, as a prime victim of the totalitarians, should be represented in the field by a distinctly Jewish fighting formation, clearly identified, placed under British command. The bulk of its personnel would come from Palestinian Jews already serving with the British Forces in the Middle East, but it would also accept Jewish volunteers from neutral countries as well as stateless Jewish refugees who wanted to strike a blow on behalf of their persecuted nation.

This offer, first made in 1939, met with prolonged hesitation on the part of the officials concerned. Lack of equipment was cited, and difficulties in obtaining the required transport. But there were Palestinian units already mobilized and in action, and the Jewish Agency continued to press the proposal.

After a lot of preparatory work by Barney, and by Joseph

Linton of the Jewish Agency and Lavy Bakstansky of the Zionist Federation, a letter over the signature of Major Victor Cazalet was sent to Members of both Houses of Parliament, inviting them to join a committee to further this project. The committee was formed at a meeting on 19 May 1942 in Committee Room 9 in the House of Commons. Major Cazalet and Jos Wedgwood were made joint Chairmen; S. S. Hammersley and Barney became Honorary Secretaries. The Executive included Lords Davies, Melchett and Strabolgi, and the MPs Creech Jones, R. D. Denman, Geoffrey Mander, Eleanor Rathbone, C. G. Ridley and Sidney Silverman. Others of the founders were Sigmund Gestetner, Simon Marks and Harry Sacher. Among the many who joined later were Lord Lytton, Vernon Bartlett, Blanche Dugdale, Sylvia Pankhurst and Sir George Jones, MP.

Barney did a lot of organizing and speaking for this committee whose efforts were co-ordinated to a certain degree with the American Palestine Committee, under Senator Robert Wagner, and the American Emergency Committee for Zionist Affairs, chaired by Rabbi Stephen S. Wise. The government was slow in yielding, and it was rather late in the war when the Jewish Brigade Group was finally formed in September 1944. It fought with distinction in Italy, France and Belgium, and did yeoman service in helping survivors of the holocaust.

We had returned to our flat in Lancaster Gate Terrace in January 1944, and I well remember a Rosh Hashanah eve dinner there in September, at which Moshe Sharett, later Prime Minister of Israel, was present. It was he who had finally piloted the Jewish Brigade project through the War Office. After dinner he told us about the Brigade, and said: 'I've been asked to recommend a Jew in the regular army who already had brigade rank. Know anyone?' My brother, Squadron Leader Alfred Cohen said 'What about Benjamin?' I do not doubt that this conversation had something to do with the fact that the British officer appointed to command the Jewish Brigade was Brigadier E. F. Benjamin.

In the spring of 1944 my parents came back from Canada, bringing Ruth with them. They had managed to get passage on a Portuguese steamer out of New York, and then flew on from Portugal to Britain. On their very first night at home there was an air raid, and bombs fell on Tyburn Convent near our home in Bayswater.

Greville remained in Canada to take his matriculation exams. He came home that summer on a British naval vessel, under a scheme to bring back schoolboys who were nearing military age. For him too there was an air raid on his first night at home, and we all went down into our shelter. Soon the anti-aircraft guns began to bark, and a boyish grin spread over Greville's face. It was plain that he was delighted to have come back in time. After all, he had not missed the War.

The war in Europe ended in May 1945 and Churchill dissolved the 'Long Parliament' that had sat for ten years. It was now time for Barney to contest the seat for which he had been the prospective candidate for so long — Leicester West. It was a constituency very different from those he had fought previously — Cardiff, where the voters were very political and vocal; and Whitechapel, where political passions ran high. Election meetings in Leicester were very quiet and orderly. People actually put up their hands to ask questions! Throughout the years, Barney had grown close to the people of Leicester and come to know their city well.

Leicester is situated in the very heart of England, a geographical circumstance responsible for much of its rôle in history and commerce. It was founded by the Romans as a fortification on the Fosse Way from Exeter to the Wash, at the point where that highway crosses the River Soar. The most prominent evidence of Roman occupation is the Jewry Wall, dating from about AD 130. It is an impressive structure about thirty feet high. The origin of its name is obscure, although there is record of a few Jews living in the area during the Angevin period. They were expelled from the district in 1231 by the Earl of Leicester, Simon de Montfort, who thus anticipated the expulsion of the Jews from all of England by Edward I in the year 1290.

The Castle, built in Norman times on a site overlooking the River Soar, was used by the Earls of Leicester, and was a favourite residence of John of Gaunt. Its Great Hall was built about 1150, and has been used as an Assize Court since the 13th century. The Leicester Crown Court sits there occasionally even today.

The timbered Guild Hall was the seat of the Town Council

from 1495 to 1874, when they moved into the new Town Hall. Of the famous Leicester Abbey, where Wolsey came to die, nothing remains except a few place-names. Another historic figure who spent his last hours in Leicester was Richard III, the last of the Plantagenets. The best-known feature of the modern city is the Clock Tower, an ornate Gothic structure built in 1868.

For many years Leicester had been an affluent industrial centre, with its principal products footwear and textiles. Until recently it was regarded as the second most prosperous city in all of Europe, ranking immediately after Lyons, in France. It is still a city with a large skilled and unskilled work-force of men and women. There is an important engineering industry, which makes a wide variety of items, notably: machine tools, castings, precision engineering products, electronic equipment, plastics, and adhesives. Leicester is also a centre for food-processing, dying and finishing, and for the printing and packaging industries.

Leicester is at the same time a city which encourages the arts in the Midlands. The de Montfort Hall, a fine concert hall sited in beautiful parkland, seats 2,750 people. The people of the city are also enthusiastic supporters of sports, both as participants and spectators. Soccer can be found at Filbert Street, cricket at Grace Road, while the famous Leicester Tigers Rugby team is at Welford Road. Athletics, cycle and motorcycle meetings, as well as regular horse races, all arouse a great deal of enthusiasm.

Leicester has always extended a welcome to people in need of sanctuary. During the depression of the 1930s over a thousand miners and their families from the north-east and from South Wales settled in the city. Again, during the war, evacuees from London and other exposed centres came to Leicester. Many of them remained, and took part in setting up industries, thereby increasing the prosperity of the city. In recent years Leicester had taken into its fold many thousands of Asians. They are a colourful, hard-working and fine community, and they do much to enhance the prestige of Leicester.

This then was the city in which Barney's constituency was situated, and where he fought the election campaign of 1945. He campaigned on the Labour platform — a blueprint for a better world after the sacrifices of the war. The programme concentrated on the needs of the people: a national health service for all; social security and adequate pensions; the building of new houses and the repair of some million and a half damaged ones; good education; public ownership of mines, fuel and power. When he was asked how all this would be paid for, Barney would answer that we had found the money to wage war for five years; surely we could find the means to rebuild the country. We must be good neighbours and act as one family.

Harold Nicolson, the previous Member, stood as a National candidate. He argued that it was wrong of Labour to insist on going back to party politics. The first priority should be to bring the war with Japan to a speedy and successful conclusion. To that end it was necessary to retain national unity under Churchill's leadership. The Tories concentrated on Churchill. His photograph was everywhere. He had won the war, and he must be given the chance to lead in rebuilding the peace. This programme completely misfired, and Labour scored an overwhelming victory.

Barney campaigned long and hard. He was a great believer in personal contact, and he spent all day and every day either canvassing or addressing meetings. He was full of energy and on the go from first thing in the morning until last thing at night. Councillor Rowland Hill, who, with his wife Mollie, was a marvellous supporter of Barney, wanted to get him into the working men's clubs of Leicester. Barney did not drink. Councillor Hill thought he would do something about it, so he suggested a compromise — a pint of lemonade with a dash of beer in it. This suited Barney; whenever he visited the working men's clubs this was his drink.

What made Barney's canvassing easier was the little loudspeaker he began to use while travelling along in his car. He would call to people he saw on the street, greet them personally and chat to them through the loudspeaker. He enjoyed this and so did the ladies out shopping and the mothers collecting their children from school.

After the poll had closed we arrived for the count at the de Montfort Hall. Harold Nicolson and his wife Vita Sackville-West were there. It was a nerve-racking moment as we entered and heard the swish-swish of the ballot papers being counted, but it was soon obvious from the piles of votes on the tables that

Barney had won. Nicolson himself said so to Barney. When the count had been completed, the totals were: Janner 20,563; Nicolson 13,348. Barney's majority was 7,215. As it turned out, Labour had won all three seats in Leicester.

Both men were gracious, in victory as in defeat. Barney thanked all the men and women who had worked so hard for him, and his opponents for a clean and distinguished fight. Nicolson replied: 'I am sure the constituency will find in Mr Janner a very assiduous and careful Member, who will be anxious to serve and help the people as I tried to do.'

5 THE MEMBER FOR WEST LEICESTER 1945–1950

After an absence of ten years, Barney returned as an MP to the House of Commons, the place he knew so well and loved so much. He was joined by 392 other Labour MPs, the product of Labour's landslide victory. As a member of the governing party he looked forward to the implementation of Labour's programme. He was not tremendously ambitious, but he *was* an extrovert and he enjoyed public life and leadership. Once he had reached the House of Commons he had no desire to gain office in Government. Arthur Jenkins, a good friend of ours, said to me that if Barney 'laid off this Palestine business, in six months he'll have office'. I told this to Barney at the time and he said, 'Tell Arthur Jenkins to go to hell.' What he wanted was to use his position in the House to help every one of his constituents, and the causes which he held so dear. Perhaps it was this attitude that brought about something noticeable — on his way up he never kicked anyone aside. But once he had attained office he hated to give it up, and he never resigned from anything.

The State Opening of Parliament was on 15 August, and we were present to hear the King's speech. The date had been fixed some weeks earlier, but as it turned out, Japan surrendered the day before, on 14 August. So the war was really over! London went quite mad. From Piccadilly Circus to Parliament Square the streets were a solid mass of humanity, including service men and women of all the allied nations. It was a thrilling day. On the Sunday following there was a Service of National Thanksgiving at St Paul's Cathedral.

Very soon after he was elected, some of the Leicester people came to seek Barney's help in connection with the New Parks Estate in his constituency. Before the war, the area had been drained, pipes laid down and roads built in preparation for housing development, but immediately fighting broke out, tanks were stationed there. When the war in Europe ended

Leicester's Housing Committee tried to persuade the War Office to remove the tanks, because the building of houses was such an urgent priority. But the War Office was adamant, the site had to continue as a tank park.

As soon as the election was over, Fred Jackson, the Chairman of the Committee, approached the three new Leicester MPs and explained the position to them. They went up to the site and agreed to do everything possible once a Secretary for War had been appointed.

On 3 August Barney was standing in the Commons watching the ticker-tape machine when it spelled out that Jack Lawson had been appointed War Minister. He saw Lawson standing beside him, congratulated him, and said, 'When can we see you?' A week later Barney, Herbert Bowden MP, and Terence Donovan MP, persuaded Lawson to give immediate and sympathetic consideration to the matter. On the following day Lawson handed Barney a little pencilled note which read: 'You can tell your people they can start building. The tanks will be removed within ten days.' He had issued instructions for the first hundred houses to be built. Barney was thrilled and delighted.

Barney was no gourmet. One of his favourite foods was filleted fresh herring. When he returned to Parliament, the Head Waiter in the Members' Dining Room said: 'I'm very sorry, Mr Janner, we cannot give you kosher herrings, we haven't the staff.' Barney couldn't understand, and the waiter explained: 'We cannot fillet them for you.' He had always thought Barney had the fish filleted to make them kosher!

In his first speech in the new Parliament, on 20 August, Barney thanked the Government for promptly providing homes for the people of Leicester on the New Parks Estate, and added:

> They have told the men and women who are returning from war, and the people of this country, 'Your homes will be provided.' What do the Jewish people ask? Speaking on their behalf, I say, do not send them to places where they will be told that there is no work for them, where they can find only temporary refuge. Send their scattered men and women, the remnants in Europe, to a place where, if there is only a crust, that crust will be shared, where there will be

no question of one Jew saying to the other coming home: 'I have no roof for you.' Give them the opportunity of restoring dignity, self-respect and humanity to those who have survived. Let us open wide the gates of Palestine. In that manner we shall be carrying out what has been said in His Majesty's Gracious Speech.

Before the war the Labour Party had been consistently critical of the 1939 White Paper, which for all intents and purposes had blocked Jewish immigration to Palestine. At the Party Conference in London in December 1944, Clement Attlee had moved a resolution which was carried unanimously, demanding that 'Jews should enter this tiny land in such numbers as to become a majority.' There was every reason, therefore, to expect that the new Labour Government would open the doors of Palestine, especially in view of the tragic events of the war years. Consequently, disappointment was all the keener when it soon became evident that the Labour Government had done a somersault, and meant to retain the White Paper policy, and to enforce it to the full.

Palestine was transferred from the Colonial Office to the Foreign Office. In the House of Commons, Barney rose to ask the Foreign Secretary, Ernest Bevin, whether the restrictions on Jewish immigration would be relaxed. Bevin's reply showed that the Government was not prepared to do anything that might antagonize the Arabs. He implied that in any case, not all Jews agreed with the aspirations of the Zionists.

The gauntlet had been thrown down. Resistance to British rule in Palestine now encompassed virtually the whole Jewish population. At the end of October the Haganah raided the detention camp at Athlit and freed 208 'illegal' immigrants held there. Meantime, many thousands of displaced persons languished in camps in Europe. The Government sent troops, planes and ships to prevent them from reaching Palestine. At a special Zionist Conference Barney said, 'We are standing at the graveside of six million Jews, some of whom might have reached Palestine and life, had there not been a White Paper.'

So the battle lines were drawn. The British Government — Barney's own party comrades — were in effect at war with the Jews of Palestine, with the displaced persons, and with the

Jewish Agency. It was a very difficult two years for my husband. Time after time he stood up in Parliament and put the case for the Jews, and got very rough treatment. He used to come home and say: 'It was awful in the House today. Everybody was against me.' But he always stood his ground, obeyed his conscience, and said what he thought. In a letter to me after Barney died, Teddy Sieff of the Marks and Spencer family wrote: 'I shall remember him as a man of great courage, and will not forget how he stood up in a hostile House of Commons at the time of the hanging of the two sergeants' (in 1947: a reprisal for the execution by the British authorities of three Irgun members).

When the military in Palestine arrested the Jewish Agency leaders one Sabbath day, Barney thundered in the Commons: 'I say today, to arrest the Jewish Agency, to arrest the socialists, the trade unionists, the very persons we have praised year in and year out, is literally nonsense.'

The Jewish community was enraged by the arrests. The English Zionist Federation organized a protest meeting at Beaver Hall on 8 July. From there a mile long march set off, led by Thomas Gould, a Jewish VC. After it passed the Mansion House, Barney, Rebecca Sieff and Selig Brodetsky led it to Trafalgar Square. They carried the Union Jack and a banner saying 'Let my people go'. Trafalgar Square was packed with thousands of people. After the demonstration Barney and 'Baffy' Dugdale headed the procession to 10 Downing Street and handed in a resolution.

When the Irgun blew up the British Military Headquarters in one wing of the King David Hotel in Jerusalem, Barney condemned the act, and said he was expressing the feelings of the Jewish Agency and most of the Jews of the world. In this connection it is a tribute to his sense of fairness that he stood up over twenty years later in the House of Lords to defend the Irgun on one point, even though he still disagreed strongly with their tactics, and with their Revisionist politics.

The Irgun had always claimed that they had telephoned a warning to vacate the King David Hotel before they blew up the Military Headquarters wing. Their claim had been frequently denied. But on 22 May 1979 Barney read to the House of Lords a note he had received from a Dr Crawford of Bournemouth,

Mother: Gertrude

Father: Joseph

Headmaster: Edgar Jones

Janners' Bazaar, Barry, 1911

Milestones: Barney as a graduate of Cardiff College, University of Wales, in 1916 — then as Private Janner the following year. He became a solicitor in 1919; and during the Second World War was an ARP warden in London

1927: Engaged and married

*A meeting in Cable Street for the 1930 Whitechapel and St George's
by-election*

Off duty: Broadstairs, 1935; Villars sur Ollon, 1946; and at his 80th birthday party on 20 June 1972. Back row, 1 to r: *Ruth (Lady Morris), Philip (Lord Morris), Barney, Daniel Janner, Greville, Myra (Greville's wife);* middle row, 1 to r: *Diane Morris, Marion Janner, Elsie Janner;* in front: *Jonathan Morris, Linda Morris, Laura Janner, Caroline Morris*

On duty: on the balcony of City Hall, Tel Aviv, in 1934 – Mayor Dizengoff is at the centre of the group – and in Westminster with a group of Leicester schoolgirls in the mid-1960s

With ex-President Harry S. Truman in 1956 and (below) *with Australian Prime Minister Sir Robert Menzies in 1963*

Barney (and Ruth in 1982) at the stone marking the Janner Forest in Jerusalem Hills

To celebrate the 60th anniversary of his becoming a solicitor, Janners gave Barney a dinner at the House of Lords on 29 March 1979

affirming that in 1946 he had received a letter from Major-General Dudley Sheridan Skelton, CB, DSO, FRCS, at the time in charge of a hospital near Jerusalem. Dr Skelton had been in the King David Hotel on the very day of the explosion, and had heard the warning passed on to the officers in the bar, but had been advised to ignore the bluff! However, he had decided to take the warning seriously, and had left the hotel. Thanks to Barney's sense of fair play, this footnote to history is now recorded in Hansard.

About these difficult years, Harold Fisch writes in his book *The Zionist Revolution*:

> During this period of 'strained relations' between the Jewish people and the British Government there was no stronger critic of the Government than Mr Barnett Janner . . . a member of Mr Bevin's own party. Mr Janner lost no opportunity to voice his solidarity with the *Yishuv* in Palestine and his abhorrence of Mr Bevin's policies. It is clear that at this time the sense of responsibility for the Jewish fate and the Jewish future rested squarely on the shoulders of Diaspora Jews, especially the leaders of the Jewish community such as Mr Janner.'

Several years later, when the 1950 election drew near and constituencies had to adopt candidates, I was told by Morgan Phillips, Secretary of the Labour Party, that he went to Leicester at that time as he expected trouble at Barney's adoption meeting. He thought that Barney's stand on Palestine might cause difficulties. He was amazed when Barney was not only chosen unanimously, but was showered with praise. This fair-minded action endeared the people of Leicester to Barney even more, and his affection for them grew with the years.

When the UNSCOP report was up for consideration at the United Nations General Assembly in 1947, he flew to New York and was present on 29 November when the historic Partition Resolution was passed, recommending the creation of a Jewish State. He and Rabbi Abba Hillel Silver danced in the corridor, hugging one another and weeping for joy. A few days later Barney was back in London, addressing an exultant meeting of the Zionist Federation at Kingsway Hall.

The next six months were touch and go for the Jews of Palestine, and Barney had a very busy time in Parliament. Britain was in the process of giving up the Mandate and withdrawing her forces, and Westminster was ceasing to be the place where the fate of Palestine would be decided. Finally, on 14 May 1948, the State of Israel was proclaimed in Tel Aviv, and recognized sixteen minutes later by the United States. Barney kept pressing Ernest Bevin to recognize the new State, but only got evasive replies.

His first visit to the new State was in August of that year, when he went to a meeting of the Actions Committee in Jerusalem. He had been in the land before; he was to visit it many times as the years went by. But this was his first sight of Israel, free and independent. In the biblical words he loved to sing after the Sabbath meal, he was 'like those who dream'.

Earlier the same year Barney had answered an SOS from the gravely threatened Jews of Aden. His mission to that city on the southern tip of the Arabian peninsula was the beginning of a long involvement in the rescue of an ancient Jewish community.

Aden was an important port and way-station straddling the sea lanes between the Red Sea and the Indian Ocean, on the way to India. It had been a British Protectorate for some time. Its Jewish community was an ancient one, whose roots go back some two thousand years. In 1947 many of the Jews in Aden lived in an area of the port called The Crater, a small quarter consisting of no more than four streets.

After the United Nations decision of 29 November 1947 to partition Palestine, a wave of anti-Jewish violence swept through the Arab world from Morocco to Iraq. Aden was no exception. Its established Jewish community, including some merchants, had always had good relations with the local Arabs. In 1947 the community had received over three thousand Jewish refugees from neighbouring Yemen, which had joined the Arab League. These refugees were concentrated in Sheikh Othman village, Camp Hashid and The Crater, and most of them were quite destitute. The American Jewish Joint Distribution Committee and the Jewish Agency were giving them some support.

On the morning of Tuesday 2 December, the Arabs in Aden

declared a three-day strike. This strike rapidly developed into a violent anti-Jewish demonstration. Stones were thrown and houses were set on fire. The Jews defended themselves with bottles and closed all their shops in The Crater and Steamer Point. They appealed to the British authorities for help, and late in the evening some British sailors were seen patrolling. All was quiet until the next day when the Governor imposed a twenty-hour curfew and sent in the Aden Protectorate Levies (APL) who were made up of local Arabs. Instead of protecting the Jews they allowed the Arab mobs, many of whom came from outside Aden, to attack the Jews at will. Armed with daggers, knives, hammers and iron bars, they burned and looted houses and shops, and the two Jewish schools. The APL were seen to encourage the Arab mobs and to fire on Jews who were trying to escape from burning buildings.

The looting and burning continued until 4 pm on the Thursday when the APL were withdrawn and replaced by British sailors. Eighty-four people had been killed and more than eighty wounded by bullets fired by the APL. Four synagogues were burnt down, thirty Jewish houses destroyed, fifty Jewish shops completely wiped out by looting and fourteen Jewish cars burnt. Seven hundred Jews were made homeless and the whole community reduced to a state of total insecurity and devastation. The damage was estimated at about £1 million.

Despite the intervention of the British forces, tension remained high and later in December there were more disturbances. This time the British prevented them from getting out of hand.

The situation in Aden remained tense. On 29 December Barney saw Mr Hartford, Mr Trafford Smith and Sir Sidney Abraham at the Colonial Office, principally to discuss the question of compensation. It developed that this would not be a simple matter, because an enquiry would have to be conducted to establish responsibility.

In the meantime, the Emergency Committee in Aden cabled Barney and asked him to come to their aid. He responded without hesitation. 'At considerable personal sacrifice and inconvenience,' wrote A. G. Brotman, Secretary of the Board of Deputies, 'Janner undertook to go out to Aden in an honorary capacity' (i.e. without remuneration).

He was met at the airport by the Governor, who had arranged for him to stay at Government House. But the Jewish community wanted him to stay with them at The Crater, which of course he did. In a recollection which he dictated some years later Barney said:

> They put me up at the home of Rahamim M. Howard in a large bare room. Access was by a ladder from the street. Some rioting was still going on. The walls were pitted by bullet holes, and in the circumstances I felt a little uncomfortable . . . I arranged for a different set of troops to defend the inhabitants, i.e. the Royal Marines who were in Aden at the time. They took over and the riots were dealt with.'

He was taken around to see the damage caused by the rioters, and visited the Jews from Yemen at Camp Hashid. Apart from what the attackers had done to kill and wound, they had also burnt the sacred scrolls of the Torah in the synagogue. 'I took some of the partly burned parchment with me,' Barney wrote, 'and I still have it at home.' I have kept those fragments, and still have them.

At Camp Hashid Barney noticed a fair-complexioned woman among the dark-skinned Yemenites. She turned out to be Dr Olga Feinberg, a physician who had come on her own to offer medical help to the Yemenite Jews. She had been brought up in Germany by Jewish foster-parents, received her medical education in Switzerland, and had gone to Palestine, where she opened a surgery in the completely Arab town of Jericho. After some years she was warned by local people that Arab extremists were coming, and she was advised to flee. She left and her surgery was burned down. In search of a place where her desire to help other human beings would not be rejected, she went to a hospital in India. After the war she felt the call of the Homeland, and decided to return to Palestine. On her way from Bombay the ship docked at Aden, where she learned that the Yemenite Jewish refugees had no qualified medical help. She decided to stay.

Barney wrote that the first thing he did was to advise the Adenese to leave. 'But as in the case of the Jews of Germany, they had been there so long they were reluctant to pull up the stakes. Besides, everything they possessed would have to be left behind.'

He conferred with the Governor, and was reassured that security would be tightened. A court was constituted to investigate claims for damages that had been put in by over five hundred people. Together with Harry Vitales of the Joint Distribution Committee Barney helped form committees to deal with rehabilitation, education, medical treatment, and food for those in need — which meant practically the whole community.

Three times he went to Camp Hashid; he saw the Poor Shelter House at the edge of the Jewish quarter; he went to Steamer Point, five miles from The Crater. He also met some of the non-Jews who had helped the Jewish community in its time of trouble, including the Medical Officer of Health, Dr Cochrane.

The Adenese Jews were deeply affected by Barney's visible concern for their suffering and by the help he gave them. They regarded him as a sort of father-figure. Oriental fashion, they saw his name as a symbol because, in the Arabic they spoke, the two words *ja'a nar* mean 'light has come'. He gave them confidence. Now they felt safe, someone was looking after them. 'I returned from Aden,' Barney wrote later, 'and they kept in constant touch with me. I tried to get compensation for them, and I appointed Mr A. S. Diamond (later a Master of the Supreme Court) to go out to Aden and take up their case. Unfortunately the law there was based on Bombay Indian law, and this prevented the granting of compensation. My firm and I took up their cases, for which we accepted no payment. The fees and expenses of the barristers were paid by the Adenese themselves.'

Barney had terribly strong convictions about not accepting any reward for services rendered in his public capacity. When the Adenese Jews sent him a beautiful Persian rug he immediately sent it back, and paid the costs of the return carriage. So he was deeply offended later, when he was pressing the government on the floor of the House of Commons to help the Jews of Aden, and the MP Sidney Silverman came up to him in the lobby and remarked that Barney was doing very well financially out of the plight of the Adenese Jews. Barney was absolutely furious, wrote him a scathing letter, and never spoke to Silverman again.

On 18 February Barney learned in the House that the Government had set up an inquiry into the events in Aden which would be presided over by Sir Harry Trusted, KC, until 1941 Chief Justice in Palestine. He asked Diamond if he would assist, and he then got in touch with Norman Bentwich, who was in Aden on behalf of the Anglo–Jewish Association, and arranged for him to represent the Aden community at the Inquiry which opened on 8 March.

The situation improved, but Barney's relationship with the Adenese Jewish community had only just begun. Two years later, in 1950, there were more disturbances and Barney was again involved in making representations to the Government. Many of the Adenese Jews had emigrated to Israel by this time, and Barney wanted loans that had been given by the Aden Legislative Council under the Rehabilitation Scheme to be converted into grants, so that more Jews could leave.

By 1954 there were only eight hundred Jews left in the colony. Many of those from Yemen had passed through Aden on their way to Israel and Barney intervened with the Colonial Secretary, Oliver Lyttelton, on behalf of a number of Yemeni Jews who had been held up at Lahej. The authorities said that the community would not be able to accommodate them on a temporary basis, but the Adenese Jews themselves insisted they could cope, as they had done for centuries. They were still experiencing problems, having never really recovered from the 1947 disturbances, and on 30 June Barney went to see Sir Tom Hickinbottom, the Governor of Aden, who was then in England. He referred to the fact that the visit of two Egyptian frigates to Aden some time before had been followed by the stoning of Jewish houses and persons. Recently there had been a visit by a Muslim emissary from Jordan who was collecting funds for the repair of the Dome of the Rock, and this had greatly disturbed the Jewish community because such visits were usually followed by an outbreak of emotion that could result in harm for the Jews. Sir Tom agreed to look into all these matters and deal with them.

When the President of the Adenese community, Mr S. M. Banin visited the Board of Deputies in December that year, he emphasized how grateful they were for the way in which Barney had drawn the Governor's attention to their problems. The Administration was now doing everything possible to safeguard peace and ensure security.

There were periodic disturbances from time to time, and the community always addressed its problems to Barney. For his part, Barney consistently advised them to leave. Even so, many remained and it was difficult to persuade them otherwise.

The final chapter in this saga came when the British Government decided to grant independence to Aden, which had joined the Federation of South Arabia in 1961. Competition between the rival nationalist groups was fierce and terrorism against the British mounted. The situation became so bad that the original date for the hand over of power — 1968 — had to be brought forward to November 1967. The Board were naturally anxious about the remnants of the Aden Jewish community, now numbering merely three hundred souls, and in June 1966 Barney had a meeting with Sir Richard Turnbull, the High Commissioner for Aden. Sir Richard said that everything possible was being done to protect Jews and their property. The disturbances were aimed primarily against the British administration and indiscriminate damage was done, but the Jews, like the Indians, were in an exposed position and sometimes singled out.

The main question was how to make arrangements for those who wanted to emigrate. Sir Richard said he had endeavoured to expedite permits for Adenese Jews to come to the UK.

Early in 1967 the situation in Aden became very grave and a growing number of British, Arab and Jewish people were killed or wounded. Many of the remaining Jews were anxious to come to Britain as speedily as possible. The Chief Rabbi in Aden, Shlomo Yehuda Cohen, had written in a letter to the Chairman of the Board of Deputies Aliens Committee, that for an Aden Jew now to wait his turn would be dangerous. He would be exposed to physical danger after the British have moved out. Mr W. M. Lee, the Commonwealth Office official responsible for obtaining immigration permits, said that the matter was being considered at a higher level, and that he would let the Board know when there was news. Meanwhile, the Adenese were getting extremely anxious. To cut through the red tape Barney went straight to David Ennals, Parliamentary Under-Secretary of State at the Home Office. He followed up with a letter asking Ennals to expedite 'the granting of permits for these unhappy applicants. I am sure that you will appreciate the terrible plight in which they find themselves'.

On 16 May, a telephone call from the Home Office confirmed that priority had been granted to those Adenese who wanted to come to Britain. Barney was thanked for intervening so quickly.

During May and June the situation became absolutely intolerable. Arab policemen looked on indifferently while Jews were shot in the street. Businesses and homes had to be deserted because of threats and mob violence. Banks refused to cash their cheques, post offices tore up their letters and looted and burned parcels intended for relatives in Israel and London.

The British moved the last 132 Jews under cover of darkness from The Crater to Steamer Point, and put them up in the Victoria Hotel and the Royal Navy Residences. They were told not to leave their places of shelter. One young man went to the funeral of an Arab friend and was shot dead.

A few days later, in the dead of night, the British took the Jews to the airfield, where a plane was waiting for them. They took off at four in the morning, the aircraft landing first in Israel, where some of the passengers disembarked, and then flying on to London with the rest. I met them on arrival at Gatwick Airport with Richard Slotover, a young cousin of ours who had been working with Barney and me on this dramatic rescue. It was an emotional moment.

They had with them only what they could carry in small worn suitcases. We took them to the Jews' Temporary Shelter in the East End. Later, Barney went down to the shelter and welcomed them to England.

Throughout this last episode, as before, Barney spared no effort to help the Adenese Jews. He would spend hours on their problems, great or small. When they called on him to help he never refused.

The Adenese Jews in England have proved to be a very fine group of immigrants, hard working and honourable. They adored Barney, for they know that without him they would all have been dead.

Barney's interests and concerns during his first years back in Parliament covered a wide range. He busied himself with causes high and low, with small and big organizations, and with the intimate concerns of his West Leicester constituents. He was on the Labour Party Advisory Committee on Legal Aid for the Poor, a subject he knew about from many years of personal experience as a solicitor dealing with the problems of people unable to pay legal fees. He spoke in the Commons many times on this issue. As Vice-President of the Board of Deputies, he took special interest in issues of defence. In 1949 he was re-elected Vice-President of the Board.

He was Chairman of the Zionist Federation from 1940, during the most tumultuous years in the modern history of the Jewish people. In 1950 he relinquished that post and was elected President. For years he was continuously re-elected President of the Association of Jewish Friendly Societies and President of its Convalescent Home. Long a member of the Council of Christians and Jews, he joined the liaison group between MPs and the Council in 1947. In CCJ circles he was very much loved and gave long and acknowledged service. He was Honorary Rents Adviser to the Labour Party, Chairman of the Anglo–Israel Club, Vice-President of the Association of Jewish Ex-Servicemen, of the Monash Branch of the British Legion, of the World Maccabi Union and of British Maccabi.

One thing that concerned Barney at this time was the resurgence of antisemitism in Britain, and the threat of neo-Nazism in Germany. In Britain, Mosley and his British Union of Fascists had been proscribed from the outbreak of war in 1939, but after the war he made a comeback with his Union Movement, which was the old Fascism in a new guise. Once again the East End experienced antisemitic incidents. In 1947 Barney went with Board of Deputies deputation to see Chuter Ede, the Home Secretary, to express the anxiety of the Jewish community at the increase of antisemitic incitement in the East End and elsewhere through the abuse of free speech.

In its legislative programme for the 1945–50 Parliament, the Labour Party had made housing one of its major priorities. In this connection, there existed a whole series of Rent Acts which had been passed over the years and which made the entire system extremely complicated — hard enough for civil servants and experienced legislators to understand, let alone hard-pressed tenants. Barney consistently argued for a consolidation of all the existing Rent Acts, to remove the anomalies and make it easier for local authorities to provide information to tenants on their rights. Reading through the interventions he made and the amendments he put down during the debate on the Leasehold Property Bill in 1951, it becomes clear that he was consistently trying to secure the interests of the tenant.

It so happened that in 1951 Barney was talking from personal experience. The lease on our home at Lancaster Gate Terrace had expired after fourteen years and we were confronted with the problem of finding somewhere else to live. In the Commons Barney mentioned our personal plight so as to give more emphasis to his argument.

In 1946 he spoke in an adjournment debate on Government assistance to university education, giving Leicester as an example. 'The universities must be placed in such a position that they can command the services of men and women of the highest and best scientific knowledge, and experience in teaching,' he said. After flying to America to visit the Leicestershire brides of United States servicemen, he opened an adjourment debate in which he asked the Government to lift the restriction on taking more than £5 out of the country, in the case of people wanting to visit relations married to American and Canadian servicemen.

In addition to the protection of tenants, his particular interests were these: all facets of criminal justice; the guardianship and adoption of children; the rights of minorities; protection of animals (he was very fond of animals); the outlawing of genocide; education at all levels, and anything and everything pertaining to his constituency.

From 1948 Barney was persistent in his questioning of the Foreign Office on future relations between Britain and Israel. As other states were affording recognition to Israel — nineteen of them by December 1948 — why was Britain not doing so? In his essay on the Parliamentary Palestine Committee, he wrote:

> I remember one particular debate on Foreign Affairs, on December 9th and 10th, 1948, that revealed the Government's unfortunate policy towards the newly-risen Israel. That debate was marked by demands on all sides of the

House that Israel be granted diplomatic recognition by this country. Within a month the Government had to accede.

De facto recognition was accorded on 28 January 1949 and *de jure* recognition on 27 April 1950. The Israeli flag was unfurled in London at Manchester House, Manchester Square, to mark the event.

Barney also sought restitution for those victims of Nazism whose property had been seized by the Nazi State. There was in addition the question of what should be done with the funds of those who had been murdered. In a Commons debate on the distribution of German enemy property Barney said these funds should be used by survivors of the Holocaust. There were signs as well of a resurgence of Nazism, and in December 1949 Barney asked the Minister what was being done about it. He received a reassuring answer but remained concerned, and when the question of German rearmament came up he asked the Government to consider the whole problem very carefully.

In his last speech in the 1945–50 Parliament, Barney returned to the theme of Israel, Middle East peace and the rôle Britain should play in the process. He drew attention to the proposed scheme for improving the economy of the whole area, schemes approved by Israel but rejected by Syria and Jordan. Moreover, Egypt was acting contrary to the Armistice agreement of February 1949 by not allowing Israeli ships through the Suez Canal. He felt that the solution of all Middle East problems depended upon co-operation between the Middle East countries themselves. Such co-operation should be economic, political and military — not directed against anyone else but for the common security and benefit of all countries in the area. 'At present,' he said,

> the Arab Governments are persisting in their policy of refusing to transform the Armistice into a permanent peace settlement. We in Britain want to encourage the development of the armistice into a peace treaty. We should realize that so far as Israel is concerned, she is prepared to do all she possibly can to create a peaceful settlement. We should support that effort. If we throw ourselves into a real determination to bring about peace and rehabilitation in the

Middle East, we shall have done something not only for the Middle East, not only for the Arab States, but for the world as a whole.

When criticized by MPs like Major Tufton Beamish (Lewes), Earl Winterton (Horsham) and Thomas Reid (Swindon), who accused him of always speaking first for the 'Israelites', Barney consistently stressed that what he was saying was to the advantage of the UK, that Britain would benefit from a prosperous and peaceful Israel.

By the time Clement Attlee called the 1950 General Election, Barney had had the satisfaction of seeing many of the social reforms he so passionately believed in implemented, though he was constantly urging improvements on his own Government. He fought the election in what was, in effect, a new constituency. A redistribution of Parliamentary seats had taken away North Braunstone Ward, much to his dismay. Some houses had been built on the New Parks Estate, so a small part of the loss was made up. The constituency was now called Leicester North-West.

The Labour Government had achieved a great deal in five years and had laid solid foundations for post-war Britain. But there were still rationing and controls and a great deal of austerity. These were necessary and ultimately to the country's benefit; but the political pendulum was beginning to swing.

This was Barney's second Leicester election, and by this time his helpers and the people of Leicester knew him well. He was fifty-seven, but with the energy and stamina of a man less than half his age. He felt keenly the value of personal canvassing and of having large numbers of Party workers mobilized to get out the vote. Colin Grundy, now a Councillor and an Honorary Officer of Leicester Labour Party, remembers being a student Labour supporter in 1950 and putting up a Labour poster in his window. 'It wasn't long before Barney was round knocking at the door asking who put the poster up. "Well, will you come and help?" he said and then proceeded to tell me all about canvassing and what he wanted doing.' Colin says that Barney always struck him as being larger than life, 'a very warm human being with tremendous compassion for people and an understanding of human problems. It was his warmth and humanity which impressed me more than anything else.'

Councillor George Billington, Lord Mayor of Leicester, who had been a prominent Party worker in Newton ward, first met Barney in 1950.

> I had always thought of him before that as someone — I don't know how to put it — I don't want to suggest that it was anything he'd done — but he seemed somewhat on a pedestal. I had known of him because my father used to talk about him long before the war when he was first adopted candidate for the old West Leicester constituency. When I met him I found him to be so pally, warm and friendly in a way that I didn't expect. . . . I found that he was easy to talk to. He would break down anybody's reserve by putting his arm round him and saying 'Look here old boy, we're in this together, we're working for the same cause and that's what it's all about.' He was concerned with everything from the most serious and important issues to the minor matters that irritated people locally.

It was during a rally at the Corn Exchange on 15 February, with Attlee there, that Barney showed his great ability to turn an embarrassing situation into a comical incident. While he was speaking his false teeth dropped out. 'Well,' he said, picking them up and replacing them in his mouth, 'good quality teeth supplied by the National Health Service and unbroken — and even if they had been broken they would have been replaced by the National Health Service!' The crowd roared.

Barney used to hold his 'surgery' in a small room above the Trade Hall. During the Election campaign a *Leicester Evening Mail* reporter interviewed him there.

> A group of constituents await interview, and as the Member for West Leicester hurries forward to greet the first, he is almost the brisk, assured doctor, trying to put his patients at ease. His dark city suit, white collar and grey tie further the likeness. But what follows reveals a shrewdness more characteristic of the advocate than of the physician. For in all his activities Mr Janner has the advantage of

that insight into human nature which comes to the trained legal mind: and from long experience of the courts and of private practice he knows the value of 'the personal touch'.

During the campaign some of the opportunities Barney had of helping people came to light. At an election meeting at Belgrave Road School, a member of the audience thanked him for his help 'in settling a legal matter in five minutes which had been outstanding for ten years.' In another instance he was able to intervene personally with Manny Shinwell, the War Minister, to arrange for an Army driver to fly home to Leicester from Hong Kong to see his father who was dangerously ill.

'We must run the affairs of the country as one runs the affairs of the home,' George Billington remembers Barney saying during the campaign. 'His emphasis on the family was there all the time. I can remember a funny occasion when he was being formally adopted as candidate when he stressed his family-man status — and the other four people at the top were all bachelors!' When Barney used the word he usually meant the family of Britain, but his real family were certainly involved when it came to canvassing. Ruth worked day in and day out at every election. She was and is very popular in the Division. Greville, studying at University, brought a party of Cambridge University students, all members of the Labour Club, to canvass during the weekend before polling day. They clambered into a coach covered with political posters and red ribbon. Barney and I were in front in a car with Ruth as we wound our way through the city centre, using a loud speaker.

When some party workers were delivering an elector to the polling station on the New Parks Estate, very close to closing time, two youngish people came out and said 'Have you got a car there? Could you fetch my mother — she's eighty-five and she's never missed voting yet.' The workers dashed off to get her, while some people they had already taken to the polling station had to wait until they fetched the old woman. They returned with her, only to find the doors of the station closed, but they heaved a sigh of relief when she said 'Damn! That's the first time I've not been able to vote for Mr Churchill.'

Barney's opponents were Nigel Nicolson (Harold Nicolson's son) for the Tories, and R. A. Burrows for the Liberals. The

98

turnout on 23 February was high — 86 per cent of the electorate. Colin Grundy remembers being at the count at the Town Hall. 'It was the first count that I attended. Part way through I got into conversation with Barney, who convinced me that he had lost, and I was completely depressed. I met another long-standing member of the Labour Party and told him what Barney had said. He answered, "Don't take any notice of him — the blighter always thinks he's lost."'

Barney polled 23,505, a majority of 7,593 over Nicolson (the Liberal lost his deposit). In the country at large Labour returned to power with a bare majority of only six seats over all the other parties in the House of Commons.

6 DEFENDING THE WEAK
1950–1955

Although Barney had already been to Israel a few times our first visit together to the new state was in 1951. We flew out on 10 May, on an El Al aircraft, leaving at 7.30 am.

My diary of the trip shows how impressed I was with Israel's new airline:

> The plane was luxurious and the best I've been in, four-engine Constellation done out in blue and grey leather and plush.

The trip took almost nine hours, including a one-hour stopover in Rome. We reached the shores of Israel at 8.15 in the evening local time. My diary continues:

> Flew over Tel-Aviv. All lit up. What a thrill! Landed at Lydda 6.15 our time.
>
> A woman came on the plane, welcomed everyone and then said, 'Mr Barnett Janner, you are welcome to Israel.' All the other passengers had to wait on the plane while we were photographed at the top of the steps. We were then escorted indoors by officials of the Israeli Government and put into a separate room. All our papers were ready for us and we were taken through immigration and customs in a flash with words of welcome from all the officials. No Prime Minister could have been given greater courtesy.
>
> Driving to Jerusalem in the dark, there was an hour's hold up because a military convoy was returning from a parade in the city. We got out and chatted to some soldiers, and Barney had a political argument with one of them in Yiddish. We reached Jerusalem at midnight and booked into the Eden Hotel.

More of our impressions of the young state, three years after its birth, are recorded. Here are some of them:

We got up late, and by the time we got downstairs breakfast was over. Had tea and an apple salvaged from the
plane. They are unobtainable here, and Maurice Rosetti,
who had come to take us to the (old) Knesset asked if he
could have a little just to remind him how they taste . . .
The weather was terribly hot as we arrived in a *hamsin*. We
were not wearing hats and Barney had on his navy blue suit
. . . Everything is rationed except bread. There are no
Jaffa oranges or grapefruit — all are exported . . . There
are no apples at all . . . The rationing is a terrible headache
for the women — much worse than we in England had to
handle during the war, and most of them are getting weary
of it . . . Went to the Ussishkins, and when Barney said he
would have a cold drink they opened a tin from America
they had been keeping, thinking it was a fruit drink, and it
turned out to be apple sauce!

We went to a construction site at the entrance to Jerusalem,
where the structure now called *Binyanei Ha-Umma* was being
built.

This is going to be a cultural and musical centre for the
country. The large hall will seat 3,500: the smaller one 750.
It is hoped that it will be ready for the Zionist Congress.

A few days after our arrival we attended the President of Israel's
Reception.

Piled into the bus and went off to Rehovot. Moshe Sharett
and Zipporah greeted us with affectionate embraces as
they got out of their car, and we went in with Sprinzak and
his wife. What a glorious place — magnificent grounds
with flowers, trees and lawns . . . Dr Weizmann sat with
Moshe, and a few people including Barney had chats with
him.
    Later in the trip we went along to see Weizmann. He and
Mrs Weizmann were sitting on the terrace outside the
long, book-lined living room. He looked old and frail, but

his brain was clear and his eye bright. Vera Weizmann kept using a flit gun to keep the flies off him. They were most friendly — in fact effusive. He enquired after all the veteran British Zionists by name and wanted to know how Britain and Parliament felt about Israel. When Barney said how wonderful it must be for him to see the realization of all his work, his face lit up and he said 'I am in Heaven here'.

After Barney's death, Harry Shine, who used to be Executive Director of the Keren Hayesod, told me that Weizmann was very happy that Barney had succeeded him as President of the Zionist Federation. Harry also told me that Weizmann set great store by Barney's opinions on the problems of the day, and always wanted to talk with him when Barney came to Israel.

Our tour took us to most parts of the country. Near Haifa, we visited a reception camp, *Sha'ar Aliya*, and met some of the Iraqi immigrants who were living in tents. Barney talked to a cinema operator who was living in one tent with ten other families. All had the same story about Iraq — as soon as they registered to leave for Israel, their bank balances were frozen, their household goods and houses confiscated, and if they had a long wait they became destitute.

One particularly enjoyable evening was spent at dinner with the Sharetts. The diary reads:

> Moshe is as unassuming as ever. He came to the door, took our coats and handed round drinks. There were 14 of us: Sir Leon and Lady Simon, the Rosettis, Dr and Mrs Berenblum and others. I sat next to Moshe at dinner, which was an austerity meal beautifully served. Moshe is a great admirer of the British Parliamentary system. He told us that in the Knesset during the previous week he shocked the members at Question Time by replying to a question 'The answer is "No, Sir"' — and sitting down. He roared with laughter as he told us of the sort of shocked gasp that greeted this reply . . . He is an excellent raconteur and kept us laughing the whole evening.

Barney was in Israel again in August 1951 for the 23rd Zionist

Congress where he urged unity on the delegates. He was aware of the great things being done in Israel and he appreciated the fact that different political parties existed there, but he deplored the factional squabbles that went on in the Zionist Movement. Especially at this early stage in the State's life, with big problems to be overcome internationally, he felt that only a united political front would achieve the desired results. He referred to the British experience, and recommended it as an example.

After the 1950 election, when the Labour Government had a majority of only six in the Commons, Parliamentary life was a veritable hell. MPs were brought in ambulances from their sick beds. Provided they were in the precincts of the House the Whips could vote for them. One night Barney had a temperature of 103, and the Whips insisted that he come down and sit in the Harcourt Room downstairs. So I wrapped him up well and put a hot water bottle on his chest inside his pullover, and drove him to the Harcourt Room. After fifteen minutes he was allowed to go home. Luckily there were no ill-effects.

The Labour Government lasted less than two years, and in October 1951 Barney had to fight another election. He had one or two rough meetings, but was re-elected to Parliament with a good majority. This time it was a straight fight between him and W. J. Heyting for the Tories. Barney polled 25,184 votes to Heyting's 19,125, a majority of 6,059. In the country as a whole, the Conservatives came to power with a majority of sixteen seats over all the other parties.

At this time Barney became particularly concerned with the United Nations Genocide Convention. He continued to argue in its favour until the British Government finally agreed, many years later, to accede to the Convention.

The Draft Convention on Genocide was adopted unanimously by the General Assembly of the United Nations in Paris on Thursday 9 December 1948. It contained nineteen articles, the main purpose being to make genocide, whether committed in time of peace or in time of war, a crime under international law. Genocide was defined as the mass extermination of groups of people on national, ethnic, racial, religious or political grounds. It had been signed by many countries, among them the United States, the USSR and Israel, but not the United Kingdom.

The question was first raised in the House of Commons on 19 October 1949 by Barney, and again on 21 October by Major W. L. Wyatt. In reply Ernest Bevin, the Foreign Secretary, stated that the United Kingdom had not signed because 'the exact implications of accession from the point of view of United Kingdom law were being studied.' The matter was raised again on 20 March 1950 when the Foreign Secretary was asked whether and when he would ask Parliament to ratify the Convention. The reply was that the question was still under examination.

Barney then raised the issue on the adjournment on Thursday 18 May 1950. He said that, as a lawyer himself, he could see that the Government would have some reservations about certain aspects of the Convention, but the British legal experts had had it under consideration even before it was adopted by the General Assembly, and they had not voted against it. Was it then already intended that the Convention should not be ratified by the United Kingdom? Barney argued that the Government could ratify in a way similar to the US Senate, where it was proposed that ratification be subject to four reservations (or 'understandings' as they are called in the US). It was important to give a lead to other countries, particularly smaller ones.

But the Government were unsympathetic. The Minister of State, Mr Younger, explained again that there were still legal difficulties which needed clearing up.

Barney was in New York in June and had intended to meet James N. Rosenberg, Co-Chairman of the United States Committee for a United Nations Genocide Convention, but it was a very rushed stay and he had to fly back to London for the opening of the Parliamentary session. Mr Rosenberg wrote to him, 'I think it would be of immense help if the British Government were to ratify. You will doubtless know, however, that Sir Henry Hartley Shawcross (Attorney General of the Labour Government) has been out of sympathy with the Convention. At least that is my understanding.' Barney replied on 20 June: 'I would be grateful to you if you would let me have information from time to time in relation to the proceedings before the United States Senate or any other steps which have been taken so that I may use them in promoting the matter here. I shall certainly do all I can to help as I feel very keenly about the need and urgency of ratification by all the Governments concerned.'

It was only in 1970 that Britain finally ratified the Genocide Convention. During those years Barney never gave up the struggle. He raised the question periodically during the 1950s but it was obvious that the Government were out of sympathy with the proposal because they maintained that certain provisions conflicted with British practice: in particular, that the extradition clause contained in the Convention might in certain circumstances take away the right of political asylum 'on which this country justly prides itself'.

In 1952 Barney raised the question in relation to Britain's support of the United Nations and its specialised agencies. He felt that there was no point in proclaiming support for the UN if Britain refused to adopt those measures for ensuring peace and security which had been agreed upon at UN meetings. In New York in October he presided at a conference of non-governmental organizations convened to discuss publicity matters (Barney was representing the Co-ordinating Board of Jewish Organizations — CBJO) and called for a world-wide campaign to stress the importance of the ratification of the Convention by all countries. And again in the House of Commons in November, Barney attacked the Government for not acting, this time discussing the problem in the light of his concern about the resurgence of Nazism in Germany. But the Government continued to insist that intricate legal questions had to be resolved before anything could be done.

In 1961 Barney returned to the issue after undergoing a harrowing experience in Israel. This was the time of the trial of Adolf Eichmann, the Nazi official responsible for carrying out Hitler's extermination programme. During the trial Barney met Gideon Haussner, Israel's Attorney General and Eichmann's chief prosecutor, to discuss some of the legal questions involved. Recently Gideon told me that Barney was very reassured by the manner in which the trial was being conducted. There had been a lot of criticism about the way the Israelis had apprehended Eichmann; it was claimed that Israel could not be impartial; that Jewish judges could not be objective, and that the trial would not be fair.

Gideon says that they discussed together the possible conclusions of the trial and that Barney asked him about the death penalty. Barney had long been opposed to capital punishment, and he asked whether it was imperative. In Gideon's words:

> I said, 'I can see no other way of this trial ending. Eichmann has put himself beyond the pale of organized humanity. This is not a case of a man blinded by greed or passion. Here is a man who has pursued nothing but crime for many, many years. There is no way of imposing on him any penalty other than death.' I believe Barney saw that and accepted it, but the trial fascinated him. He was there at several sessions watching, observing, and it shook him to the core. He had to confront it and listen to the witnesses one after the other telling the terrible, terrible story . . . I don't believe he was there during the evidence of Eichmann . . . he was here when we led with our evidence for the prosecution. He was very interested in all the legal points that were raised at the trial. We had opportunities to exchange views on what went on. There was a lot of turbulence during those conversations and Barney was always calm, dismissing with a quip or with perfect humour those very disturbing aspects which at that moment were causing a stir among people . . . and later of course were unimportant. Barney knew it from experience, from his sense as a Parliamentarian.

When Barney raised the genocide issue on the adjournment in June 1961, he began by referring to efforts he and other MPs had made in the 1930s to make the House aware of the atrocities being committed by the Nazis. An MP had intervened, so shocked was he by what Barney was saying at that time, and asked him to give his authority for the facts he was quoting. 'Even the information which was available at that time was too horrible to believe.' He continued:

> Last month, about twenty years afterwards, I remembered that incident while I was sitting in the solemn atmosphere of the courtroom at Jerusalem, overcome by the evidence to which we were listening from men and women who had witnessed such scenes as the crushing out of the brains of men and women, and even children, by so-called human

beings who were worse than the most brutal beasts of the field. Tears came to the eyes of all who were in that court, including the Foreign Secretary of Israel. It was impossible to suppress the emotional reaction which the recounting of these horrific incidents aroused. How was it possible that six million men, women and children could have been tortured and done to death in this age by such diabolical methods? Clearly, the civilized world has to ask itself how this was possible and what can be done to prevent any recurrence.'

Barney surveyed the history of the Convention and explained that there were more ratifications to it than to any other United Nations Convention adopted under the Charter. He argued that any reservations the Government might have could easily be upheld by amendment of the Extradition Act or by taking a disputed matter to the International Court of Justice. He concluded:

In spite of the limitations on the effectiveness of the Convention and the possible need for improving or strengthening of its articles, it is undoubtedly a great step forward in the struggle of the United Nations to secure universal respect for human rights. This is a struggle in which this country should not drag behind, but should give that leadership for which particularly the free and newly independent States of the world look to us in all matters of progress, humanity and international co-operation.

Joseph Godber, the Joint Under-Secretary of State for Foreign Affairs, said in reply: 'I am sure that no one who has listened to the Hon. Member for Leicester, North-West, most carefully, as I have done, could fail to have been touched by the very real emotion and sincerity with which he brought forward this tragic subject to the attention of the House.' He tried to reassure Barney that in most of its aspects the crime of genocide was already covered by existing law. The Government were not prepared to alter legislation, which would have to be done to accommodate the problem of extradition. Nevertheless, Godber said that since a decision had been delayed so long and was thus liable to misinterpretation, the whole question was being re-examined. When Barney again raised the issue on the adjournment in November, the other Joint Under-Secretary, Peter Thomas, said:

> I am grateful for the way in which the honourable Member has presented his case this evening and I can assure him, as did my honourable friend some weeks ago, that we have all the points he has so eloquently urged very much in mind. The House will be informed as soon as we reach a decision and, if that decision is that we should accede to the Convention, the necessary legislation will be brought in as soon as the legislative programme permits.

But disappointment was to come for Barney in the following year when he received a letter from Edward Heath, Lord Privy Seal, in the Tory Government:

> Foreign Office, S.W.1.
> July 4, 1962.
> *Dear Barney,*
> In the adjournment debate on November 8 last year on the Genocide Convention, Peter Thomas promised that the House would be informed as soon as a decision had been reached on the question whether the United Kingdom should accede to the Convention. This decision has now been taken and we are proposing to make an announcement in the House in the near future that the United Kingdom will not accede. In view of the interest you have always shown in this question I felt it right to inform you before the announcement is made.
> I will not go into a detailed explanation now, as you will be familiar with the difficulties from the two adjournment debates we have had . . . I need hardly add that the very nature of the crime of genocide is so appalling that the decision not to accede to a Convention intended to outlaw it was only taken after the most exhaustive consideration of every aspect of the question. We concluded, with the most regret, that

the difficulties in the way of accession are over-riding.

We consider that the Government's decision would be best conveyed to the House in the form of an answer to a Question. It occurred to me that you might yourself wish to put down a question for this purpose and I enclose a draft question which, in that event, you might like to make use of. I should explain that a detailed statement of the reason for the Government's decision would be too long for an Oral Answer and so I would propose to circulate it in the Official Report.

Yours sincerely,

Ted Heath.

Barney replied that he was very disappointed and hoped that 'after examining your full reply I shall be able to convince you of the importance of our acceding to the Convention.' He put down the question which was duly answered on 18 July, but the House was not happy with Heath's answers to the supplementary questions. *The Times'* leader referred to the decision on the following day, and argued that if the British Government did not like the present Convention they should present a new one to the United Nations.

There was no budging the Conservative Government. Barney tried again to get them to reconsider, in a 4 am speech later in July, but while reiterating the Government's 'utter abhorrence of the crime of genocide and their determination that those who commit it should be brought to justice', and giving 'an unqualified assurance that Her Majesty's Government would never themselves violate the principles embodied in the Convention', Peter Thomas insisted that that was that.

There was a rise in anti-semitism in 1960. An example is the threatening telephone call I received at night from a man calling himself 'a member of the British Nazi Party'. He said he was 'going to kill me and all my family'. I had these calls on several nights. My au pair was so frightened that she ran to her sister's home. I telephoned the police, and said that Barney was abroad. They stationed a police guard outside our flat in Albert Hall Mansions. The press found out and numerous newspaper reporters telephoned me. They all wanted to know where Barney was. I said to them, 'I will tell you; but it is my life and the lives of my children that are at risk, so please don't disclose that he is in Israel. It will only rouse these lunatics further.' Not a single newspaper revealed that he was in Israel — they all said he was 'abroad'.

Neo-Nazis like Colin Jordan and John Tyndall were achieving publicity with their organizations. In July 1962, a rally had been held in Trafalgar Square where, as Barney put it, 'We had in Britain the amazing spectacle of people declaring themselves to be Nazis and saying that Hitler, the arch-criminal, the high priest of the doctrine of torture, murder and destruction, was a man whose policy we should continue to follow.'

Barney tried once more with the Tory Government in June 1964, but Peter Thomas refused to reconsider. The position changed with Labour's success in the 1964 General Election. The new Government was more sympathetic, and soon after Barney had asked the usual question in the Commons about the number of States which had so far ratified the Convention, George Thomson, (now Lord Thomson of Monifieth) Minister of State at the Foreign Office, wrote to him confirming that the Government was considering the matter. On 15 November 1965, in reply to a question from Barney, Thomson said that the Government had decided that it *would* accede. Patrick Armstrong, Honorary Clerk to the Parliamentary Group for World Government, wrote to Barney, 'I think this is a real triumph and am so glad your work for this has been rewarded.'

The change of heart involved a reconsideration of the extradition problem in Article VII of the Convention. George Thomson said

> . . . where a person has in fact committed an act of geno-cide of the kind which the Convention requires to be punished, even if he can be shown to have been inspired by political motives, it would in our view be wrong in principle that he should be able to claim asylum on these grounds.

Legislation would be introduced to bring domestic law into line with the Convention.

Nevertheless, it took five more years for the Government to

find the necessary time to put its decision into effect. Barney pressed Dick Taverne, Under Secretary at the Home Office, in 1966 and 1967, but it was only on 2 February 1970, in Barney's last year in the Commons, that the UK's Instrument of Accession to the Genocide Convention was deposited with the Secretary General of the UN.

The UK's accession to the Convention was a tribute to Barney's persistence and to his belief in the moral gesture. His relentless campaign became such a feature of the House that the Convention was jocularly described in the Commons as the 'Jannercide Convention'.

His many interests and responsibilities kept him on the move. The development of air travel made it far easier to fit in all the international meetings and conferences he was invited to, but sometimes he would still travel by sea. In January 1953 he flew to New York for a meeting of the Policy Committee of the Conference on Jewish Material Claims Against Germany. He returned, in time for the opening of the Parliamentary session, in the *Queen Mary* together with Winston Churchill. Hearing that Barney was on board, Churchill invited him down to his cabin to have coffee with him. He was wearing his famous 'siren suit'. As soon as Barney entered the room, Churchill stood up and said 'Janner, I am a Zionist' . . . as if to say, 'Now that's that, let's get on with something else.'

Another Churchill incident occurred outside Barney Baruch's house in New York. Churchill was inside with his friend Baruch, and a crowd had gathered outside waiting for Churchill to come out. Barney passed by, and some of the people said 'Wait. Churchill is coming out.' Barney replied 'I can't wait. Besides, I see him every day.' They looked at him as if he were mad!

For Israel, the early 1950s were years of consolidation and the absorption of many thousands of immigrants who were arriving from such Arab countries as Yemen, Iraq, Morocco and others. But the survival of Israel was still under threat, and Barney was as vigilant as ever in expressing concern for her security in the House of Commons, no matter what others said about his consistently pro-Israel speeches. In February 1953 he was worried about the sale of jet planes by Britain to the Arab countries.

He went to Israel regularly to attend the meetings of the

Actions Committee, as a delegate for the General Zionists. His constant plea was for others to learn by the experience of the Zionist Movement in Britain where all the factions co-operated in the Zionist Federation (as they did until recently). He wanted the Movement to 'change the system of severe Party business', to concentrate on practical work. He would use himself as an example of non-political Zionism — a traditional Jew and a socialist, belonging to the General Zionists!

Barney knew that the US and Israel were now great centres of Jewish life, but he was adamantly opposed to the idea of running down Zionist activities in Europe, something which was on the agenda at the 1952 meeting. 'What was the good of taking the main offices in Europe away?' he asked. 'Why have you not got the good sense to realize that you must have some kind of regional organization in Europe itself? Don't you think that we in England are capable of guiding such work, when we have achieved such a great deal, when we have been able to persuade our community to be about 80 per cent Zionist?'

This was a theme he referred to in the following few years. He believed that the Movement was understanding what could be achieved in Europe. He was also a strong advocate of what he called 'middle-class agricultural settlement', of the kind we had seen at Kfar Mordechai during our 1951 tour. Since then Barney had worked hard to help that 'Anglo-Saxon' community. In the Actions Committee Barney argued that more money should be allocated for loans for this kind of settlement — it was a way of broadening the base of Western *aliyah*.

During our trip to Israel in 1953 we saw that immense changes had taken place in two years. Barney was always keen on projects that promoted *aliyah*. One such plan was called *Shnat Sherut*, which brought young people from abroad to spend a year in Israel studying Hebrew and working. We visited such a group from Britain, at Kibbutz Usha, and he sat with them for over an hour. They were all grateful for his advice and encouragement. He always enjoyed being with young people.

At Nahalal we called at the WIZO Agricultural Training School, founded and run by Canadian Hadassah. The children were at their classes and Barney was introduced to them in each classroom. One child whispered to me in Hebrew 'Is he Bevin?'! Barney spoke to them for a couple of minutes about

Parliament and then asked if anyone had any questions. One immediately jumped up and said 'Can I have your autograph?' He was instantly surrounded by some forty boys and girls all waving their exercise books or pieces of paper at him. At Kfar Mordechai, where the electricity Barney had worked three years to get them could only be used in the few wooden houses, we went into the little village office where they had a radio. They turned it on and were thrilled to have Barney dance with one of them to the tunes of a dance band.

During the war Jewish organizations had been considering what to do about property expropriated by the Nazis. In 1951 the Conference on Jewish Material Claims Against Germany was established by twenty-three national and international Jewish organizations. Its aims were 'to obtain funds for the relief, rehabilitation and resettlement of Jewish victims of Nazi persecution, and the rebuilding of Jewish communal life; and to obtain indemnification for injuries inflicted upon victims of Nazi persecution and restitution for properties confiscated by the Nazis.'

After Barney died, Saul Kagan, Executive Director of the Claims Conference wrote from New York:

> Barney — as he was called among his friends on this side of the ocean — was one of the founders of the Claims Conference in 1951, who played a major leadership rôle during the first ten years of our existence. These were the years of basic decisions and accomplishments of the Claims Conference. He was deeply involved in the formulation of the policies for the distribution of the funds which were obtained as a result of our agreement with the German Federal Republic. As you know, the allocations of the Claims Conference were vital for the rebuilding of the Jewish communities which were occupied by the Nazis and for the resettlement and rehabilitation of the survivors. I have very warm personal memories of my dealings with him. He brought to our work not only his broad grasp of the Jewish problems following the Holocaust, but a fine sense of humour which helped to see us through difficult moments.

Barney became a Vice-President and Director of the Claims Conference, and was a member of the Executive Committee.

He was also instrumental in the establishment of the Jewish Trust Corporation (JTC) whose main purpose was, according to an official history of the JTC, to 'discover, claim, acquire, receive, hold, maintain, manage, administer, hire, liquidate and otherwise dispose of' heirless and unclaimed Jewish property in the British Zone of Occupation in Germany and the British Sector of Berlin, and 'to use such property for the benefit of Jewish communities of Germany and victims of Nazi or other persecution or discrimination'. The British Government agreed in 1949 to the establishment of this body and Barney chaired the meeting of Jewish organizations interested in the problem, convened by the Board of Deputies on 17 October 1949. The relations of the JTC to the post-war communities in the British Zone of Germany had to be clarified, and an understanding arrived at with them regarding the property of the former Jewish communities. Negotiations took place and the result was the 'London Agreement' reached at a meeting chaired by Barney and signed on 3 March 1950.

The German Federal Government agreed to pay compensation to victims of Nazism, but attempts to negotiate reparations from Austria were less successful. In October 1952 Barney was appointed the Board of Deputies' representative on the co-ordinating committee of Jewish organizations for negotiations with Austria. Talks were held with Austrian Chancellor Julius Raab in June 1953 and Barney, as a member of the eight-man delegation, reported to the Board of Deputies on the results, which were disappointing. Barney discussed the problem with Nahum Goldman in Paris after the negotiations were stopped and the Austrian Government failed to resume them.

The *Jewish Chronicle*, commenting on a meeting of the Board of Deputies when the Austrian problem was discussed, said:

> The deplorable failure of the Austrian Government to meet the just claims made on it for restitution to the Jewish victims of Nazism was rightly condemned. A welcome lead in this regard was taken by Mr Barnett Janner MP. He led a joint deputation of representatives of interested Anglo-Jewish organizations to Mr Selwyn Lloyd, Minister of

State at the Foreign Office, to ask the British Government to use its influence with the Austrian Government to secure a just settlement. It may be hoped that this energetic action will help towards removing the present deadlock in the negotiations with Austria.

Unfortunately, the Austrians never co-operated in the same way as the Germans. Barney wrote to *The Times* in 1955 on the anniversary of the *Anschluss*, drawing attention to the fact that the Austrian Government had still not paid compensation to former Austrian citizens who were dispossessed during the Nazi period. In the same year, during the Commons debate on the Austrian State Treaty Bill, Barney raised the matter and said that it would be in Austria's interest to pay compensation. He felt that the British Government could have been more helpful in securing such compensation from the Austrians. In reply Harold Macmillan, then Foreign Secretary, said Barney had acted very properly in raising the matter, which was of great concern to the Government. He hoped that Article 26 of the State Treaty would provide the machinery for solving the problem and that signing the Treaty would mean a new start for Austria. The reparations agreement, concluded with Austria in 1962, fell far short of what might fairly have been expected.

In the 1931–35 Parliament, Barney had often appealed to the authority of the League of Nations when discussing world problems. When Hitler began implementing his anti-Jewish measures, Barney had urged the Government to take the matter to the League. The League had proved impotent, but Barney believed that the United Nations, which was designed to overcome the weaknesses of the League of Nations, could be a major force in the post-war world, particularly when it came to upholding and securing human rights. And this, to be sure, became one of the main activities of the UN and its specialized agencies.

Immediately after the war, Barney, through his Chairmanship of the Foreign Affairs Committee of the Board of Deputies, became involved in the human rights activities of the UN, and of other international organizations. In November 1948 he went to the third session of the Human Rights Commission at Lake Success. He addressed the Commission on behalf of the Co-ordinating Board of Jewish Organizations, and emphasized the need to exclude incitement to racial or religious hatred from freedom of expression and information.

In October 1952, at a session of the UN Sub-Committee on the Prevention of Discrimination and the Protection of minorities, Barney said that implementation of the principles of non-discrimination enunciated in the Charter should constitute the primary objective of all UN institutions. The Sub-Committee had been set up in 1947 because the Commission on Human Rights was so occupied with the drafting of the Bill of Human Rights that it had no time to deal with the intricate aspects of discrimination, and the protection of minorities.

In an article he wrote for the *Jewish Chronicle* in 1955 Barney referred to the work being done by the UN in this field, adding:

> That is not to say that human rights have been secured in practice in the world. Far from it; progress, if any, has been very slow; in some respects, the world has even taken retrogressive steps. But it remains an important fact that the question of human rights has been placed on the agenda for all time, and that the Governments of the world are not allowed to forget about it.

In subsequent years Barney watched the high hopes which had been invested in the UN's work against discrimination fade, but he maintained a realistic approach throughout the whole process. There were no easy answers; it was not a simple process to develop internationally applicable anti-discrimination laws which countries with vastly differing social, political and legal systems would accept. But the problems of discrimination, the rights of asylum, and the curse of statelessness, were all issues of such importance that they should be continually pressed upon Governments.

In 1952, Harold Lever, MP for Manchester Central (now Lord Lever), introduced a Private Member's Bill to amend the law of defamation so as to afford greater protection for the individual. John Fortune, the editor of the *Leicester Mercury*, wrote to Barney urging him to support the Bill and Barney replied: 'I have supported the Bill all along and I was on the Committee which dealt with it. I shall certainly do whatever I

116

can to help further.' In fact Barney had not only supported the Bill, he had tried, together with Sir Leslie Plummer, Labour MP for Deptford, to get provisions incorporated into the Bill outlawing the defamation of groups. Barney said,

> If the law affords protection to individuals, I cannot see a logical ground for not extending the same protection to groups or communities. I agree that there may be some difficulty — indeed, there is some difficulty — in defining a group or community. The type of vilification particularly against the section of the British community of which I happen to be a member, and the type of statement that is made at times today which is not acceptable, is something which every decent citizen would revolt against if only he knew the consequences that might ensue. I am not talking about a trivial matter: I am talking about a subject in which similar activities on a large scale in Nazi Germany were materially responsible for causing the death of six million innocent victims. Nobody here at that time realized what effect that kind of vilification would have.

Barney's proposal attracted much sympathy in the House but the Government argument was that it was impossible to legislate satisfactorily on the problem, and the proposal to amend failed. Harold Lever's Bill passed into law.

On 12 July 1952 we celebrated our Silver Wedding with an 'At Home' at our flat, 69 Albert Hall Mansions. On Saturday 19 July we held a big Silver Wedding and Victory party for 850 Labour Party members in Leicester at the de Montford Hall. (The 'Victory' was for the General Election — a little late.) During the evening two of Barney's oldest constituents, Mr Charlie Saxton and Mr Will Crookes, both members of Leicester Labour Party for more than fifty years, presented us with a chiming clock. It was a great evening — dancing, food and jollity. Throughout the years, and still today, people who had been there have told us how wonderful it was and many have kept their invitations.

In May 1953, Edgar Jones died. At the funeral Barney paid a moving tribute to the man who had been such a formative influence on his life. A former pupil of the school wrote to

Barney a few days later:

> Immediately . . . I read in the *Western Mail* the next morn-
> ing the tribute you paid to Major Jones we wished that
> 'Edgar' could have been spared to have read it himself. I
> spent a few hours at Eryl [the home of the Jones family] on
> Sunday following his passing, and I was thrilled that not
> only had our beloved Head Gwyneth [his daughter] read
> his 'best epitaph', but that you had followed it by your
> personal visit the morning after. You will never be able to
> realise what your loyal friendship has meant to those dears
> at Eryl. It would be impossible for me to tell you how many
> old Barrians of our village were moved by your inspired
> tribute to our dear friend and I assure you that because of
> your unbroken loyalty to Dr Jones and Barry all down the
> years we do now feel that you are a tremendously strong
> link between Edgar Jones and the old boys and girls of his
> school.

Many years later, in a 1974 radio interview, Barney spoke of
Edgar Jones's influence: 'He was fifty years ahead of his time in
the scholastic profession and he had a great effect on me, as he
did on the other students at the school.'

In Parliament Barney was anxious to protect the rights of
tenants. There were two Rent Acts in the post-war Parliament,
in 1946 and 1949. The first created rent tribunals to fix the price
of furnished lettings, and the second authorized rent tribunals
to determine 'reasonable' rents, on the application of the tenants. This Act applied to unfurnished houses and flats. Barney
was worried that this system of protection for the tenants might
be eroded by Tory legislation. During the thirteen years of Tory
Government, from 1951 to 1964, two Acts were passed which
decontrolled many houses and permitted increases in controlled
rents.

From the very start Barney went on the offensive to prevent
the Tories from tampering with the Rent Acts. In July 1952 he
accused the Government of encouraging landlords to charge
exorbitant rents and thus circumvent the Acts, and he drew
attention to other abuses: houses were standing empty and the
Tories were objecting to their being requisitioned; agents were

charging £5–£20 for finding accommodation, and so on. He was worried for the future of the Rent Tribunals because he saw that the measures proposed by the Government would weaken them. Throughout the Parliament he consistently opposed Tory plans to weaken tenants' rights, calling the 1954 Bill 'pernicious' and saying it was 'a pure travesty' to name it a Leasehold Reform Bill.

He was still dealing with housing problems on a day-to-day basis, in Leicester and in his solicitor's practice. To give one example, in October 1954, in a case widely reported in the national press, he acted on behalf of a Mrs Eliza Dorrell, a 60-year old woman from Stockwell, who was being sued for £57, said to be arrears of mortgage payments. The plaintiffs in the case were a firm called Rojan Ltd, an estate company belonging to one Arthur Bertram Walters. In the Lambeth County Court Barney said, 'It was their system, as fraudulent swindlers, to come together under the alias of Mr Walters, or of Mr Brady — the man whom no one can discover, who is kept behind a façade.' They used the courts to get possession orders, on which they tried to get tenants to buy their houses rather than be evicted.

The judge in the case said that Rojan Ltd was a collecting agency into which money passed. 'Once it had gone over to the other side, that money disappeared.' In his judgment the judge said, 'The whole organization is nothing but a wholesale fraud, designed to cloak the activities of Walters. There may be a remedy which will overtake Mr Walters in the long run. It is contrary to public policy that the judgment of this court [a possession order] should have been used as a lever to wrench out of Mrs Dorrell the money she paid.' The judge ordered that the mortgage should be set aside, and gave costs to Mrs Dorrell.

Before women's rights became a big issue in this country Barney was supporting a Private Member's Bill on Women's Disabilities. He argued that women should have the opportunity to obtain from errant husbands the payments to which they were entitled. He spoke on industrial safety, and on food hygiene in an adjournment debate where Dr Charles Hill, Parliamentary Secretary to the Ministry of Food, and later Lord Hill, thanked him for the public service he had performed by raising the issue. He also discussed legal aid; he argued against the importation of foreign horror comics which he believed were having a harmful effect on the young; and supported a Private Member's Bill which aimed to stop the sale of toy guns that could be made into lethal weapons.

In a motion he moved in March 1953, he urged the Government and hospital authorities to establish a comprehensive geriatric service to cover the whole country. He drew attention to the fact that the proportion of the population over sixty-five was growing all the time. Many families do marvellous work, but many old people are lonely and miserable. He argued that within the present Acts it was possible to do much more, to set up geriatric units in each group of hospitals.

'There is a duty upon the community as a whole', Barney said, 'to make the last years of its elders pass in happiness and tranquillity, with as little pain to them as possible, either mentally or physically.' After a lengthy debate the motion was passed. The Parliamentary Secretary to the Ministry of Health, Miss Patricia Hornsby-Smith (now Lady Hornsby-Smith), said: 'This has been a most helpful and constructive debate. I join the congratulations offered to the honourable Member for Leicester NW, not only on the terms of his motion but on the full and constructive speech he made. He set the pace of the debate.'

7 PRESIDENT OF THE BOARD OF DEPUTIES OF BRITISH JEWS 1955–1964

In April 1955 Sir Anthony Eden took over from Churchill as Prime Minister, and called a General Election for Thursday 26 May. It was not an easy fight. The Tories had been reaping the economic benefits of Labour's post-war austerity programme. They had been able to end controls and rationing.

In Leicester it was a straight contest again between Barney and his Tory opponent. This time the Tories selected Frederick Arthur Tomlinson, a Nottinghamshire trade unionist lorry driver, to oppose him.

Election meetings were usually decorous affairs, but not always. For example, Barney often dwelt on the number of letters he had from constituents and how carefully he dealt with them. At one meeting a lady heckler accused him of ignoring a letter she had sent him in 1953 about her son in Korea. He asked her to come back the next evening and he would reply after consulting his files. She did not turn up, but he informed the gathering that not only had he dealt with the case, but he had also sent an airmail letter to Korea.

As part of their election coverage the *Leicester Evening Mail* produced pen portraits of the candidates:

> If they dubbed him the 'Persistent MP', Barnett Janner would smile and take it as a compliment. For his perseverance has often transformed matters parochial into items of national interest. Whether it be from telephones on Stocking Farm to allowances for parents who visit GI brides, he will repeat his question in the House until justice, he feels, has been done. An expert on housing and rent problems, Mr Janner is Honorary Advisor to the Labour Party on both subjects. He gave evidence before the Government Committee set up some years ago to enquire into the Rent Restriction Acts.

121

At a Leicester May Day rally Barney was on the platform when Arthur Deakin, General Secretary of the Transport and General Workers Union, collapsed and died while delivering a speech. Barney and two other Labour MPs rushed across the platform to help him but there was nothing they could do.

Not all the memorable incidents from that election were quite so dramatic. Barney canvassed door to door, making speeches with his usual speed and energy. Councillor Colin Grundy, who canvassed with him in that election, remembers one incident when he and Ron Simmons, Assistant Area Organizer for the East Midlands, were with Barney in Haddenham Road.

> Barney went into a house and Ron and I finished off the rest of the road and then came back and Barney was nowhere to be seen. Ron said, 'Where is he?' and I said 'Well, he went into that house,' and Ron said, 'I'll go and get him out.' Ron knocked at the door and went into the house. He was back out in about ten seconds and said to me that Barney was in there playing hell about the Tories and their lack of house building. Sitting in front of the fire in a zinc bath with a towel around her was a young woman. Barney was completely unconcerned about that — he was more concerned about the housing. He was taking notes and condemning the Tories!

Colin told me another story about canvassing one evening in the Haddenham Road. They knocked on a door and when there was no reply

> Barney said, 'Well, let's go down the entry.' We did so and we saw an old lady passing across the yard. He shouted out in his usual exuberant way, 'Hello there!' and then shone his torch vertically upwards across his face and on to his hat, which must have been a horrible sight. The woman just screamed and ran. Then he said, 'Come on, let's go.' But the lady's son came out and on being told we were canvassing for Barnett Janner was quite happy.

Ruth, Barney and I worked terribly hard at canvassing, as at all elections. Barney did try to rest a little every day. He would come into the hotel at about half past two, have a bite to eat and then sleep until about five when he would go on his 'evening shift'. Many political people used to say, 'You can't canvass at lunch time, people are eating and don't want to be disturbed,' but we found that meal times were the best times to catch them in. Barney drove his helpers hard but, as they recall, he never asked anyone to do something he was not prepared to do himself, so they did not mind.

He would attack the Tories on their politics and the mistakes they made, but he was always very fair to his opponents. One story is told of a Party meeting when Barney made some complimentary remarks about a Tory Minister, and a local Party member said to him 'I don't know how you can talk about these people like this . . . you know they're offensive to us.' Barney said

Look Tony, it's like this, we're working with these people all day long. If we weren't a little bit civilized at times life would be unbearable. When they are wrong in some political matter don't expect that I will take it lying down. But when they are doing the decent thing, which may not be very often, they ought to be congratulated.

The Tories were returned to power with a fifty-eight seat majority. Barney held his seat with a majority of 3,510, his second smallest margin of victory as a Leicester MP.

With one election over, Barney was thrown immediately into another. He had been Vice-President of the Board of Deputies of British Jews since 1946. In June 1955, after thirty years as a member, first for Cardiff and then for Leeds, he stood against Dr Israel Feldman for election to the Presidency. Immediately before the election the *Jewish Chronicle* wrote:

If service to the Board is to be the criterion — and it must be a very important, if not the determining factor — none can doubt the prior claims of Mr Janner on this occasion. He has for many years, in the true sense of that usually overworked word, been indefatigable in his attention to the business of the Board and, through it and in many other ways, especially in Parliament, to the welfare of the community. Assiduity, even if naught else — and there is, of course, very much else — would seem to demand Mr Janner's promotion.

The election was on 19 June and Barney won by 187 votes to Dr Feldman's 82. He pledged himself to do all he could to cement relationships in the community as a whole.

He was an inspired leader who pulled the Board up to new levels. His predecessor, Dr Abraham Cohen, had unfortunately suffered from heart trouble. Barney was the first President of the Board to be received by the Prime Minister of the day. He went to No. 10 Downing Street on 5 August 1955 for talks with Harold Macmillan. They discussed a whole range of matters of importance to the Jewish community in Britain and overseas. It was such an unprecedented event that the *Jewish Chronicle* sent a photographer to take his photograph outside No. 10.

Even before he was elected he was fulfilling many important presidential functions. The second Commonwealth Conference of Jewish Leaders was held in June 1954 at Woburn House. Attending the conference were delegates from Aden, Australia, Canada, India, New Zealand, Rhodesia, South Africa and the UK. Barney presided at the opening session, welcoming the delegates with a speech which dwelt on the achievements of the 1950 conference. At that conference, the first in the series, Barney had chaired the sessions which dealt with foreign affairs, having been elected Chairman of the Foreign Affairs Committee in 1949. His opening theme was the securing of effective respect for human rights, through the Human Rights covenant of the UN. He had harsh words for the World Jewish Congress for handing in its memorandum on the covenant without consulting other Jewish organizations. Barney felt that the promotion of the welfare of Jewish communities abroad could best be done by co-ordination. At the 1954 conference he emphasized that the purpose was to discuss the problems of overseas communities, not to establish a 'Commonwealth bloc of Jewish communities, or in any way to separate ourselves from Kelal Israel'.

The problems he considered important were the diminishing size of the Commonwealth communities through inter-marriage, and the loss of ties with the Jewish religion. Such

124

activities as combating antisemitism and assisting less fortunately placed communities were only useful in the context of a full Jewish life.

It would be impossible to record all that Barney did in his capacity as President of the Board, the very many representations he made to British Government Ministers; his travels on behalf of oppressed Jews; and the representations he made to the Heads of foreign states. He breakfasted with Harry Truman in London in June 1956; he had an interview with the Prime Minister of Australia, Sir Robert Menzies. While President he tried to improve the finances of the Board. He travelled throughout the country and raised £150,000 for the Trust Fund which the Board set up.

There were some memorable occasions during Barney's Presidency of the Board which will be remembered as outstanding events in the life of the Jewish community. They are tributes to his energy and his vision of the proud rôle he wanted the Jewish community to play in British life.

On 5 November 1958, the Board gave a glittering dinner and ball at Grosvenor House in honour of Eliahu Elath, Israel's Ambassador to the Court of St James's, to mark the tenth anniversary of the establishment of the State of Israel. There were more than a thousand guests. The speakers were the Prime Minister Harold Macmillan, Hugh Gaitskell, Leader of the Opposition, the Liberal leader Jo Grimond, Barney (who was Chairman) and Lady Megan Lloyd George.

Eliahu remembers the dinner as:

> The great event in our lives in the nine and a half years we were in London . . . The BBC transmitted it to Israel. Many of our friends listened to it. The next morning I received a very nice cable from Golda Meir.

Macmillan made a fine speech, treading delicately around the contentious aspects of British policy in the Middle East, and succeeding in being humorous as well.

Many of the guests wrote to us afterwards expressing their thanks for the evening.

Two years later the Board held a Banquet and Ball on 4 April 1960 to celebrate its two hundredth anniversary. His Royal

Highness The Duke of Edinburgh was the Guest of Honour. Barney presided, and responded to Prince Philip's toast to the Board. The Chancellor of the Duchy of Lancaster, Dr Charles Hill, and the Leader of the Opposition, Hugh Gaitskell, made excellent speeches. The former President of the Board, Judge Neville Laski, proposed the toast to the Jewish communities of the world, and Arthur Lourie, Israel's Ambassador, responded. James Orr, The Duke of Edinburgh's secretary, wrote to Barney that the Duke was

> delighted with the most enjoyable evening and the excellent dinner he had yesterday as guest of the Board of Deputies of British Jews. The whole occasion was a great success and the abbreviated speeches appeared to bring out the best in both speaker and audience.

In his speech Barney said:

> We are tonight holding a family party and our joy is complete by having you with us. You, sir, are a man who is the embodiment of the true spirit of the age and if I may say it without presumption, you take a deep interest in everything which concerns the people, irrespective of class or creed, and bring to all you say and do a spirit of adventure and excitement that inspires us all.

HRH Prince Philip later turned to Barney several times on matters involving Jews. His Royal Highness asked Barney to come to Buckingham Palace as he wanted to discuss something with him. Barney went, and Prince Philip explained that he wanted a portrait painted of Professor Sir Solly Zuckerman, Secretary of the Zoological Society of which Prince Philip was President. The Duke said he did not want to make a public appeal for such a person, but thought that some members of the Jewish community might like to honour Sir Solly in this way. Barney privately raised the several thousand pounds required.

On 18 May 1966 Prince Philip paid a private visit to the Zoological Society to accept the portrait on the Society's behalf. Barney made the presentation. The portrait now hangs in the Headquarters of the Society at Regents Park. At that time

Prince Philip and Sir Solly Zuckerman interested Barney in the work of the Zoological Society, and he remained active on its behalf.

When Barney was awarded his Knighthood in 1961 it was the proudest moment of his life, especially as it was awarded for his work as President of the Board of Deputies. He was in Israel attending the 25th Zionist Congress when the announcement of his Knighthood was made on January 1st 1961. He was deeply touched when at the opening of the session that day Moshe Sharett said from the chair:

> I am sure I am expressing what is in the hearts of all of you as I say from this platform of the presidency of this Congress, to our dear and honoured friend, a veteran and dedicated Zionist of many years, a Jewish public servant and an honoured leader, one who has fought for us with extraordinary courage on the political scene for all these many years, that for the honour which has been bestowed on him by his Government I extend our heartiest felicitations to Sir Barnett Janner. We are happy in the honour that has come to him, not only because we hold him in such affection and esteem, but also because the recognition which has been given to him is an honour to the Jewish people.

The *Jewish Chronicle* paid him this tribute:

> Mr Janner is rightly esteemed for the human and kindly qualities, the sympathy and warmth of heart, which have always typified him throughout his career. For many years he has been a Member of Parliament who has zealously furthered the promotion of social and democratic causes. But Mr Janner has won general admiration also by the tireless way in which he has devoted himself to the leadership of Jewish causes. He has shown in no uncertain manner how the duties and obligations of a good British citizen include loyalty and service to his own religious community.

In 1963 the Board became involved in the Mancroft Affair. In

December, Lord Mancroft, a Jew, resigned under Arab pressure from his directorship of the Advisory Board of the Norwich Union. The Arabs proposed to do business with the huge insurance company, but objected to Lord Mancroft's Jewish business connections, particularly his link with Great Universal Stores. As the *Daily Mail* put it, 'Norwich Union referred the threats to Lord Mancroft and accepted his resignation. They said their business would be seriously prejudiced by an Arab boycott.'

The resignation brought a storm of protest and publicity all over the country and in all parties. Barney tabled a question in the House, and the Board of Deputies intervened with the Norwich Union. As President of the Board, Barney issued a strong statement deploring the incident. The Company replied in a totally unsatisfactory manner and Barney said to the press: 'It is hard to believe that the conduct of a body of such standing should be conditioned by the irresponsible and hostile attitude of the Arabs towards Israel.'

The President of the Norwich Union, Sir Robert Bignold, issued an invitation to the Board to meet him and Barney agreed. They met on 10 December together with other Board and Norwich Union representatives, as a result of which the Company invited Lord Mancroft to resume his seat on the London board. After the meeting the Company issued a statement:

> They assured [the Board of Deputies] that the Norwich Union have never had the intention to aid or comfort the Arab boycott of Israel and absolutely refused any suggestion that they intended to encourage it. The Norwich Union representatives also made it clear that they write insurance business in Israel as well as in many other parts of the world, and they propose to do their best to encourage and expand this business.

The Government issued a statement strongly disapproving of 'pressure from any source on British firms to discriminate between British subjects on any grounds.' Although Lord Mancroft refused the invitation to rejoin the board of the Company, the representations made by the Board of Deputies under

Barney's leadership achieved the desired effect. In the House of Commons, and through Board deputations to the Home Secretary, Barney was active in pressing the Government to ensure that the police did everything they could to deal with resurgent antisemitism. In 1964, the activities of the neo-Fascist groups had become more worrying, particularly after the Trafalgar Square rally in 1962, organized by the 'National Socialist Movement' under the slogan 'Hitler Was Right'. Following that meeting Barney went with a delegation to the Home Office to try to persuade the Government to ban the Fascist groups. He said:

It is our opinion that the law greatly needs strengthening and that the Board, in co-operation with other organizations, organize and present to the Government a petition signed by thousands of citizens asking for suitable legislation to be passed against incitement on racial and religious grounds.

His activity on behalf of *shechita* twenty years earlier had to be re-enacted in the 1950s, when Robert Crouch MP introduced a Private Member's Bill to remove the exemption of *shechita* which had been written into the 1933 Slaughter of Animals Act, from the requirement of stunning. The Board was very active in putting the case for *shechita* to the MPs concerned and the Bill failed to get a second reading. Referring to the Crouch Bill in his President's report in 1958 Barney said:

The fact that this legislation was not proceeded with, has not removed the menace of the continuing endeavours of the antagonists of *shechita* to promote legislation prohibiting the Jewish method. Their attempts are made in every possible direction and they seize the smallest opportunity that may present itself in any measure, however remote on the surface from the Slaughter of Animals Act, to further their ends. This aspect of defence has been constantly watched both in and out of Parliament.

In 1963 there was a further attempt, this time by David Ensor MP, to abolish the exemption of *shechita* and other forms of ritual slaughter, from the various Acts. The Board again mounted a vigorous campaign, using the testimony of experts to show that *shechita* was a humane way of slaughter, and the Bill was overwhelmingly defeated in December. Bernard Homa, Chairman of the Board's Shechita Committee, wrote to Barney:

> I know that the work you did in Parliament and outside in connection with the recent anti-Shechita campaign was motivated entirely by your own sincere devotion to the cause. Nevertheless I feel that I must express to you my sincere admiration and, I feel sure, that of the whole of the Anglo-Jewish Community, for the splendid way in which you were able to muster so much support to counter Mr Ensor's intentions.

One of Barney's duties as President of the Board was to represent the Board on the Co-ordinating Board of Jewish Organizations (CBJO) and then on its successor the Co-ordinating Committee of Jewish Organizations (COJO). Both organizations had consultative status with the United Nations as non-governmental organizations with the Economic and Social Council. Barney and Philip Klutznick, now President Emeritus of the World Jewish Congress, were co-chairmen of the CBJO.

The way in which one honour came to Barney always remained something of a mystery to him. In May 1957 he was awarded an honorary Doctorate of Law by Leeds University. The degree was conferred by the Princess Royal, Princess Mary, Chancellor of Leeds University, and Barney was presented by the Pro-Vice-Chancellor Professor Whetton who, in his address, said: 'In honouring Barnett Janner we acclaim the paramount work of his life for Israel — for He that keepeth Israel shall neither slumber nor sleep.' In their profile of Barney before the ceremony, the *Yorkshire Post* called him 'a vigorous and outstanding personality in general public life'. Barney was very grateful to be so honoured. In his letter of thanks to the Vice-Chancellor, Sir Charles Morris, he said, 'The ceremony on Friday was one which I shall never forget, nor will my family and friends who had the privilege of being present.' Others honoured on that occasion were Sir William Ivor Jennings, Professor Gunnar Myrdal, Dr Margaret Mead and the then

Archbishop of York, Michael Ramsey (later Archbishop of Canterbury).

Barney was re-elected twice to the Presidency of the Board at the triennial elections of 1958 and 1961, and he stood again for a fourth term in 1964, at seventy-two years old.

In March 1964 the *Jewish Chronicle* published an editorial in which they called on Barney and other septuagenarians to stand down and make way for new blood.

> The Board's leading members can proudly claim to have rendered it lengthy and distinguished service. They are exemplified by Sir Barnett Janner, who has already devoted nine intensive years to the Board's Presidency and an even longer period to lower office and committee membership. He has always found time for everything and everybody — nothing is too big or too small for him, no one too important to be bothered for help, no one too unimportant to be seen personally. But the question inevitably arises whether the time has not come for these elderly statesmen of the community to become elder statesmen and make way for the younger men, while they are still in a position to advise from the sidelines.

Not everyone agreed with the Editor of the *Jewish Chronicle*. One reader's letter in response to the editorial said,

> I cannot readily call to mind any other Anglo-Jew who has played such a useful and energetic rôle in every facet of Jewish life in this country and to such good effect. I can think of no one who is held in greater esteem and authority by all Government departments in this country and in the field as well. He is a great Parliamentarian and fearless in speaking frankly on every occasion when the interest of the Jewish community is concerned.

The election took place in June 1964. Alderman A. Moss, Senior Vice-President, and a former Lord Mayor of Manchester, defeated him by fifteen votes. Naturally Barney was upset, but he took his defeat well. The *Jewish Chronicle* reported:

Sir Barnett made a brief and moving speech which earned him an ovation. Addressing the Board as President for the last time, he wished his successor luck. 'As far as this community is concerned the Board has always been my first allegiance and I propose to continue my public work. . . . But I am sure the Board will realize that I could no longer do it in the same manner. My doors will always be open to every person and organization in the community at all times, and I shall remain entirely at the disposal of my friends.

It is typical of the greatness and depth of Barney's character that even after he lost the Presidency of the Board he continued to work there with all his heart and soul, as Chairman of the Foreign Affairs Committee and then as Chairman of the Eretz Israel Committee, which office he had to relinquish in 1979 after the Board had passed new rules limiting the number of years one could be a Chairman or a specific Honorary Officer.

The *Jewish Chronicle* editorial of 19 June 1964 said:

As Sir Barnett Janner hands over the reins of office to his successor, the whole community will join in unstinted recognition of his nine years of selfless service as President of the Board — the culmination of many decades of service to the community. Sir Barnett has been indefatigable in furthering the interests of Anglo-Jewry, and it is devoutly to be hoped that neither he nor any member of the community will interpret his defeat in the presidential election as implying ingratitude or lack of appreciation. . . . The retiring president will remain with us as elder statesman; his invaluable experience and gifts will undoubtedly still be at the community's service. While electoral victories and defeats are forgotten, a record of achievement endures.

Alderman Moss died a month after the election, and Solomon Teff took over. A few days later, in a portrait of a Board of Deputies meeting Chaim Bermant wrote:

On the platform the familiar faces, among them, the most

familiar of all, Sir Barnett Janner, the People's Barney, like a somnolent crag topped with silvery moss. He is to a Jewish gathering what a *mezuza* is to a Jewish home — it isn't quite kosher or complete without him. And the Board of Deputies without Sir Barnett is of course inconceivable. He may no longer be president, but his presence is still presidential. He is still up on high and, indeed, one cannot imagine him elsewhere. Sir Barnett was made for the platform.

When we visited Israel in 1953, we found that many of our friends in Government and the diplomatic service were worried about what would happen after the British withdrew from Egypt. Already the armistice agreement was being flouted, for Israel's ships were not allowed through the Suez Canal, in defiance of an explicit provision that there was to be freedom of navigation. There were fears that once the British had left, Nasser would find the earliest opportunity to attack Israel.

In fact, he was making his intentions known, and not by rhetoric alone. Terrorists were being trained on Egyptian soil, and then infiltrating into Israel and inflicting death and injury on civilians, not to speak of property damage. The Arabs called them *fedayeen*, and treated them as heroes. President Gamal abd-el Nasser gave them his full support.

Britain pulled her troops out of the Canal Zone in June 1956, and in July Nasser nationalized the Suez Canal. Anthony Eden, who had become Prime Minister, saw this seizure of 'a vital artery of world commerce' as a threat to British interests.

In the meantime, Israel had her own reasons for reacting to the escalating violence against her population. On 29 October 1956, she launched 'Operation Sinai' and in a hundred hours had reached within hailing distance of the Canal. Some four days later Britain and France landed troops in the Canal Zone. President Eisenhower expressed disapproval of all military action, which also aroused considerable opposition within the UK. A ceasefire went into effect on 7 November, and UN observers entered the area.

Barney first responded to Nasser's seizure of power in Egypt in a debate in the Commons in November, 1954, drawing attention to Nasser's threat to deal first with the Canal and then with the problem of Palestine. He told the House that he remembered reading words similar to Nasser's in the 1930s in relation to Jews in Germany. People said then that what was being threatened was unbelievable. The Egyptian Jewish community was now in jeopardy. Barney argued that no more concessions should be made to the Arabs. Britain should stand up to Egypt over the Canal and force them to allow Israeli ships through.

Writing in the *Western Mail* a few days later Raymond Gower MP described that debate and said:

> One who spoke with unusual power was Mr Barnett Janner, once a schoolboy at Barry and for some years a Cardiff solicitor. Both sides were moved by his impassioned appeal on behalf of the State of Israel. The whole House approved when he condemned the action of the Egyptians in preventing Israeli ships from using the Suez Canal.

After the debate Barney told a reporter, 'I found other Jewish leaders surprised at the Foreign Secretary's confession that he did not know of the serious attacks which are being made upon Jews in Egypt and elsewhere. He has promised to inquire into them.'

In March 1955 Barney questioned Eden about the *fedayeen*: 'Is he aware that on March 24 an attack was made on a wedding party in the west Negev where a woman was killed and 90 injured? Will he do something about enforcing the armistice on the Egyptians?' Eden replied: 'I am aware that the account you have given only gives the wrongs on one side and not the wrongs on the other. I am indeed aware that wrong exists on both sides. We are doing what we can.'

Throughout 1955 and the first few months of 1956 Barney kept on pressing the Government about the danger of supplying arms to Egypt. In January 1956, after the arms deal between Czechoslovakia and Egypt, he insisted that the balance of power between Israel and the Arab states had been upset. When the Jordanians dismissed General Glubb in March, a sign of their wish to rid themselves of British influence and draw closer to Nasser, Barney regretted that policies of economic advancement for the whole region had not been adopted, rather than policies of military aggression and blackmail. The Suez Canal was the main route for the increasingly important Persian Gulf oil. 'I deliberately say "blackmail",' he told the House, 'because the truth is that what has been practised upon us is plainly blackmail. Of course oil is important to us; but we must not imagine that if a blackmailer is appeased to a certain extent, he will be satisfied.'

In some ways Barney and Anthony Eden, Prime Minister since April 1955, viewed the problem similarly. Eden felt that since failure to stand up to the dictators in the 1930s had led to war, failure to stand up to Nasser's dictatorship would also lead to the shattering of world peace. Barney too likened Nasser's plans to those of Hitler in the 1930s. As far as he was concerned both the rhetoric and the intention were the same.

After the nationalization of the canal in July 1956, and after meetings of the nations who used the canal failed to resolve the crisis, Barney argued that some kind of economic action should be taken which would 'prevent Colonel Nasser and others like him from violating international laws'. The Egyptian boycott of Israeli ships was a violation of human rights.

Before the Suez invasion both Labour and the Tories had been united in their condemnation of Nasser's actions. But once the invasion was launched, Labour condemned the Government's decision. They were against the use of force, and felt that the United Nations should have been called on to solve the problem. Since the Israeli invasion of Sinai was linked to the British and French action, Labour policy also involved the condemnation of Israel.

This situation created extreme difficulties for Barney, who approved of Israel's operation to rid herself of the danger of the Egyptian border, yet decided, along with sixteen other Jewish Labour MPs, to vote against the Government's action in a censure motion. An anonymous writer in a *Jewish Chronicle* silhouette of Barney in 1960 put it this way: 'As a Labour backbencher who leads a non-socialist wing of the General Zionists, in November, 1956 he was hoisted on the horns of a dilemma that has become a classic.'

In the Commons debate on 6 November Barney explained his position. 'I think it is unfortunate that the Israeli action has been mixed up with the movement of British and French troops into the Suez Canal Zone. It is better to analyse these two points separately.' Israel, Barney said, was not interested in intervening in the Suez dispute.

> There is nothing at all to show that Israel has now taken a stand on the Canal issue which makes her move in Egypt an endorsement of Anglo-French policy. . . . I categorically reject the notion that Israel is the aggressor. I am sorry to say that even the official Government spokesman at the United Nations has referred to Israel's 'flagrant aggression'. The fact is that Israel went out to protect her nationals from the armed forces of another country. She went out to establish the rights for her ships to use the Suez Canal. I do not think that she intended to go right across the Suez. I must say that I have no confidence in the Government's policy. They have a heavy responsibility for the present tragedy. The Government built up Nasser as a statesman, as a moderate man with constructive ideas.

The Times commented on the 'Voting problems of Jewish MPs' in its 14 November issue. After saying that Barney 'found himself apparently bound to vote for motions and resolutions by implication condemnatory of Israel's actions', the paper obtained the comments of some prominent Jews. Mr Leonard Stein said that 'the most to be expected of an MP was to vote as his conscience bade him — but he did not think that entitled someone else to tell the MP what his conscience bid him to do. Mr Janner was put into Parliament to support the Labour Party.' Mr Ewen Montagu QC agreed that:

> Nothing could be more harmful to the Jewish community than to call an MP to account for his vote in the House of Commons. But any intelligent member of the Board of Deputies could raise the point that, when an MP held office in the Jewish community and that office clashed with his duty to his constituents, he should at once resign one of the offices.

There were those in the Jewish community who gave Barney a

very hard time over this parliamentary vote. Some even called it a betrayal of Israel. But at the Board of Deputies' meeting on 18 November a resolution was passed expressing full confidence in him. During the debate, which was heated, there were frequent interruptions. In an emotional speech Barney defended his actions:

> Looking back on the forty years of my public life I have a clear conscience that I have done my duty to my country and to Jewry. During this period I have found no difficulty in reconciling both these responsibilities. Not only is there, I believe, no inconsistency between the offices I hold, but I venture the hope that my membership of the House of Commons has enabled me to render some additional service to the Jewish people without in any way affecting my obligations to my constituency, my Party and my country. What I have done in the past I shall continue to do. My conscience is clear.

There was more trouble to come. In March 1957, he attended the Executive of the European Confederation of General Zionists in Paris, where he found himself in a lions' den. The Confederation's executive finally adopted a motion of confidence in him, with three members of the right-wing faction abstaining. They had called for his resignation from the Confederation because of his vote in the House of Commons. But they backed down from their demand when Barney gave his explanation. While approving the Israeli Sinai Campaign, which was launched in self-defence, he objected to the military action of the British Government, the more so as only a fortnight earlier, the same Government had threatened to bomb Israeli cities if Israel found herself at war with Jordan.

Despite the political controversy Barney applied his energies to the problem of the Jewish refugees from Egypt. At almost the same time there was also the problem of the refugees who left Hungary after the 1956 uprising. In his 1958 report to the Deputies Barney said: 'I would put in the forefront the relief and rehabilitation work which again came within the scope of the Board's work and the general tasks of the community.'

Over the years we entertained at our home most of the

important figures of Israel, many of whom Barney had worked with at the offices of the Zionist Organization at 77 Great Russell Street before the establishment of the State. With Weizmann he remained on intimate terms until the latter died in November 1952.

A particularly good friend was Moshe Sharett, Foreign Minister and later Prime Minister of Israel. For years whenever Moshe was in London he would spend Friday evenings with us, and Barney would invite Ministers of the Crown, Members of Parliament and others to meet him either at dinner or afterwards. We did this for many prominent Israeli politicians, and I look back with pleasure to those Friday evenings. They gave an opportunity for MPs of all parties to get first-hand news of what was happening in Israel, and to speak in a friendly and intimate atmosphere with the heads of Israel's government. We both considered this a useful and enjoyable thing to do.

Barney was always very friendly with Golda Meir, and she too spent many evenings with us, meeting members of both Houses of Parliament and other people in British public life. Among those whom we entertained at our home were two future Presidents of Israel, Yitzhak Ben Zvi and Zalman Shazar. Many years earlier, in Egypt during the First World War Ben Zvi, the a volunteer in British uniform, had been a tent-mate of my oldest brother Henry, then a private in the Royal Fusiliers. The third man in the tent was Corporal David Ben Gurion.

Barney saw Ben Gurion more often in Israel than in London. Recently, when Harry Shine was reminiscing to me, he said:

> Once there was a project which I discussed with Ben Gurion for over an hour. I put a suggestion to him, which he did not accept. Then he said, 'Barney Janner will be here in a day or two, and I'll see what he thinks.' He said that he often discussed with Barney what was going on in England and in Europe. He would ask him what should be done and what should not be done, and he often took his advice. That was really a great thing — Ben Gurion taking somebody else's advice!

In the summer of 1957 we spent several weeks on holiday in the United States with our friends Rabbi and Mrs Gershon Levi.

They said: 'You showed us Old England, let us show you New England.' So we took to the road. Barney asked if we could make a stop at Leicester, a small place near Worcester, Massachusetts and said to have been founded by men from Leicester, England. Gershon thought, correctly as it turned out, that the place would be governed by an old-fashioned town meeting, and told Barney to telephone and ask for the First Selectman, and tell him when to expect us. Barney did just that, little realizing that the date he proposed was the actual evening of the Town Meeting!

The voice at the other end of the phone said, 'You'll be welcome!' 'Is there a hotel in town?' 'Sure!' So when we got to the drug-store in Leicester, we stopped to ask where the hotel was. There was none! The nearest was at Vernon, several miles away. We checked in, and then returned to the combination Town Hall-Fire Hall-Police Station. In trooped the Board of Selectmen, warmly welcoming and a little red-faced.

What had happened was this. The First Selectman had a neighbour who was a practical joker. When he heard a booming British voice on the telephone, someone introducing himself as a 'Member of Parliament from Leicester, England', he was sure he was having his leg pulled. He decided to teach his neighbour a lesson by playing along.

Once they realized the true situation, the good people of Leicester could not have been nicer. They actually produced a police escort, and took us to the Town Library, which they opened, although it was night-time, so that we could see the flag of Leicester, England, presented to them by a former Lord Mayor. They rounded up their one British war-bride, and took us all to supper.

We celebrated Barney's seventieth birthday in 1962. At a dinner which the Zionist Federation gave in his honour, tributes were paid to him by, among others, Arthur Lourie, the Ambassador of Israel, Sir Andrew McFadyen representing the Liberal Party, and Selwyn Lloyd, the Chancellor of the Exchequer. When the Chancellor remarked that we had been married for forty-five years, I had to interject that that was a slight exaggeration!

The next speaker was Harold Wilson, who could not let the opportunity go by. He referred to the error as 'The Chancellor's usual coefficient of inflation.'

Two years later Barney led a British delegation on a sombre mission — the commemoration of the twentieth anniversary of the uprising in the Warsaw Ghetto. There were very few Jews left alive in Poland. On the Sabbath, the Jewish delegations went to the only synagogue in Warsaw. Recently, in a conversation I had in Jerusalem with Gideon Haussner, he remembered meeting Barney on that occasion.

That year Barney was honoured by the Government of Belgium. The Belgian Ambassador made him a Commander of the Order of Leopold the Second, in recognition of his work in furthering Anglo-Belgian relations; Barney had for years been Honorary Secretary of the Anglo-Belgian Parliamentary Group. The same year King Baudouin and Queen Fabiola came to London on an official visit, and we had the honour of meeting them.

It was in that year that the two of us attended a ceremony in the Judaean Hills near Jerusalem, where the first saplings were planted in a forest that bears Barney's name. Amongst those who paid tribute to him were Arthur Lourie, and Yaacov Tzur, former Ambassador of Israel, Chairman of the Jewish National Fund. The forest was planted as a tribute to Barney by the Zionist Federation and other friends.

We were both very pleased and excited when, in 1957, our daughter Ruth qualified as a solicitor and became the third partner in the firm. When Barney's nephew, Major Gerald Davis, had returned from his war service in the Royal Artillery, he had become a partner, and the firm's name had been changed to 'Barnett Janner and Davis'. Now it was changed again, and became 'Barnett Janner, Davis and Janner'. It remained so even after Ruth became Lady Morris of Kenwood on her marriage in 1958. She had always taken an interest in the law firm. From the age of fifteen she used to come in and work at the office, making herself useful wherever needed. When she finished her schooling at St Paul's she studied law.

With Gerald and Ruth extremely busy and devoted to the firm, Barney was able to spend more time on his public work . . . However, he continued to go to the office every morning until the summer of 1981.

In 1978, Barnett Janner, Davis and Janner amalgamated with

the firm of solicitors Rees Kon Freeman & Co. Gerald and Ruth and the other partners were pleased when someone suggested a single name for the new firm: 'Janners'. What a compliment to the respected name my husband had earned throughout his life!

The year 1979 marked the completion of sixty years of practice as a solicitor for Barney. The firm of Janners planned a wonderful dinner for him in the Cholmondely Room in the House of Lords, but kept the plans a strict secret from him. I got him there on a pretext, and will never forget the look of astonishment on his face as he walked into the room and beheld all the partners and executives with their husbands and wives. It was an evening to remember. The Law Society took note of this unusual anniversary by giving a celebration luncheon in Barney's honour.

8 THE PARLIAMENTARY PROCESS
1955–1964

No one ever accused Barney of lacking persistence. That quality stood him in good stead in his long campaign to outlaw the weapon called the flick-knife, known across the Atlantic as the switch-blade.

In the 1950s flick-knives became popular among teen-age gangs and teddy-boys. It was a sign of toughness to own one. It looked harmless enough when held closed in the hand; but the speed with which the murderous razor-sharp blade sprang open made it very frightening and dangerous.

The flick-knife danger was brought to Barney's attention by the *Illustrated Leicester Chronicle* and the *Leicester Mercury*. They supplied information to him, and he decided to raise the question in Parliament. On 14 July 1955 he asked Major Gwilym Lloyd George, the Home Secretary, whether he was aware that flick-knives were being sold openly, and were carried by teenage groups; and whether he would take steps to prohibit the import, manufacture and sale of these weapons. The Minister answered that he had no evidence that flick-knives were carried to any extent by teenage groups.

Barney was not happy with this answer, and he pressed the point again on a number of occasions during 1955 and 1956. He also asked Peter Thorneycroft, President of the Board of Trade, to ban the import of these knives. The answer was that it could not be done. Besides, it was pointed out, 'it was already an offence to be in possession of an offensive weapon in a public place without lawful authority or reasonable excuse'. The trouble was that it was usually impossible to obtain a conviction on those terms. The prosecution frequently had great difficulty in proving its case until after the damage was done.

It was on a tour of America in 1956 as President of the Board of Deputies that Barney discovered the problem had been tackled in the State of New York. Inquiring closely into the difficulties experienced there with teenage gangs, he found that in New York and certain other States, the switch-blade knife had been banned. The New York Penal Law defined the weapon very successfully. In July 1956, after describing the New York law, Barney asked the Home Secretary whether he would consider the advisability of introducing similar legislation. Gwilym Lloyd George said he would look into it. Meanwhile, young people could still walk into a shop and buy these knives over the counter for 27s 6d.

But the Government insisted there was really little public anxiety about flick-knives. The Board of Trade made some attempt to influence retailers not to sell them, and a statement was supposed to be issued to this effect in 1957. It was not issued, and in November Barney brought the matter up again with the new Home Secretary, R. A. Butler. He asked whether the Minister was aware that more cases had been occurring of the use of flick-knives for the commission of assaults. Butler, who said that the police had adequate powers to deal with the problem, told Barney that the knives were used by such people as blacksmiths, electricians and fishermen.

When a *Leicester Mercury* reporter went to find out whether flick-knives were actually used for these purposes, he was told a different story. A Leicester blacksmith said: 'I don't know a blacksmith in Leicester or the county who has such a thing.' A partner in a firm of tool merchants in the city said: 'We supply most trades in the area — and we don't sell any flick-knives. We have not even been asked for one in this connection.' Travellers did call and offer to supply his shop, 'But we will have nothing to do with them.' The head of a firm of cutlers in Leicester commented: 'I don't know any trade which uses them. We get tough guys in here sometimes who ask for them. They are told that we do not stock them.' But at a shop where flick-knives were sold, the reporter was told 'They are used by telephone linesmen, gardeners, farmers and market men. Many miners also use them.'

In February 1958 Barney told the House that a thirteen-year-old boy had recently pressed a flick-knife against the heart of another boy, and had also stabbed a thirteen-year-old Leicester girl. Again he asked the Minister to ban the import of these knives, because there was considerable alarm in Leicester and elsewhere. But he was still a voice crying in the wilderness.

In 1959 he decided to introduce a Private Member's Bill. That is no easy task. Of the few procedures available to a back-bencher, all of them strewn with obstacles, Barney chose the Ten-Minute Rule. It is a system whereby, immediately after question-time on Tuesdays and Wednesdays, an MP, after asking permission of the House, is given ten minutes in which to explain his proposed Bill. If the House agrees, the Bill takes its place after other Private Members' Bills. Even so, if it does not get government support, it has little chance of success.

Leave to bring in Barney's Restriction of Offensive Weapons Bill was granted without opposition. The Bill was supported outside Parliament by the Association of Municipal Corporations and many other organizations. However, it failed to get a Second Reading.

On 5 March 1959 Barney tabled a motion to the effect that the House would welcome an opportunity to consider a motion that the Restriction of Offensive Weapons Bill be read a second time. Fully aware of the shock value to be obtained by breaking an ancient rule of Parliament, he suddenly produced a flick-knife and pressed its spring-button. The gleaming long blade shot out with a menacing click. There were shocked cries of 'Order! Order!' from all parts of the House. The Speaker rose from his chair, 'If that is a dangerous weapon, the honourable gentleman should not have brought it into this chamber.' Barney replied: 'With respect, Mr Speaker, if it is such a dangerous weapon the Government should do something to stop its manufacture and sale.' Probably as a result of this demonstration of how an unseen knife could become a murderous weapon in a single second, more than three hundred MPs signed the motion, and the Government waived its objections. On 13 March the Bill got its Second Reading. In committee, Philip Goodhart, a Tory MP, kindly allowed the Weapons Bill to take precedence over his Night Baking Bill, a controversial measure. After only eighty minutes of discussion, the Bill passed the Committee Stage with two small amendments, on 14 April 1959. Three days later it got its Third Reading. It was piloted through the House of Lords by our son-in-law, Lord Morris of Kenwood, and was carried on 12 May. It received the Royal Assent on the 14th of that month.

In March 1961 a case came before the courts which revealed a

144

small loop-hole in the Bill, and Barney was speedily able to get through all its stages the Restrictions of Offensive Weapons Act 1959 (Amendment) Bill. So ended four years of hard work.

All along, Barney had been supported by the Leicester newspapers that had first brought the problem to his attention. He appreciated very much the rôle played by the *Illustrated Chronicle* and the *Leicester Mercury*. The latter called his war against the flick-knife 'one of the most persistent and unremitting campaigns ever waged in the House of Commons by a private member.'

The arrival of Egyptian and Hungarian refugees in 1956 made Barney look more closely at legislation relating to aliens. In November he argued for liberalization of the law in the spirit of the Declaration of Human Rights. In the following year he supported a motion introduced by Maurice Orbach which proposed to lift the restrictions on the length of time political refugees can stay in Britain. In 1958 he made a similar point when the Commons discussed renewing the restrictions on the landing, registration and stay of aliens. 'The problems of the admission of men and women from other places into the country, and their subsequent treatment, is not novel to this generation. It involves the most important principles of humanity . . .'

Among the numerous issues Barney raised in the 1955–59 Parliament, transport figured quite prominently. He was particularly concerned about the road link between London and Yorkshire because it directly affected Leicester. There had been a great deal of talk and planning about producing a motorway network, and Barney was very persistent in his questioning of the Minister of Transport as to when he would proceed with and complete the London–Yorkshire motorway, the M1.

The fate of animals — from rare birds to warthogs — also concerned him. He asked about the increasing destruction of wild animals in British Colonial Africa. Interest in animal welfare became even more important to him as the years went by.

Harold Macmillan called a General Election in October 1959. This was the 'You've never had it so good' election, and the Tories took advantage of increased living standards. Barney's majority at the 1955 election had been 3,510, but with the

Tories in a strong position generally there was likely to be some swing towards the Conservative candidate, who was once again F. A. Tomlinson. However, Barney always had working in his favour the great fund of goodwill and affection he had built up among the people of Leicester of all parties.

It was a close fight. We canvassed long and hard to bring out the Labour vote. Polling was on 8 October and the turnout in N.W. Leicester was seventy-nine per cent. Barney's majority was cut again. He won 21,515 votes to Tomlinson's 19,742 — a majority of 1,773, his smallest as a Leicester MP. Throughout the country, Labour slumped. The Tories increased their majority in Parliament to ninety-nine seats.

There were one or two lively meetings, but otherwise the campaign followed the usual Leicester pattern — interested, concerned people who behaved in a polite and civilized way. Some of the uncivilized were Mosley supporters who interrupted a Labour rally at the Corn Exchange. At another meeting Barney was listened to in silence, but when it came to questions he was subjected to a non-stop barrage from political opponents. He greatly enjoyed these interruptions. In a lighter moment, not at the same meetings, Barney was told by a heckler: 'You haven't got a leg to stand on.' He retorted, 'All the more reason why you should give me a seat.'

When Parliament re-assembled Barney returned to some of the issues he had been concerned with in the previous Parliament. But there were always new problems to be considered. Individuals and organizations were continually approaching him about injustices, bureaucratic mistakes and insensitivities, the need for speedier Government action in various fields and the necessity of introducing reforms especially in the country's legal system.

He remained worried about developments in post-war Germany, where there were manifestations of neo-Fascism. He drew attention to the Nazi backgrounds of individual Germans who came to England on official business. He felt that everything possible should be done to rid Germany of the remnants of the Nazi evil. Unrepentant former Nazis should not be given responsible positions in the German Government, civil service and judiciary.

It was important for the German people to recover from their awful past, for German society to be rebuilt on democratic lines.

When in the early 1960s the Government announced that facilities for training on the Welsh hills would be afforded to the German Armed Forces, he thought this an insensitive move, fraught with dangers. In March 1960 the Board of Deputies passed a resolution against the whole idea. From then on Barney regularly tackled the Government on the issue in Parliament.

When he first opposed the move in the House, a distressing incident occurred. There was a debate on the issue one evening and Barney made his feelings known. Coming through the Members' lobby afterwards, Aneurin Bevan came up to Barney and said, furiously, 'Thank you, Mr *Jew*.' Barney was astounded and did not reply. When he got home he told me about it — he was terribly upset. He said, 'Nye was very red in the face. He had obviously been drinking. But it is when they are in that condition that people say what they really think.'

Barney asked the Government to vet the German troops thoroughly, so as to ensure that there were no Nazis among them. When he put this to Harold Watkinson the Defence Minister, in July 1961, the response was that no such steps were being contemplated. Barney responded:

> Surely the right honourable gentleman is not saying that anybody, whether he has a Nazi background, happens to have been of high-ranking order in the Nazi set-up or is a neo-Nazi, will be allowed into this country in order to spread that sort of vicious doctrine? Is not something going to be done about it? Will the right honourable gentleman consult the Home Office or the Foreign Secretary about what is to be done?'

Watkinson was unsympathetic. The Government could not do such a thing, he said. When similar training facilities were afforded in France there had been no objections.

In November, during a speech urging the Government to accede to the Genocide Convention, Barney came back to this problem. 'Many of us are deeply offended by the granting of training facilities for German forces in this country,' he said. 'Not having adhered to the Genocide Convention, we cannot take steps against a member of the German forces who was a violent Nazi or member of the SS.

Barney told the House of Commons that if the warnings issued by Winston Churchill in the 1930s had been heeded,

> We might have avoided a considerable part of the tragic circumstances which resulted from people not realizing what it meant for men and women to be driven not only from their homes but into places which eventually led to many of them — including some six million of my own co-religionists — losing their lives. Even today, fifteen years after the war, there are still some ten thousand people living in refugee camps in Europe. I doubt whether anyone can realize what it means for a person to be stuck for fifteen years in those camps, or under even worse conditions outside.

The experience with refugees from Hungary, he said, had shown that once the imagination of the world was fired, even great problems could be solved fairly rapidly.

Barney wanted the Government to increase the amount of aid it was granting for the resettlement of refugees, in order to give a lead to the rest of the world.

> If our country has not now the power of arms and the strength of arguments which at one time it had, it has a much greater asset — the force of conscience, the outlook which believes in treating human beings as human beings and in fostering human rights. Here is an opportunity for us to show in a modest way that this country in this respect stands where it always stood, and that we are anxious that the world should follow us. I believe they will if we take the lead.

Barney showed this same concern when he was dealing with social issues which affected the lives of ordinary people in Britain. He attacked the Government for its housing policy, which was aggravating the problem of the homeless. He said this was not a party issue. 'Human lives are at stake and it is difficult to talk about this subject without being emotional.'

148

In all those areas where the Government should be responsible for maintaining a stable society and looking after the interests of the people he demanded action. When the Albemarle Report on the youth service was published, he wanted the Government to implement it immediately. He argued that play facilities should be provided for small children when tall blocks of flats are built. ('There must be a little soul in the provision of housing accommodation.') On the probation service he accused the Government of dealing it 'almost death blows because of the parsimonious way' they were treating the pay of probation officers.

Barney's interest in the welfare of animals came to the fore during this Parliament. He was concerned about the international transport of animals after he learned of a consignment of tortoises which had arrived in a 'dead or dying condition'. Apparently there was no law under which the person responsible for exporting animals in such conditions could be punished.

On the other hand, there seemed to be an excessive amount of bureaucratic red tape surrounding the importation of some animals. It was in this connection that he asked in Parliament what had been 'the cost of preparing and presenting an Order authorizing the landing of two more wart hogs at Bromborough.' The wart hogs were for Manchester Zoo, and the cost of preparing the Order and presenting it to Parliament had been £14. This was an expensive operation. Barney then ironically asked the Government Minister: 'While we appreciate the commendable object of bringing wart hogs into this country, is it not rather a heavy and costly piece of machinery comparatively in order to bring in two pets?' The Minister said he was considering making a standing order to allow such animals in.

During discussion on a Private Member's Bill to bar anyone under fourteen from owning an air-gun, he tried unsuccessfully to move an amendment to get the age limit raised to seventeen. Speaking of the need to stop the abuse of guns, he said:

> The minds of young people today are being directed to the idea that violence is not really a serious matter. They look at pictures, they read books that one would not consider as particularly desirable reading, they see cartoons, watch

television, and all the rest. To them violence is a matter of no concern at all because practically from the cradle they are trained to regard it as natural . . . How many parents ever find their children sitting down to a really classical book? Our children want to look at the television. Very many of their games are based on the use of firearms . . .

His amendment was turned down, although he had the support of the Association of Municipal Corporations, of which he was a Vice-President and of the National Farmers Union, which was worried about the shooting of livestock by young people with airguns and similar firearms.

In June 1964, only a few months before the General Election, Barney saw the passing of the Law of Property (Joint Tenants) Bill, a measure originated by the Law Society, which he piloted through the Commons, since he was Vice-Chairman of the Lords and Commons Solicitors Group.

In January 1964, Barney introduced another important Bill under the Ten Minute Rule. It was called the 'Highways (Straying Animals) Bill'. It provided for the payment of compensation for injury or damage caused by animals straying on highways. He said that as the law stood, owners of straying animals which caused calamities were not liable to pay compensation for their lack of consideration for the safety of others; adding that he had received messages and petitions about this from individuals and organizations. He later handed in a petition with seven hundred signatures. Unfortunately, this Bill failed to get a Second Reading, due to the opposition of farming interests.

Barney continued his pressure but it was not until 1969 that he finally had his Bill put on the Statute Book.

This had been an eventful time for our family. There were proud and happy moments such as Barney's investiture as a Knight at Buckingham Palace on 7 February 1961; the marriages of our children, Greville and Ruth, in 1955 and 1958; the birth of our first grandchildren, and Barney's nine years as President of the Board of Deputies.

Towards the end of its term the Conservative Government of Harold Macmillan was rocked by the scandal of the Profumo Affair. Macmillan resigned and Alec Douglas Home became Prime Minister.

In January 1963 Labour suffered a grievous loss through the death of its leader Hugh Gaitskell, after a short illness. He was only fifty-six years old. Harold Wilson was elected Party Leader. He succeeded in putting across an image of Labour as a modern party ready to govern, and sensitive to the technological changes taking place in society.

In one of Barney's last speeches before the election he had spoken about the implications of increased automation in industry. He was already looking beyond the new technological revolution to the problems of increased leisure. His words seem even more appropriate today than they did then.

In the opinion polls Labour had been consistently ahead of the Tories since February 1961. However, by September 1964, one month before the election, that lead had been cut from 11.5 per cent in the previous May to 1.5 per cent. Because of Barney's relatively small majority in 1959 (1,773), North West Leicester was considered a marginal seat. The electorate had fallen by over two thousand following continual industrialization of the centre of the city. The biggest loss was from St Margaret's, traditional Labour territory. The Tories were therefore optimistic. George Farnham, a company director, was the Tory candidate.

For Leicester, this election was the biggest battle since 1950. A strong Liberal intervention meant a large number of candidates contesting the four seats. In Barney's constituency there was no Liberal candidate. A former Liberal agent wrote to the *Leicester Mercury* advising Liberals to vote for Barney:

> The only vote a true Liberal can cast in the absence of a Liberal candidate is for Sir Barnett Janner, the man who has served all people of North West Leicester, irrespective of party, for the past 19 years. No man could do more for us all than 'Barney', as he is affectionately known to his 'family of constituents'.

The Times wrote:

> If there is such a thing as a personal vote it will go to Sir Barnett. He is universally liked and has a reputation for 'getting things done'. His successful Bill to ban the sale of

flick-knives is seen as a first-class example of this.

In Leicester he was becoming a legend.

As Barney always said, the elections are won on the doorstep, and the hard work we put in paid off. The local newspaper commented on our readiness to get on with the job:

> So keen were agents for Sir Barnett Janner to get on with their campaign in Westcotes ward, part of his division, that they started it by candlelight. Campaign workers, including Lady Janner and city councillors Bob Trewick and Mrs E. Brewer, moved into their committee room before conversions were complete. The electrician had not had time to complete the lighting — and so out came the candles.

Barney was returned with an increased majority: he won 21,134 votes to his Tory opponent's 16,740 — a majority of 4,394. There was a swing to Labour throughout the whole country, giving the Party a narrow majority in the House of Commons of five seats. Barney had no expectations of office (though a *Daily Mail* political columnist called his absence from the Government 'a genuine surprise'), nor any wish for it. But in the new Parliament which reassembled on 27 October, he was appointed to the Chairman's panel. This gave him the opportunity of taking the chair when Bills were discussed in Committee Stage. He was elected Chairman of the All-Party Parliamentary Solicitors' Group (he had been Vice-Chairman for the past three years), and also Vice-Chairman of the East Midlands Labour Parliamentary Group. As the *Jewish Chronicle* said, 'the coming months would be a busy time for Sir Barnett.'

9 LAST YEARS IN THE COMMONS 1964–1970

Labour's slim majority meant that the 1964–66 Parliament was a hectic one for all Labour MPs. For those like Barney, who was already doing enough to occupy two men half his age, it was a period of especially intense activity.

Before the election he had been in Australia, assisting in an appeal for the King David School of the Sydney Jewish community. He flew out by the Australian airline Qantas. When he arrived, he discovered that the company had cancelled its previous arrangements for appointing its own representatives in Tel Aviv. He raised the matter with the Prime Minister, Sir Robert Menzies. Barney called on Qantas to reverse their decision as soon as possible 'since this fine airline had become part and parcel of Arab attacks on Israel in the form of a boycott'. Senator Henty agreed to take the matter up with Qantas.

With the Labour Whips keeping a close watch on the whereabouts of every MP, travelling became a little more difficult. But Barney was able to fly to Israel in January 1966 for a session of the Zionist General Council as well as for a much sadder mission. As he told the delegates:

> I came here for the funeral of our old and cherished comrade, Moshe Sharett, whose name was known and revered not only in English Zionist circles, but was so well respected generally that the Parliamentary whip permitted me to leave the country at a time when our Government majority is very small. Even the opposition, many of whom knew the late Moshe Sharett, was prepared for one of them to accompany me to the funeral. This signifies the profound admiration which Moshe merited. We deeply mourn his passing.

One of the problems which Barney tackled was the expected application of the Federal German Statute of Limitations to crimes against humanity. This meant that from twenty years after the cessation of hostilities on 8 May 1945, proceedings could no longer be instituted against Nazis responsible for the crimes of the Hitler régime. Pressure of world opinion had led the Federal German cabinet to review the question at the beginning of March 1965, and this was to be followed by debates in the German Parliament. Fortunately, some groups in Germany — a number of members of the governing Christian Democrats and of the opposition Social Democrats — were opposed to the application of the Statute of Limitations. Barney and others therefore did their best to strengthen the resolve of these groups, and to encourage enough German members of Parliament to vote for the extension of the Statute. Apart from signing petitions from both Houses of Parliament, organized by David Ennals and sent to Dr Erhard (the German Chancellor), he was very active in the Jewish community's effort to persuade the German Government to extend the Statute. In February he was part of a Board of Deputies delegation to the Federal German Ambassador in London, stressing how important it was to continue bringing Nazi criminals to justice. This campaign succeeded, and the Statute of Limitations was extended where crimes against humanity were concerned.

In 1969, there was great worry for the small Iraqi Jewish community when so-called spy trials resulted in the public hanging of Jews and the displaying of their bodies. Barney had already played a rôle in helping the Iraqi Jewish community in the dark days of 1951. After the failure of the Arab armies in Israel's war of independence, the Iraqi authorities subjected the Jewish community to harsh treatment. In March 1950 a law was passed permitting Jews to renounce their Iraqi citizenship and leave the country, and in the following months thousands left. Meanwhile, there had been an ever-growing campaign of incitement, resulting on several occasions in violence, bloodshed and loss of property. In March 1951 another law was passed which in effect meant that property of Jews who registered to emigrate to Israel was confiscated.

After my husband's death I received a letter from Mr Davide Salman-Salah, a prominent member of the Iraqi-Jewish community in this country, in which he writes:

> I would like to put on record our gratitude for all that your late husband did, not only in the dark days of 1948–53, but in the 60's as well.

A great deal of information on what was going on in Baghdad at that time was passed on to Barney, through various people and channels, and as a result he used his influence in Parliament and with Government departments to alleviate the hardships of the Baghdad Jewish community, and of the hundreds of Iraqi Jews who sought refuge in England during those troubled times.

> Needless to say, hundreds of Jews of Iraqi origin living now in England owe their refuge, residency and even citizenship to your late husband, for which they are ever grateful. The name of Lord Janner has been on the lips of almost all the leaders of the Iraqi Jewish communities inside and outside of Iraq for several decades.

In January 1969 Barney wrote to Goronwy Roberts, Minister of State at the Foreign and Commonwealth Office, expressing his concern. Goronwy replied that he had raised the matter with the Iraqi Ambassador in London but, 'Needless to say, it would probably make this intervention entirely counterproductive and it would gravely jeopardize the likelihood of any futute similar interventions, if any publicity at all was to be made about this approach to the Iraqi authorities.'

This attitude was again apparent when Barney went with a deputation to Michael Stewart, the Foreign Secretary, at the end of January. Barney demanded public condemnation, but Michael Stewart thought it preferable to make representations behind the scenes. This satisfied neither Barney nor the other members of the Board of Deputies delegation, who proceeded with a petition to be sent to U Thant, General Secretary of the United Nations, appealing to him to intervene. A statement was circulated to many people, including Parliamentarians of both Houses. One who responded very positively was Anthony Eden, the Earl of Avon, who wrote to Barney:

I have much sympathy for this appeal and if you think it would be helpful I should be ready to write to U Thant saying I have learnt of your petition and support it. I would add that any action of this kind that can be taken would be serving a truly humanitarian cause.

Later in 1969 Barney was in correspondence with Lord Goodman about the setting up of a Committee for Jews in Arab Countries. The small remnant of the Jewish community in Syria especially was facing serious difficulties and at this writing it still is.

In 1968 when the remnants of Jewry in Poland were subjected to virulent antisemitic attacks, Barney did his best to make his fellow Parliamentarians aware of the situation. He sent a note about the problem to Arthur Blenkinsop MP, a member of the Anglo-Polish Group, asking him to do what he could to help. Arthur replied that he and others of his group had met with Polish representatives in London, who told the British MPs that any antisemitism in Poland was entirely unofficial and that Jews in Poland had full rights. 'We have . . . made clear the anxiety that we all feel but I think we were all also partially reassured by the vigour and firmness of assurances that we were given.' Barney replied to Arthur:

> I am greatly surprised at the cynicism of the replies given to you by the Poles about the current campaign. For months now the British press — i.e. the *Guardian, The Times* and other responsible newspapers and journals — have given concrete details showing a substantial majority of those imprisoned or arrested in Poland are Jews. Many responsible experts in this country, as can be seen from the press, are in no doubt whatsoever that this is the result of casting the tiny Jewish population of Poland in the rôle of scapegoat for internal problems.

In his capacity as Chairman of the Foreign Affairs Committee of the Board of Deputies from 1949, the condition of Soviet Jewry was a subject Barney had to deal with continually. He raised it with Prime Ministers and leading politicians who went to visit the Soviet Union. On 11 March 1959 Harold Macmillan wrote to him. Part of the letter read:

> You will remember that you came to see me at your request before I went to the Soviet Union to tell me of the interest felt among British Jews in the position of Jews in the Soviet Union. This is just to tell you that I was able to mention this interest informally during my visit.

Hugh Gaitskell was to go to the USSR in the winter of 1962–3, and Barney wrote to him asking him to raise the position of Soviet Jews with the Soviet leadership. The reply said:

> Thank you for your letter of the 18th December and for your note on Soviet Jewry. Alas, as you will have seen, I have had to postpone my visit to Moscow but certainly hope to go in the spring. Should I do so, I will, of course, bear in mind what you say should there be any opportunity of discussing the matter. Yours ever, Hugh.

Unfortunately, Gaitskell died before he could make the trip.

Barney told the Board that the position of the Jews in the Soviet Union was deteriorating.

> This arises from what appears to be the definite policy of the Soviet authorities to put every obstacle in the way of the Jews continuing as a religious, cultural and ethnic entity forming a national group within the USSR . . . The Jewish world which has lost so many of its members in the Nazi holocaust cannot but be gravely concerned with the fate of three million Jews, with whom many outside Russia are connected by ties of blood and tradition.

Barney always had a special relationship with Harold Wilson on the question of Soviet Jews. It began in 1947 when Harold Wilson was Secretary to the Overseas Trade Department of the Board of Trade, and then President of the Board of Trade. He was negotiating at that time with Mikoyan, who was Minister of Foreign Trade and later President of the Soviet Union. Barney gave him a list of four or five people whose relatives in Britain hoped that Harold could persuade the Russians to let them out.

157

This sort of thing happened quite often until 1951, and even more frequently after that. The Soviet Ambassador would be given the names, and the wheels would be set in motion.

Harold went to Israel at Barney's instigation in 1950 for the first time. After he returned, he met Barney in the Lobby, put his arm around him, and said:

> Thank you very much, Barney, for making me go to Israel. It has been the greatest experience of my life. I was given a Christmas surprise party, and there I met some of the Russian women whom I helped get out of the Soviet Union.

From that time until the present day, Harold Wilson has been one of the greatest friends of Israel. When he was Prime Minister, he was again able to do much to help Soviet Jews. In July 1966 a motion, sponsored by Barney, was signed by 180 MPs from both sides of the House, expressing concern at the continuing difficulties confronting Jews in the Soviet Union. Harold was due to go to Moscow that month and was therefore able to carry with him the desire of the House that he should raise the issue with the Soviet leadership.

In April 1968 Barney sent another list of names to Harold, who passed it on to the Home Office, where officials were supposed to get in touch with the sponsors in Britain. In this set of cases there was a delay, and the sponsors heard nothing for some months. Barney wrote again to Harold who discovered that the Home Office officials had not acted. The matter was immediately put right, and in November Merlyn Rees wrote to Barney saying that visas would be issued to the six families whose names had been submitted for settlement in Britain.

Harold acknowledged Barney's rôle in helping Soviet Jewry when he spoke at Barney's eightieth birthday celebrations:

> Every time I have been to the Soviet Union from 1947 onwards, he produced for me the most formidable brief on some of the problems which really needed sorting out. If I have achieved anything on these visits, and the less we say about that outside the better . . . it really depends on what Barney said when he tackled me in the Tea Room of the

House of Commons now twenty-five years ago, and subsequently.

Barney either helped to form or joined practically all the major national and international committees — Jewish or non-Jewish — set up to help the plight of Soviet Jewry. He read out the *Appeal* at the World Conference of Jewish Communities on Soviet Jewry, held in Brussels in 1971; and he was a patron of the all-Party Parliamentary Committee for the Release of Soviet Jewry set up in 1972. He never lost the opportunity to attend a march or demonstration for Soviet Jews, no matter what the weather was like, or to speak on their behalf at rallies and meetings. He led the march of fifteen hundred people in July 1978 from Hyde Park to the Soviet Embassy, calling for the release of Anatoly Shcharansky.

Greville tells a story about this march. He was walking alongside Barney, and became concerned that the distance might be too much for his father. He said, 'Rather a long march, Dad, don't you think?'

'What's the matter son?' Barney replied. 'Want a piggyback?'

He was eighty-six years old at the time.

When I was in Jerusalem quite recently I was told a similar story by Zev Suffot of the Israel Foreign Ministry, a former Consul General at the Israeli Embassy in London. In the mid-1970s there was a great deal of anger when the French authorities released Leila Khalid, the PLO terrorist hijacker, after having apprehended her at Orly airport and having held her for only a few days. I quote Zev:

> In London a demonstration was held outside the French Embassy. It was a cold day in January, actually snowing. The weather was appalling. I drove by Hyde Park to see the dozen or twenty good fine men who had turned out, and amongst them was Lord Janner. He wasn't a young man in those days — he had no right to be there. He should have been at home, or possibly in the House of Lords, doing whatever he should have been doing. There were other people to do that sort of thing — but Barney had to be there. When he felt deeply about something he didn't leave

it to other people.

In June 1980, just before his health began to deteriorate, Barney was a delegate to the meeting in Paris of Members of European Parliaments, at which a committee was set up to co-ordinate effort on behalf of Soviet Jewry.

In the House of Lords he made a number of speeches on the plight of Soviet Jewry in the context of human rights violations. A closely detailed speech in May 1977, in which he demonstrated how the culture of Soviet Jews was being severely repressed, led Baroness Seear to pay tribute to Barney 'and his family for the remarkable work they had been doing in keeping in touch with Soviet Jewry'.

Soviet Jews have no democratic Parliamentary institutions to which they can appeal, so Barney and others had to act as their 'representatives' in the councils of the world. This was a cause Barney devoted himself to with unflagging dedication until the end of his life.

Barney was keenly interested in the Inter-Parliamentary Union and gave considerable time to it. The IPU came into being in the latter years of Queen Victoria's reign, when some Members of the House of Commons thought of a new form of international collaboration — personal contacts and discussion, between members of various Parliaments, to promote common legislative action and to exchange ideas. This proposal, revolutionary at the time, arose from various peace movements and societies which flourished throughout western Europe. These movements included a number of British, French and German parliamentarians. In 1885 the Liberal MP for a Hackney constituency, William Randal Cremer, founded the Inter-Parliamentary Union in collaboration with a French Member of Parliament, Frederick Passe. They called a meeting which was attended by five French MPs and nine Members of the British House of Commons, and decided to convene a larger conference the following year. In March 1889 the Inter-Parliamentary Union was founded.

From small beginnings the Union has grown until today the vast majority of Members of both Houses belong to the British

Group. The President is always the Prime Minister of the day, the Chairman has to be a member of the party in power. After the Honorary Officers, the Executive Committee consists of an equal number of Government and Opposition members, including five members of the House of Lords.

Barney was first elected to the Executive in 1962. Before that he had visited Belgium, Luxembourg and The Netherlands and in 1960 he was elected Honorary Secretary of the Anglo-Benelux Group. In 1963 he was re-elected a member of the Executive. Despite the many calls on his time, he attended that year five out of six Executive meetings. Indeed the whole time he was a member of the Executive and an Honorary Officer he was seldom absent for more than one meeting a year.

In 1964, the Anglo-Israel Parliamentary Group (which replaced the Parliamentary Palestine Committee) became affiliated to the IPU. At that time Barney was Chairman, Gilbert Longden was Vice-Chairman, Sir Stephen McAddem was Honorary Treasurer and Mr E. Popplewell was Honorary Secretary. The Annual Report for that year says: 'During the year the Group maintained close contact with the Israeli embassy and entertained a number of visitors from Israel including the Foreign Secretary.'

Barney was a delegate to meetings in, among other places, Rome, The Hague, and Delhi. Lord Murton of Lindisfarne, formerly Oscar Murton the Deputy Speaker, told me of the time when they were both delegates to a Conference in India.

As soon as we arrived, all the staff of the Ashoka Hotel went on strike. The workers thought it was a good opportunity, with such an important international gathering, to improve their industrial relations. So we had to put up with a Major-General to run the hotel. Taxis were a problem. At that time they were very rickety. Five were allocated to the British, and Barney immediately pinched the best one and went off to see the synagogue in New Delhi. While there, he bought a number of black ivory elephants for his grandchildren. These elephants made his own baggage too heavy, so he made each one of us take an elephant in ours!

In 1966 Barney was a delegate to the annual meeting which was

161

held in Teheran. Delegates' wives were allowed to attend, provided they paid their own expenses, so I went with him. This was an interesting conference, and I found Iran a fascinating country.

At that conference there were 450 representatives of fifty-nine national groups. Barney spoke about the need for economic planning and the way parliamentary control of planning should be conducted. He explained how in Britain, public opinion and Parliament can influence the Government, and that a Government cannot with immunity flout the wishes of the people for any length of time. Whilst precautions must be taken against the assumption of undue arbitrary power by the Executive still, without some delegation of power to the Executive, little can be effected.

In 1966 Barney was Chairman of the Anglo-Israel Group. The projected 1967 Moscow meeting was cancelled because the Russians would not guarantee to give visas to all national groups which really aimed at Israel. The 1967 annual meeting was held in Geneva where there was an acrimonious discussion over resolutions condemning Israel. At all ensuing conferences there were anti-Israel resolutions and the emergence of the Soviet-Arab bloc became more and more apparent.

In 1969 Barney was elected Chairman of the British Group for the year 1970. His period of office was cut short by the General Election when the Tories won and the Chairman had to be of the other party.

After that he was elected Vice-Chairman. He continued to serve as either Chairman or Vice-Chairman of the Benelux and the Israel Groups until 1980.

In 1974 the annual meeting took place in Japan. This coincided with the February 1974 General Election. There were thus no Members of the Commons, because when Parliament is prorogued there are no MPs. So the delegation consisted entirely of Members of the House of Lords. As Barney was a previous chairman he was chosen to lead the delegation. En route they were warmly welcomed by the Vietnamese Parliamentary Group and by the British Ambassador. After the Tokyo Conference the delegation went to South Korea and met President Park who prepared lavish entertainment for them.

In 1975 the Annual Conference was held in London. It was at

162

this meeting that the Palestine Liberation Organization, in the form of the Palestine National Council, was first admitted as an observer to the IPU. The Executive Committee voted to exclude them, but the Council, in contravention of the rules of the conference itself, decided to admit the PNC as an observer. The Arabs insisted that if the PNC's admittance was contrary to rules and regulations, the statutes should immediately be changed instead of waiting two or three years. This proposal was carried with the British delegation abstaining. When Tom Williams, QC, the Labour MP who was presiding at the Conference, invited Khaled al Hassan, the PLO representative, to speak, Barney walked out together with the Israeli delegation. The British Group were very much on his side and were equally dismayed to find that no matter what they said or did, nothing made the slightest difference to the vote. A rally was held in Trafalgar Square to protest against the admission of the three PLO representatives to the Conference. Barney spoke and told the protesters that the PLO formed part and parcel of a system of terrorism which was threatening the fabric of civilization.

Since then IPU meetings have become worse and worse. In 1982 Arafat spoke, ironically enough at the same time as Natanel Lorch, Clerk of the Knesset, was presiding over a meeting of parliamentary clerks. The British clerk wished Lorch a happy New Year.

Photographs in the various Annual Reports of the IPU include many of Barney, who was then a heavy man of some fourteen stone. Despite this he continued to have boundless energy, as can be seen by the close attention he gave to the IPU at a time when he was very fully occupied with Parliament and Jewish affairs.

At a meeting on 11 March 1981 the Honorary President, George Thomas, then Speaker of the House of Commons, said, 'May I say what a particular joy it is to see that Lord Janner who has been very ill, and who I know has reached his eighty-seventh year, has made the effort to be with us. We are all very, very pleased indeed' — and there was warm applause.

In 1970 Barney was created a Commander of the Order of Orange Nassau by Queen Juliana of the Netherlands. When she visited England in April 1972, Barney and I were invited to the magnificent State Banquet given in her honour by Her Majesty

Queen Elizabeth at Windsor Castle. A few people were taken up to talk to Queen Juliana and Barney was asked to sit with her for a while. He did so, and needless to say he talked to her about Israel. He thanked her and her people for the help they had given to Israel and for her keen interest and support.

The opinion polls in 1966 were consistently in Labour's favour and Harold Wilson decided it was a good time to go to the country. There had not been time for much legislation, but one or two major measures close to Barney's heart had been introduced: the 1965 Rent Act, which provided security of tenure and the Race Relations Act of 1965 which outlawed racial discrimination. Barney congratulated the Government on introducing that Bill and looked to the past for its ultimate justification:

> The Weimar Republic in Germany, under the plea that freedom must be respected, took no heed of the vile abuse and the principles or lack of principles of those who were exercising those freedoms. Thus the biggest disaster — I speak categorically about this — which has befallen the world, civilized or uncivilized, gained impetus and became a grim reality.

He also spoke in the debate on the Government's White Paper setting out proposals for leasehold reform. The aim was to afford the leaseholder living in his own home greater security by ensuring that his house would not revert to the freeholder when the existing lease expired. This was a measure Barney had been seeking for years, and in the formulation of which he had played his part as honorary rents advisor to the Labour Party.

> The measure which we are contemplating deals with the situation where some leases have existed for ninety-odd years, ground rent has been paid, and the tenants have kept the houses in repair. They have built up communities. The result has been not just bricks and mortar, but a worthwhile life for those who are living in the communities.

The leasehold reform debate was on 1 March 1966, and the

General Election was on 31 March, so it was back up to Leicester to fight for the seat again, with Labour leading by 9.5 per cent in the opinion polls. The local papers did not expect much change; the bookmakers were offering heavy odds on Labour to win. Barney had a new opponent again: Mr Carol Mather, an old Harrovian and a member of the Conservative Party's research department. By this time Barney had won six consecutive elections in Leicester. As the *Leicester Mercury* put it: 'There are few people in his constituency he does not know by now.'

The poll was much smaller than in 1964 but Barney's majority went up from 4,394 to 7,807. In 1945 Barney had had the lowest Labour majority in Leicestershire, but now in 1966, his majority was the biggest of any candidate of any party in the county. He polled 60.8 per cent of the votes recorded. The *Leicester Mercury* greeted the result with a banner headline:

JANNER TOPS THE MAJORITY STAKES

In the country as a whole the Labour Party came back to power with a majority in the Commons of ninety-seven seats.

Barney was still President of the Zionist Federation, a post he held until his death. This involved him in various committees of the World Zionist Organization, in numerous speaking engagements and tours for the Jewish National Fund, the Keren Hayesod and the American United Jewish Appeal. He made regular trips to the US during these years — San Francisco, Los Angeles, New York, and elsewhere. At Zionist Congresses and meetings of the Zionist General Council he continued to plead for less political bickering and more political co-operation, as at the January 1967 Zionist General Council:

> It isn't that Zionism has failed; it isn't that the Jewish people aren't Zionists — whether they know it or whether they don't. It isn't that people don't realize on reflection that the Zionist Movement was instrumental in creating the State of Israel. Zionism has succeeded, but our public relations have been bad — and that's where we have failed so far: we have failed in putting the whole of the position forward in such a way as to make it clear that we have

165

excellent goods to sell; but we are bad salesmen!

What led Barney to these harsh conclusions about the movement he had spent his life fighting for, was Israel's deteriorating international situation. In the United Nations Israel was coming under attack, as the Arab and some Third World countries were becoming increasingly prominent. Across Israel's borders terrorist attacks were causing consternation and Egypt's Colonel Nasser was adopting a threatening posture. In the Commons at the end of 1966 Barney had stressed that Israel only wanted to live in peace, but it was not surprising that she could no longer tolerate the kind of incidents that had been taking place. Israel carried out a reprisal raid on the village of al-Samu in Jordan which was condemned at the UN.

> If the Arab nations were given to understand firmly that Israel has come to stay, then I think that the Arabs who are now carrying on this aggression will discuss around a table the problems which face both peoples.

Tension mounted. Nasser became increasingly aggressive in his speeches and pronouncements. In May 1967 he asked the UN Secretary General to remove the UN peace-keeping force stationed on the Egyptian side of the border. Egyptian troops were massing even before the UN troops left. Nasser then closed the Straits of Tiran to Israeli shipping, thus cutting off the port of Eilat, Israel's vital southern lifeline. Israel's efforts to stimulate international action to get the Straits reopened produced no results.

On 31 May Barney made a speech in the House of Commons, reviewing Israel's great achievements and warning of the dire consequences if the country were to be destroyed. Israel was putting into practice the principles of the UN, and yet the Secretary General had seen fit to remove the UN force from Sinai. Israel was setting an example to the world:

> a humane, civilised, cultured country, one which believes in democracy and humanity . . . if ever there was a State in which Socialist idealism irrespective of what may be felt polemically in this House, were brought into effect not in

any aggressive sense, but in the hope that the nation as a whole would prosper and everyone would have the benefit of communal life and common understanding, that State is Israel.

He urged Harold Wilson and George Brown to do all they possibly could. He begged them to understand that 'this embattled nation of two and a half million brave and courageous men, women and children cannot stand the strain of prolonged deliberations'.

In June Israel launched pre-emptive strikes against the air forces of Egypt, Jordan and Syria utterly destroying them. With complete mastery of the skies, Israel's forces occupied all of the Sinai Peninsula to the east bank of the Suez Canal, all of Palestine west of the Jordan river, and the Golan Heights. She agreed to a cease-fire on 10 June.

The Anglo-Jewish community threw itself body and soul behind Israel. Ten thousand people marched from Hyde Park to the Israeli Embassy and there Barney handed in a message of solidarity to Ambassador Aharon Remez. Thousands of young men and not so young people volunteered to go out to Israel to help. Jerusalem was unified and the Western Wall made accessible again.

At the United Nations Abba Eban eloquently offered the Arabs the opportunity to negotiate all outstanding disagreements. But the only response was a series of negatives.

In July Barney again put Israel's case to the House in emotional terms. What upset him was the double standard being applied to Israel and the Arab countries. Israel had done what she set out to do from the moment of her founding. In June she stood alone, as Britain did in the Battle of Britain:

> The battle of Israel in most respects resembled the Battle of Britain. The Israelis were alone. We did not help them. We are falling over backwards to explain to the rest of the world that we did not go anywhere near them, that we did not want to have anything to do with the matter, but let them fight their own battle.
>
> That is true, but not having gone near them in the time of their trial and trouble we have no right now to warn

them about what they are to do in the future.

Barney reminded the House that Israel had always offered to negotiate with the Arabs, but the Arabs had only offered violence. Israel had absorbed half a million refugees from Arab countries but the Arabs only used their refugees as political pawns.

> The Jews honour every religion and give full facilities for everybody to worship according to their will. Yet for nineteen years, with practically not a murmur from anybody, no Jew could go to the holy places of Jerusalem. Where is the decency of the world? How do we expect to have a world in which men and women will live in peace if we are not prepared to take sides on the question of morals?

Vigorously responding to the pro-Arab interventions by Christopher Mayhew and Sir Harry Legge-Bourke, he insisted that the Arabs had paid for their threats and their aggressive intentions. The British Government should now try to help achieve a peace settlement, to 'get the Israelis and Arabs together to sink their differences and make a settlement so that the peace of the whole area may be established to the advantage of all'.

In July Barney went to Israel to see for himself the results of the Six-Day War. In October he was officially invited by George Brown, the Foreign Secretary, to lead an all-party delegation to the Balfour Declaration celebrations in Israel. He was impressed with what he saw, and said he believed that people in Britain were on Israel's side: 'After the victory it was impossible to walk down the streets of Britain without someone saying, "Don't let the Israelis move out of Jerusalem. Don't tell the Israelis what to do."' Barney saw this as a golden opportunity to put Israel's case to the world, to improve Israel's public relations. 'It is important that our "goods" should speak for themselves. What we lack are agents to distribute our "goods", whilst on the other hand the Arab world adopts the tactics of Goebbels and his ilk and they do so most successfully.'

Hopes that the Arabs would negotiate with Israel in the wake of the Six-Day War were never fulfilled. The war of attrition set in and there was more than ever a need for the friends of the

State of Israel to stand up in the House and put Israel's case. In one of Barney's last speeches in the House of Commons he repeated the arguments in favour of the existence of a Jewish state. He paid tribute to Israel's citizen army: 'They are defending their right to exist and that is all that they want,' he said. It was Israel's right to act as a haven and a home for Jews from the Soviet Union. Describing the vision of co-operation which he believed in all his life, Barney concluded: 'In my view, the genuine interests of Israel, of the Arabs and Britain all coincide.'

Although busier than ever with all his political involvements Barney found time for other activities. He was still making his Yom Kippur tours of the East End synagogues, but the Jewish life of the area was beginning to disappear. A few years earlier Barney had talked of the change to a *Jewish Chronicle* reporter:

> Today, the Jewish people have an easier life. Their views and habits have changed. In the East End, though, I still feel the grip of the friendly, warm, homely Jewish life about me — something which is irreplaceable. In some parts outside East London, where Jews now congregate in better surroundings, they maintain a traditional Jewish life, but I am not sure that they always retain that full warmth and camaraderie of the old days.

In March 1970 Barney and I were jointly awarded the B'nai B'rith First Lodge of England Award, for valuable services to Anglo-Jewry. Roy Jenkins, then Chancellor of the Exchequer, made the presentation on behalf of the Lodge at a diamond jubilee dinner at the Royal Palace Hotel, Kensington. When the award was announced Mr Robert Brodtman, President of the Lodge, said that since we had done so much both individually and together 'it would have been most invidious to have chosen one rather than the other. The award is given to someone who has made a major contribution to the Anglo-Jewish community, and their whole life's work is ample testimony to their eligibility.' Roy Jenkins said: 'I can think of no other two people more deserving of this honour.'

The 1966–70 Parliament saw the passing of another Race Relations Act which Barney wholeheartedly supported. In 1968

169

he and Edward Lyons were among the Labour MPs appointed to a select committee on race relations and immigration, charged with supervising the operation of the Race Relations Act. Barney called on the Jewish community to 'throw itself into the job' of assisting the integration of Commonwealth immigrants into Britain. He felt that Jews ought to take a greater interest in the problem, 'in view of their built-in capacity and desire to help their fellow-men'.

The Labour Government also introduced radical plans for educational reform. Barney took an interest in this, not least because he always believed so strongly in the importance and the value of Jewish education, and of education in general. In 1966 he explained to the House the workings of the various Jewish schools in Britain and the valuable work they were doing. He said that:

> For a Jewish child a Jewish education means an education in the highest moral standards. It is essential that a child of the Jewish faith should understand what it means to be a Jew, and should then be in a position to face his fellow men with a sense of commitment to the moral doctrine. This had, indeed, happened. The new ecumenical spirit does not relate only to the various denominations of the Christian faith. It includes understanding between that faith and other faiths.

In this Parliament Barney was given the responsibility of piloting through the Commons the Solicitors' Bill, which extended the powers of the Law Society.

Barney never had any luck with the ballot (essentially a drawing of lots) by which the limited time available for Private Members' Bills was allotted in the House of Commons. Nevertheless, he was able to see a few measures introduced which he personally had sponsored. To be sure, not all these measures succeeded all the way to final passage, but even when a Bill of his failed to get a Second Reading, he sometimes had the satisfaction of seeing one of his ideas taken up by the Government and included in a piece of Government-sponsored legislation. This happened with the Justices of the Peace Bill. He had been campaigning for years for lay magistrates living within three miles of their courts to claim travel and subsistence allowances. In 1968 the Government wrote this provision into its own Bill.

Barney loved being in the House of Commons, and after so many years of devotion to it and to the democratic ideals it represented, he became a master of its procedures and entirely at home in its precincts. He communicated this love of Parliament to the numerous groups he invited to see the Commons: school children, college students, workers from Leicester factories, friends, Israelis and so on. During the Lords debate on the establishment of the Ministry of Technology, Colin Grundy had a party of boys from his Leicester school in the Strangers' Gallery. He pointed out to Barney that C. P. Snow was sitting in front of them — he was Lord Snow and Parliamentary Secretary to the Ministry of Technology, and he was an old boy of the school. 'Barney didn't hesitate,' says Colin. 'He went down and told us to meet him in the central lobby, and in about five minutes he had Snow out to have a chat with the boys from Alderman Newton School.

In another of Colin Grundy's parties which Barney took round the House was a boy called Barratt.

> He was as Tory as you could wish, and he came over to me and asked who the gentleman was who had taken us around, and when I told him it was Barnett Janner he said, 'Conservative, of course.' So I said, 'No.' And quite honestly it was a really traumatic experience for the boy to be convinced that this man, whom he described as a gentleman, was actually a member of the Labour Party — he couldn't believe it . . . he was very taken with Barney and couldn't understand that this man was a Labour man.

Barney would often entertain guests in the Commons dining room or give them tea on the Terrace. George Billington recalls one occasion:

> I particularly remember him standing there at tea in the House of Commons in the dining room, and I'd got this something and chips, and he sat down at the table with me and placed himself over the table, talking away, and every

few minutes he would be picking up a chip from my plate and eating it . . .

Barney did indeed love chips.

Councillor Janet Setchfield, currently Chairman of Leicestershire County Council told me another amusing story about Barney and the Commons. He used to act as solicitor to the Boxing Board of Control and to a number of boxers, including Randolph Turpin.

Barney said 'Come down to the House of Commons and I'll give you tea on the Terrace — strawberries and cream and all that.' . . . I went into the House of Lords — I couldn't get into the Commons — and I listened to a debate on Sewage in Scotland. Then Barney came and rescued me. 'Come on,' he said, 'we'll go and have tea on the Terrace.' That was marvellous. I remember him sitting down at this table and there were all these 'Bruisers' . . . They all had cauliflower ears. Another time I was at the House of Commons I met Barney and he said, 'We'll have tea in the Lords.' Crumpets and these cream cakes — well, we sat there and he said, 'Don't you tell Elsie what I have been eating,' and we were munching away, it was lovely. We really enjoyed ourselves, all those crumpets and cream.

Barney adored crumpets and he was very disappointed that, during certain months, they did not make them.

Speechmaking, an essential part of the life of any politician and public figure, was one of Barney's great strengths. But when it came to preparing a speech, he had an infuriating habit. As Cicely Merry, the wife of one of his agents reminded me:

He would get very enthusiastic about something and everyone around him would be drawn into researching it; but he could just as easily reject the whole thing, leaving everyone in the air. On one weekend he was invited to address the local association of Nigerians (he always involved himself with the overseas groups). He asked me what I knew about the Nigerian problem, which unfortunately was very little. He then asked me to ring Denis

Healey who was, I believe, the Foreign Secretary and get him to give me a run-down on the present political situation. As it was Saturday, and Denis's only time off that week, he was not too pleased and raced through all the ramifications at breakneck speed while I tried to take it all down in shorthand. I then typed it all back, worried to death that I would not have done it in time. Barney scooped it up on his way to the meeting and *never mentioned any part of it* in his speech. Perhaps he thought it more tactful not to, in view of the divisions in that country then and now.

This was certainly one of Barney's habits. Many a time I or other people have typed out information for him which he urgently needed for a speech — and then he never used any of it. The reason was that he liked to have masses of papers spread untidily before him, which he could refer to if he wanted, in addition to the part which he had himself prepared, and then when he got on his feet he would speak as the spirit moved him, using very little of what was on the table. In fact he made a much better speech off the cuff than he did when it was meticulously prepared.

He had enormous reserves of stamina which enabled him to pack so much into his life, and he was physically very strong. In July 1970, when he was already seventy-eight years old, he went to Israel to a meeting of the Actions Committee (the Zionist General Council), of which he was a member of the praesidium, and he caught the 8 am plane home. This meant he had to leave Jerusalem before 6 in the morning. I met him at 1.30 at Heathrow Airport, drove him straight to the Lords, and that afternoon he made his maiden speech — on the subject of Israel. Apart from his chest — the after-effects of being gassed in the First World War — he had a nose operation in 1932, and a hip replacement in 1975. Other than that he never ailed. Consequently he had no idea what it meant to be under the weather. You were either ill or well. If he had the 'flu, the moment his temperature was normal, he was up and out.

Shonie Levi, our friend for many years, told me recently about the breathtaking pace Barney kept up when he stayed with her in Jerusalem in 1980. He was eighty-eight years old by then, and was attending a Zionist Congress. Shonie says:

> Shortly after his arrival he was taken to visit a JNF project
> somewhere in the Aravah. He was picked up practically at
> dawn, and told me he would be back in the evening to
> attend a wedding. I asked: 'Where's the wedding taking
> place?' and he said, 'Somewhere near here.' I realized that
> the trip to the South would take four and a half hours each
> way, and would be very hot and tiring, so I was sure he
> would get back late and miss the wedding.
>
> I came home that evening sure he would not be back yet,
> and found the living room filled with people who were
> going to the wedding, while Barney was getting his clothes
> changed. I said to one who was going to take him, 'Where
> is this wedding?' He answered, 'Somewhere outside the
> suburbs of Tel Aviv.' I couldn't help exclaiming, 'What!
> After that long trip through the heat?' He came home at
> midnight and was up fresh and bright the next morning
> ready for an eight o'clock meeting. When the session
> ended it took half-an-hour to leave the hall — because
> everybody wanted to shake his hand. People came and
> said, 'Lord Janner, I mean Barney,' or 'Barney, I mean
> Lord Janner.' I was tired but he was not.

This was his last visit to Israel.

For the last thirty years of his life Barney invariably wore a
carnation in his buttonhole. It started this way: he used rather
to hanker after having a buttonhole, so one year I gave him a
birthday present of three carnations a week, which were deli-
vered by a local florist to his office in High Holborn. The
following year I had to keep this up, but of course he expected a
birthday present in addition! So this practice continued for very
many years until the shop stopped delivering. After that either
he or I used to buy a carnation en route to or coming from
Parliament. Even when he was in Israel the manager of the King
David Hotel in Jerusalem sent a red carnation to his room every
morning. At St Stephen's hospital, where he was for his last
three weeks of life, the nurses pinned a carnation or a red rose to
his pyjamas.

Early in 1970 there was every indication that a general election was in the offing. Barney fully intended fighting North-West Leicester again, although he was nearly seventy-eight years old. Finally the date was fixed for June, and immediately after the election was called, Bob Mellish, the Labour Chief Whip, telephoned and told Barney he would be elevated to the House of Lords. Barney told him that he had already given his word to fight the Leicester seat. 'I am committed to Leicester,' he said.

This happened while Barney was in bed suffering from an attack of bronchitis. The doctor came, and told him that he would have to give up his vigorous style of electioneering.

Barney agonized over his decision for the next twenty-four hours, but was finally persuaded to accept a peerage. His announcement that he would not be standing in the fast-approaching election caused consternation in Leicester. The local Labour Party had to begin immediately the process of adopting a new candidate. Greville, who was well-known to the Party workers up there, was keen to fight the seat, but there were others who had the same idea, and there were many contenders. So Greville had to work hard, and as a result his name was among those put before the Selection Conference. He handled himself well, speaking and answering questions, and we were all delighted when he was chosen to be the candidate.

As in the past, the whole family trooped up to Leicester to help in the canvassing. When it was all over, Greville had won the seat. Afterwards, many of his colleagues in Parliament quipped: 'Now that we have done away with hereditary peer-ages in the Lords, the Janners have started a hereditary House of Commons!'

A peculiar circumstance arose in connection with Barney's status as a voter in this election. Under the law, peers, lunatics and criminals cannot vote. All through the campaign Barney expected to vote, because the Queen had not yet sealed the Letters Patent. But three days before the poll, he received a telephone call from the Lord Chancellor's Office. For the first time since he had grown to manhood, he was ineligible to vote.

The tributes when Barney left the Commons were generous. The *Jewish Chronicle* wrote:

The granting of a life peerage to Sir Barnett Janner on his

retirement from the House of Commons will be most warmly welcomed by the entire Jewish community. For several decades he has been a tower of strength and an indefatigable worker for communal causes and for Israel. Whatever the issue, domestic or foreign, large or small, Anglo-Jewry's premier parliamentary spokesman has invariably found the time and the energy to put himself at the service of the community, in addition to fulfilling his normal parliamentary and professional duties. His move from one Chamber to the other and the well-deserved honour accompanying it, is not in any sense the end of a career but simply a milestone. Everyone will hope that he will remain active for many years to come in the Upper House where his experience and his courage will certainly be appreciated.

There were numerous messages of congratulation, as might have been expected, but what made so many of them stand out was the extraordinarily warm recognition of what Barney had achieved in the Commons, and in his life generally. To quote from only a very few of the very many, the Israel Ambassador, Aharon Remez, wrote: 'Nothing can so dramatically change the whole picture of the House of Commons for me, and I am sure for all my colleagues, as the thought that you will no longer be there. For so many years, you have been the very pillar of trust and the source of wisdom and inspiration.' Selwyn Lloyd, who was standing again as Tory candidate for Wirral, congratulated Barney on 'a deserved tribute to all that you have done' and wrote amusingly: 'Last time, in July '62, when I said nice things about you at that dinner [Barney's 70th birthday celebrations], I got the sack a week later! I hope this letter will not involve me in losing my seat!!'

From Leicester Cathedral the Provost John Hughes sent this message: 'We feel we have a very special greeting for you because over the years you have always been so kind and co-operative to the Christians you have represented in Parliament. We have felt, when you have honoured us with your presence at the Cathedral, that we are hewn from the same rock, sons of the same God.' The Secretary-General of the Law Society, with which Barney had been associated for so long, wrote: 'Their [the Council of the Law Society] association with you has always been a close one and they much appreciate the way in which you have dealt with the Solicitors Group in Parliament throughout your Chairmanship of that Group.'

The Haham, the spiritual leader of the Sephardi community, Rabbi Dr Solomon Gaon, said:

> It is no flattery to say . . . that while serving faithfully this country you served the Jewish people and the State of Israel also in a most loyal and inspiring fashion. When some Jewish Members of Parliament might have been reluctant to express their views your voice, very often alone, was heard loudly and clearly defending the cause of the Jewish people throughout the world and especially in Israel. As a student I remember listening to you in the Shoreditch Town Hall giving clearly the message of the Zionist Movement to the crowds who had gathered from the whole of the Metropolis. In those days it might not have been very popular to be a Zionist or to think of a Jewish State but you were never afraid of expressing your beliefs not only in private but in public for all the people of this country to hear.

The Chairman and Managing Director of the *Leicester Mercury*, A. W. Peake, called Barney's peerage 'a worthy tribute to your work as the Member of Parliament for Leicester. This has given considerable delight to local people irrespective of the party to which they belong.' And the Editor, John Fortune, said: 'As far as a Member of Parliament is concerned you have always been an ideal of what an MP should be.'

Apart from the many friends who wrote, from all over the world as well as from Britain, there were letters from people and organizations Barney had helped as an MP, from Golda Meir and Nahum Goldman, from Horace King, the Speaker of the House of Commons, from the Bishop of Leicester, and many, many more.

And from a former Conservative Prime Minister, this message: 'Many congratulations on your peerage. I am sure you will enjoy the House of Lords. I shall always remember with pleasure our talks when I was in Parliament. Yours sincerely, Harold Macmillan.'

177

10 IN THE HOUSE OF LORDS 1970–1982

On 30 June 1970 Barney was sworn in as a Member of the House of Lords. It was a glittering short ceremony. I cannot describe the emotion that filled me when I saw him enter the Chamber in his red robes, flanked by his sponsors: his old colleague in Leicester, Terence, Lord Donovan, and our son-in-law Philip, Lord Morris of Kenwood. I thought to myself: 'There is a man who has pulled himself up from his ankles to such a day as this,' and I wept silently.

For the first six months in the House of Lords he was not very happy. He missed the hurly-burly and the cut-and-thrust of debate in the House of Commons. But he gradually got used to the quieter atmosphere and he gained a great respect for debate in the Lords. Once when I asked him why he was not going to speak on a certain day he said: 'I am not going to get up in the House of Lords if I don't know the subject well.' He also found that he was still serving on the same committees and held the same offices with the Lords and Commons Solicitors' Group, the Anglo-Benelux Group, the Anglo-Israel Parliamentary Group, the Inter-Parliamentary Union and the Joint Committee on Consolidation Bills with the Commons, on which he had sat for years and continued to do right up to his death. So he came to enjoy the Lords, was able to carry on with his communal and Parliamentary work, and could still speak on the causes which he held dear. His voice continued to be heard in the corridors of power. He was not only highly respected in both Houses but was very much loved and admired.

Barney's interests in the House of Lords were as wide as they had been in the Commons, but the dreadful terrorist attacks and hijackings of this period aimed at the State of Israel and at Jews, the 1973 Yom Kippur War and the beginning of the peace process between Israel and Egypt meant that he often had occasion to address the House on Middle East issues. In the last decade of his life he continued to work for the Zionist Federation as President, and he would often go down to the Federation's offices in Regent Street to carry out his duties and attend meetings.

Israel and the Middle East situation was the subject of his maiden speech in the Lords. He alerted the House to the problem of Soviet penetration in the area, the massive arms shipments to Syria, Iraq and Egypt, and argued that Israel should play a rôle in preventing this Soviet involvement from increasing: 'Indeed, I go so far as to say that Israel itself stands in the position of being able, with the help of the civilized world, to protect not only itself but the civilized world against this kind of penetration.' Barney also dispensed with the proposal that the Jerusalem problem should be dealt with as a preliminary step to solving the whole Middle East crisis. He had seen how beneficial Israel's administration in Jerusalem was; and that it was visible proof that she only wanted to live in peace.

The world was becoming an increasingly hostile place for Israel and it was more important than ever to present her case in the public arena. At the 28th Congress in Jerusalem in 1972, Barney submitted the resolutions of the Political Committee to the Plenary, and made this point:

> We live in a small world and cannot disregard the world around us. Therefore to attain our objectives we have to convince others — the non-Jews — that our cause is just. We cannot bury our heads in the sand and imagine that without the help of civilized people we shall succeed in freeing our brethren in Russia or attain our other Zionist objectives.

Again he argued for better public relations to put Israel's message across.

There was a rowdy session when Barney reported for the Resolutions Committee and his political experience was put to good use. At one point, there was much noise and confusion when the Herut group proposed a motion demanding an increase in settlements in the occupied territories. Barney had to give Menachem Begin some firm advice: 'Please Mr Begin, you know full well that there is no point in passing a resolution in this forum telling the Government of Israel what to do.'

The September 1972 massacre of Israeli athletes at the Munich Olympics outraged decent-thinking people everywhere. Speaking in Liverpool Barney said: 'The world must condemn or the world will perish' and at a Zionist Federation public rally in London he declared that acts against Jews were acts against the whole world. He had already spoken out in the Lords against the establishment of a Palestine Liberation Organization office in London. This was the organization responsible for the hijacking of planes, and the massacre of pilgrims at Lod Airport. Replying for the Government, Lady Tweedsmuir said that such organizations could not be refused permission to set up offices in Britain. Barney argued that the rise of international terrorism had to be combatted with concerted international action. He wanted the Government to agree to proposals being put forward at the Conference of the International Civil Aviation Organization, to stop airline services to states which harbour hijackers. What was happening in the air, he said in the Lords, was 'piracy, the piracy of modern times which is just as violent as the piracy of old on the seas'. States which freed terrorist murderers, as West Germany had done, were giving in to blackmail. If sanctions imposed on such countries did not work, there was another method — flushing out the criminals from their training dens.

Barney flew to Israel with two hundred leading Jewish industrialists, businessmen and communal leaders on a special trip to commemorate the twenty-fifth anniversary of the State. Together with Chief Rabbi Immanuel Jakobovits, Rabbi Dr Solomon Gaon, Nobel Prize Laureate Ernst Chain, Edmund de Rothschild, the Israel Ambassador Michael Comay, and members of the Marks and Sieff families, he met Golda Meir, Moshe Dayan, Pinhas Sapir and Ariel Pincus to discuss Israel's problems.

In January 1973 Barney joined Golda Meir at the University of the Negev in Beersheba for the dedication of the Sherman Institute of Applied Research. The Sherman Foundation had been created by Harry and Abe Sherman, founders of Sherman's Football Pools, who lived in Merthyr Tydfil, South Wales. These generous men had put aside a considerable sum of money, and on 13 January 1958 had formed a charitable foundation. Barney was invited to be a trustee, and he readily agreed to his friends' request. He remained a trustee for the rest of his life. The Foundation has donated vast sums for good causes in Wales, England and Israel. The delightful Sherman Theatre at Cardiff University is one of their projects, and is a permanent memorial to these two splendid men.

When Harry, the first Chairman, died, he was succeeded by Abe. After he too passed away, the chairmanship was handed to Dr Alec Lerner, who lives in Israel. He has carried out his duties in that capacity just as the founders would have wished.

During 1973 there were some ominous signs in the Middle East, but these went largely unnoticed, until in October President Sadat of Egypt launched his long-prepared surprise attack against Israel on Yom Kippur Day, while Syria attacked from the north. Israel, strained to the hilt, soon faced a shortage in military supplies, including spare parts and ammunition for her British Centurion tanks. Some of this material had already been ordered and paid for, but the British Government declared an embargo on shipments of arms to both sides, and refused to deliver. The embargo scarcely affected the Arabs, since most of their supplies came from the Soviet Union, but it put Israel in a difficult position, until an American emergency airlift enabled her armies to continue fighting and to counter-attack.

Barney was furious with this one-sided act of the Tory Government. He called the embargo 'shameful. A more despicable thing could not have happened.' Soon Britain was rewarded when the Arab oil-producing states declared an embargo of their own, but favoured the UK by exempting her from it. Barney coined a new word for this: he called it 'blackmoil'. Judging by the twenty thousand people who turned up at Speaker's Corner to march to the Albert Hall in solidarity with Israel, the whole of the Jewish community and most of the non-Jews agreed with him.

In December, with Israel's armies still in the field, David Ben Gurion died at his Negev home. Barney flew over for the service

181

in the Knesset, and was airlifted to the burial at Side Boker. When he returned he walked straight into a conflict with the Labour Party's front bench in the Lords. The Party spokesman, Lord Kennet, went contrary to Labour policy when he spoke of the Arabs as the 'world's underdog having at last risen up and imposed a cut-back on its sole export commodity, oil'. Together with a number of other peers and peeresses Barney deliberately walked out of the Chamber while Lord Kennet was speaking.

He constantly argued that Arafat and his organization should be outlawed by all civilized states. The massacre of schoolchildren at Ma'alot in northern Israel confirmed his argument. For many years he had looked to the United Nations as a source of moral authority in the world, but as time had gone by he had seen the international body become dominated by countries which condoned international terrorism under the pretext of 'struggles for national liberation'. So when Arafat was allowed to speak to the General Assembly in December 1974, with a revolver at his hip, it was a sad day for Barney. He said in the Lords, echoing the words of Sir Edward Grey at the outbreak of the First World War,

> . . . the lights have gone out at the United Nations. They have gone out because the United Nations have allowed a declared assassin — who has practised every conceivable kind of attack on human beings, who has sent his people to shoot children one by one in a schoolroom — to speak. . . . Today the UN presents to the world not an image of the original UN with its Charter, but a distorted figure as in a concave mirror. It is our duty, I think, to try to bring a moral outlook to bear on the position. If we look at it that way, we will see that the PLO is an instrument of the Devil, which should not be a participant in discussions even on behalf of the Arabs themselves: because it is as much a disaster to them as it is to the rest of the civilized world.

The PLO terror continued and Barney became even more disillusioned with the United Nations. He told the Lords that 'Subversion and extremism are being used by the destroyers of the morals of the world by devious, evil methods; some horribly visible, and others using every device in an attempt to cover their evil designs.' Action against terrorism has to be taken

> together with the other civilized nations of the world. We will not be able to do it through the United Nations Organization, because most of their members are in fear of blackmail pressure of those Arabs who wish to exterminate the State of Israel.

Things went from bad to worse. In late 1975 the UN passed a resolution equating Zionism with racism. For Barney this kind of language was a way of encouraging antisemitism:
He told the House that

> Those who voted for the resolution clearly wished to drag the United Nations into becoming a party to what I call a diabolically-conceived programme, examination of which will show it to be akin to that adopted by the Nazis. Millions are being spent on a type of propaganda similar to that advocated by Hitler in *Mein Kampf*. The destruction of Israel is its aim and it has the ultimate object of destroying the Jewish people. The attempt to defile Zionism by attributing racism to it clearly means the fanning of antisemitism, just as the Nazis demonstrated by similar actions.

Although Barney had ceased to be Chairman of the Foreign Affairs Committee of the Board of Deputies in 1973, he was elected Chairman of the Board's Eretz Israel Committee, which seeks to act as a liaison between Israel, the Government and the Jewish community here. Already eighty-one years old, Barney fulfilled all his duties with vigour, and continued attending Zionist General Council meetings in Jerusalem. In December 1973 he attended the Conference on Jewish Solidarity in Jerusalem — the Jewish people's response to the UN's 'Zionism equals racism' resolution.

His fifty years of devotion to the Zionist cause as an officer of the Zionist Federation were honoured in March 1976 with a dinner at the Café Royal in London. Abba Eban praised the singlemindedness of Barney's Zionism, and Gideon Rafael, the Israel Ambassador, described Barney as 'a man of independent mind, whose Zionism was liberal, whose politics were Labour, whose Judaism was Orthodox and whose whole being was humanistic.' There were wonderful messages of tribute from, among others, Harold Wilson, Israel's President Ephraim Katzir, Yitzhak Rabin, Yigal Allon, Golda Meir, Shimon Peres and Teddy Kollek.

Despite all of Israel's trials and the election of its first non-Labour coalition Government in 1977, there was a dramatic move toward peace in November 1977 when it was announced that President Sadat would go to Israel. Barney was agog with excitement and very keen to attend the Knesset when Sadat spoke. The Clerk of the Knesset at that time was Natanel Lorch, a friend of ours. He remembers Barney phoning him from England on the Thursday night before Sadat was due to speak on Sunday, 19 November.

> I got a call from Barney saying that he was leaving London. 'I'm on my way. Make sure there is a ticket for me for the Knesset.' Needless to say he was not the only one! There were only seven hundred seats, including Members of the Knesset and about fifty seats in both galleries. Everyone wanted to come, dignitaries, rabbis, ex-MPs, MPs' wives. A thousand journalists were there and they were housed in a Jerusalem theatre with thousands of television cameras and telephones. I had to refuse to get a ticket for anyone except Barney. I got him one because I thought he deserved it for his decades of work for Israel. When it was all over there was an unscheduled meeting between Begin and Sadat. Everything was then agreed in outline but it took two years for it to be brought into force. On the way back I saw Barney standing in the corridor when I was on my way with Sadat's entourage. He followed me into my office, we had coffee and Barney expressed his thanks and had a chat with Mustafa Khalil [later Egypt's Prime Minister]. Needless to say, the Egyptians all knew who he was.

When the Treaty was finally signed Barney was able to say in the Lords that it marked 'a new era of civilized conduct towards each other by neighbours in the Middle East, achieved by negotiations — not by war — led by men of great courage, ability and statesmanship.' Barney saw the peace between Egypt and Israel as the basis for peace in the whole region. As he told the Lords in 1980 the State of Egypt contains half the Arabs and they had now made peace. This should show the way to the rest of the Arab world.

When the European Community issued its Venice Declaration of June 1980, going further than ever before in calling for a Palestinian State, Barney saw this as encouraging the PLO to indulge in even more international terrorism. But he was also aware of other dangers in the Venice document:

> We are opening a door for enemies of our country and of European countries which may, I am afraid, result ultimately in having possibly — I will say probably, though I hope not — a further pro-USSR State in the Middle East.

It was necessary to support the Camp David Agreements, not to encourage the PLO.

Barney always stressed how important Israel was to the whole world — 'a jewel in the crown of the world' he once called it — but it was wrong to expect all the concessions to come from her in order to achieve peace. 'Does anyone suggest . . . that if little Israel, which is not the size of Wales, did not exist, everything would be calm, collected and without difficulties?' It was the Europeans who wanted impossible sacrifices from Israel and all because they were giving in to Arab 'blackmoil'.

One of Barney's last speeches in Parliament in February 1981, was on the EEC's Middle East initiative. He was nearly eighty-nine years old, and becoming increasingly frail. Once again he called the Camp David agreements an 'outstanding diplomatic achievement', and urged their Lordships to realize that 'the security of a state like Israel, a small state, should not be regarded as being just a detail, but should be right at the heart of any negotiations that take place'.

Barney attended the 29th Zionist Congress in Jerusalem in 1978 and the Zionist General Council in June 1979. July 1980 saw him at the Egyptian Embassy with Ambassador Shlomo Argov of Israel and other members of the diplomatic community, as guest of the Egyptian Ambassador, General Hassam Abou-Seeda, for a reception to mark Egypt's National Day.

He had the satisfaction, during the 1970s, of seeing the arrival in Israel of many thousands of Jews from Soviet Russia. This did not prevent him from raising the issue of discrimination against Jews inside Russia at every suitable opportunity and at the end of the decade, when emigration was even more restricted, he made sure that his fellow Lords knew just how serious were the antisemitic attacks in Soviet newspapers. He continued to press the claims of Jews persecuted under the Nazi regime, urging the East Germans to pay reparations for their part in that persecution.

In 1972, with the problems of contemporary antisemitism in mind, he hit out strongly at Hutchinson, the publishers who were bringing out a paperback edition of Hitler's *Mein Kampf*: 'Let people who wish to study the period of Hitler', he said, 'do so in museums and libraries. To want to publish a popular edition of what is the worst kind of pornography is beyond my comprehension.' Some years later, in 1977, when there were fears that the National Front would attract support in the forthcoming local elections, Barney warned that a few dozen votes here or there for the extremists could expand, and bring disaster, not only on the Jewish community but on the country itself. Speaking at the annual conference of the Association of Jewish Ex-Servicemen and Women, Barney said that Parliament itself did not have the slightest idea of how big a menace was facing them.

In 1971 he had spoken out against the Government's Immigration Bill, which deeply disturbed him. On its third reading he said: 'I think this is a sad occasion. It has been pointed out that this legislation is bound to have an effect on the immigration into this country of coloured people as distinct from those who are not coloured.' He believed the Bill would exacerbate racial tension and that it was based upon 'ideas and principles which are not liberal ideas and principles. In my view it is a Bill that ought not to have been introduced.' Racial tensions certainly increased over the decade Barney was in the Lords and in 1978 he had occasion to compare the activities of the National Front against Bengalis in the East End of London with similar acts against Jews in the same area in the past.

186

When in 1979 a teacher was killed at Southall, as police tried to keep National Front marchers and Anti-Nazi League demonstrators apart, and the matter was discussed in the Lords, Barney said:

> There are many people who are considerably perturbed by the fact that, among those who are in the National Front at present, are people who were actually in the Mosley movement when he was perpetrating some of the most serious actions against liberty, when they were against the policy of the Government altogether and when they were pro-Nazi, as obviously the National Front is at present.

He had other interests: some serious, some less so. In the debate on the Solicitors' Bill in 1972 he said:

> I think the Bill once again alerts the public to the special relationship which a solicitor has towards his client. The man in the street is, all too often, misled into placing legal affairs into the hands of unqualified persons who have not had appropriate training, and whose activities and funds are not supervised by a responsible authority. This is a risk which should obviously not be taken by any reasonable person. It is like placing his affairs in the hands of somebody who can be compared to a quack doctor.

He defended the Law Society in a debate on legal aid, a service he believed in very strongly, saying: 'It is a mistaken idea that lawyers really have not got consideration for their fellow men. Many years ago lawyers gave their services free of charge, but they could not possibly cope with all the demands made upon them by poor people.'

He became very concerned about the plight of the homeless. In 1977, after having urged the year before that the Government take urgent action to help homeless young people, he said that the problems of such people were being made by Government cuts in aid to housing associations. Later that year he proposed that single homeless young people be given priority under the Housing Bill, which was getting its second reading in the

Lords. In 1980 he had shuddering evidence of the problems of the homeless, when the weeks-old dead body of a tramp was discovered in the area in front of Janners' offices in Upper Brook Street. He told the House of Lords:

> It was obvious that this man had been coming to the basement of our office to seek shelter for the night, although we had never seen him coming or going. It was a horrible thing to find, and although I have been involved in organizations for the homeless, I was shocked to find someone like this right on my doorstep. This sort of discovery indicates the problem of homeless people in London.

Barney was a patron of the Intake Project for the single homeless for seven years. When he died, the Chairman of Intake, Martin Davis, wrote: 'He gave us valuable advice and assistance, and we will always feel it was a privilege for us to be associated with him.'

On questions relating to rents and leaseholders he remained as concerned as ever he was in the Commons. As usual, we ourselves were continually being reminded of the problems facing private tenants. The new landlords of our flat in Albert Hall Mansions were Arabs whose registered offices were in Abu Dhabi, Liberia and Jersey. They had paid £500,000 to extend the lease on the block and were now forcing up the rents. Their demands were exorbitant, and even after we went through the rent tribunals procedure, our rent was raised by four hundred per cent. So we had to move.

Referring to this experience, in a June 1980 speech on the Tory Government's Housing Bill, Barney said:

> The situation that exists for private tenants is extremely unhealthy: anonymous landlords, often registered in Liechtenstein or some offshore island with tax advantages, buy and sell blocks of flats and properties over the heads of tenants, refuse to do repairs, ignore environmental health orders and attempts by local authorities to protect tenants, harass tenants by non-provision of essential services, ignore planning regulations and so on.

He deplored the fact that private landlords were leaving accommodation empty, and advocated a policy of temporary municipalization which would allow local authorities to buy such properties. 'If the Government honestly wants to see increased home-ownership,' Barney said, 'why are we not seeing an extension of the Leasehold Reform Act to enable millions of private tenants to buy their homes at realistic prices?'

Barney always loved animals and enjoyed going to the Zoo, so it was not difficult for Prince Philip and Lord Zuckerman to interest him in the work of the Zoological Society. In *The Times* of 20 May 1982 Lord Zuckerman, President of the Zoological Society of London, wrote:

> Your admirable obituary notice of the late Lord Janner rightly emphasizes his concern with Jewish and Zionist causes, and with various social reforms of wide significance.
>
> What is not so well-known is that he was also deeply interested in animal welfare. The Zoo Licensing Act 1981, passed with the support of the Government, has now brought all zoos in Britain under legal control. Long before this Lord Janner was aware of the wretched conditions in which exotic animals are often kept in captivity and in 1971 he had introduced a Private Member's Bill in the House of Commons to regulate the management of all zoos. This Bill was withdrawn, but with some amendments was brought forward again the next year and this time it passed through all its stages before being taken over by the Home Office for redrafting.
>
> He presented the amended Bill again in 1973 when it went through all its stages before being brought to the Commons, where it ran out of Parliamentary time at the end of 1973. On this occasion its progress was stopped by the General Election of early 1974 but Lord Janner then reintroduced the Bill, which again passed through all its stages in the Lords, only to be objected to in the Commons.
>
> Lord Janner's persistence in the full knowledge of the opposition of the majority of the country's purely commercial zoos to control of any kind was well rewarded when the

Government took up the cause and saw to it that the kind of Bill he wanted found its way into the statute book.

That was typical of Barney — he was indefatigable in the service of the causes he championed. In his last years he was often invited to address audiences in the United States. Many of his visits were to raise money for the Jewish National Fund. He went to Los Angeles, Boston, Cleveland, New Orleans, Dallas, Phoenix, Detroit and New York, also appearing on radio and television. He was welcomed on these occasions like an international statesman and was often given a standing ovation. In 1979 he was part of a Joint Israel Appeal Mission to Israel and in March 1980 was the guest of honour, together with Teddy Sieff, at the sixtieth anniversary celebrations of the UIA-Keren Hayesod in Antwerp.

11 LOOKING BACK

Many honours were bestowed on Barney during his later years, but the one that gave him the most pleasure was being made an Honorary Freeman of the City of Leicester. (He had taken the title of Baron Janner of the City of Leicester when he was awarded his life peerage in 1970.) Only twenty-six others had been so honoured since the dignity was first instituted in 1892. There has to be unanimous approval by the Council of any nomination. The ceremony was held in the Council Chamber of the Town Hall on 8 February 1972 with a celebratory banquet at de Montfort Hall afterwards. The other Freemen were Alderman Sidney Bridges, Alderman Sir Ernest Oliver, and Mr Mac Goldsmith, who had come to England in 1937 from Germany and was a well-known Leicester philanthropist. Each of the Freemen was presented with an illuminated certificate of admission to the Leicester Roll of Freemen and a magnificent silver rose bowl, specially designed and executed by the Leicester College of Technology, bearing the City coat of arms, and an inscription. At the banquet the Lord Mayor, Alderman Percy Watts said '. . . Never afraid to upset those who disagreed with him, yet sensitive to people's feelings, Lord Janner could always be relied upon to persuade rather than force others to his point of view.'

Barney had remained close to the City and its people long after he ceased to be MP for N.W. Leicester. He was elected honorary life-president of the Leicester West Constituency Labour Party and he returned to Leicester during the 1970, 1974 and 1979 General Elections to help our son Greville's campaign. In October 1979 he was guest at the *Leicester Mercury* celebrity author's lunch with Sir Charles Curran (former Director General of the BBC), Patrick Moore, Sandy Gall and Lady Isobel Barnett. The city had taken him to its heart. Barney deeply cherished Leicester's spirit of democracy and its religious tolerance. Yet Leicester could hardly have been more dif-

191

ferent from Barney's first constituency of Whitechapel and St George's. There was no deprivation on the scale to be found in the East End of London, and a rather small Jewish community. Nevertheless, there was much to be done for Leicester immediately; there was a feeling that through their sacrifices in the war people had earned for themselves the right to a better life: better housing, health care, insurance, social security and a safer, fairer world. Barney wanted to see these reforms implemented, and in working to achieve them for the benefit of the people of Leicester he earned their loyalty and great affection.

He knew that being a member of the House of Commons imposed on him a great responsibility. From the bottom of his heart he wanted to help people and he saw himself doing this as much by arguing for years for the ratification of the Genocide Convention, as by badgering a Government Minister to allow a sub-post office to be opened on a new city estate. Barney was practising community politics years before the phrase ever became popular. It was second nature to him.

What happened in Leicester was the stimulus for very much of his parliamentary work. Although many of the speeches he made in debates were on issues of national or global importance, the greater part of his time in the House of Commons was devoted to his constituency. Much of this work was visible publicly, in the form of questions and the written or oral answers provided by Ministers, but he devoted an enormous amount of time and energy to activities which did not catch the public eye: the endless sending of letters or making of phone calls; representations to Ministers and private meetings with them; contact with Government officials and so on. Barney helped Leicester people in many different ways, as the hundreds of 'thank you' letters which he received during his twenty-five years as a Leicester MP so clearly show. Of course, he was not always successful; but even when the outcome was not what the constituent had hoped for, Barney would still get a letter of thanks. To quote from only one example: 'All I can do is thank you for the prompt way you dealt with my complaint. That you remain our Member for many years is the sincere wish of Yours Truly.' There were matters of a very individual nature: helping servicemen to get release on compassionate grounds; securing pensions for the old and the disabled; assisting young people to get into college and university; arranging for relatives to join refugee families already settled in the UK. There were local problems like getting pavements repaired; pressing for more telephone kiosks; helping tenants' associations, schools and local firms.

Societies and unions would write to him with their concerns. The Leicestershire and Rutland Federation of Women's Institutes contacted him about proposed new ice-cream regulations: 'It was very good of you to follow up our request — I remember you were equally helpful a few years ago when we wrote to you about the sewage pollution of rivers and streams'. The Amalgamated Union of Engineering Workers often thanked Barney for sending their resolutions to the relevant Government departments and securing replies from them. In 1953 the University College of Leicester thanked him for asking a question in the House about the danger that the University's grant would be cut by 10 per cent. The cut was restored.

Two particularly epic struggles involved Leicester. The first, the eventual passing of the Flick-Knife Act which banned spring clip knives, has been described earlier. But not all were happy. Those who wanted to own such knives would say, 'He doesn't know what he's talking about, we need these knives to defend ourselves.' After the Act was passed, a Teddy boy at Leicester market tried to buy one from one of the knife stalls, and was refused. He asked the stallholder what he could do about it and was told to go and see Barnett Janner. The Teddy boy's immediate reaction was 'Which stall does he keep?'

The second was the problem of the sub-post office on the Mowmacre Hill housing estate. Barney was very involved with the building of new housing in his constituency. He argued for it constantly in the House of Commons and kept in very close touch with the progress of the building, and with the tenants, once the estates were completed. He was concerned about the provision of full amenities on these estates. It was all very well building the houses, but if the shops, pubs, bus routes, post offices, schools, community centres and youth clubs were not also made available the job was only half done, and social problems would be created.

In July 1959 old people, pensioners and mothers with young children on the new Mowmacre Hill estate complained to Barney that they had to walk up and down a very steep hill to get to the nearest post office for their benefits. It was a tiring and strenuous walk for them. There was a bus only every forty minutes, and anyway the pensioners found it hard to afford the fare. In the winter the frozen roads made walking dangerous. There had been several accidents.

Barney asked the Assistant Postmaster General in the House whether the building of a post office could be authorized. After two months' consideration the Minister turned down the request. There was already a post office, he said, situated only a mile from the estate and regulations forbade the building of another so close. Barney called the decision 'shocking' and said, 'I propose to fight it.' And fight he did. He suggested that as an alternative, a sub-post office be opened in a shop on the estate. This was refused because it was claimed this would add to costs without bringing in extra revenue.

After the General Election in October 1959 a new Assistant Postmaster General was appointed, Miss Mervyn Pike, Conservative MP for Melton. The Mowmacre Tenants' Association and Old Folks' Club prepared a petition. Barney told the House of the 'misery and frustration' of residents and recited:

Jack and Jill went down Mowmacre Hill
To fetch their old age pension.
Jill fell down and broke her crown
But the Minister paid no attention.

He challenged Miss Pike to walk with him up the hill for herself and then decide whether the building of the post office was justified. Miss Pike agreed, and on 16 March 1960 they set off up Border Drive accompanied by women pushing their children in prams. Crowds saw them off. Miss Pike was unimpressed and announced in May that permission would not be given for a post office on Mowmacre Hill.

Barney did not give up. He asked again in July 1960 after new building plans for the estate had been proposed; and again in February 1961. In May that year he urged residents to flock to the House of Commons, lobby the Postmaster General and demand a sub-post office. In June he presented a petition from residents and said in the House that old people were becoming desperate about the position.

Finally, on 7 November he returned from Leicester to London to find a letter from Miss Pike. She was happy to tell him that they had been able to accede to his request for a sub-post office at Mowmacre Hill.

Barney was asked to perform the opening ceremony for the new post office. As he cut the tape, a loud cheer arose from the assembled local residents. This is perhaps the only time that a Member of Parliament has officiated at such an occasion.

It was not only the post offices that Barney fought to obtain. Insufficient telephone lines and kiosks posed a problem he often worried the Postmaster General about, as well as asking him why letters from Leicester should take two days to reach nearby destinations. But even more important to his constituency were schools, community centres and youth clubs. On New Parks Estate (the former War Ministry tank park) progress towards providing adequate schooling facilities was slow, and as early as 1948 Barney was helping the tenants' association by writing to the Minister of Education. This was an issue he came back to on a number of occasions in later years.

In 1953 Barney opened the New Parks Social Club and Institute's new building, which the people of the area had worked for three years to provide. Barney did a lot to help the young people there, as well as those at Mowmacre and Stocking Farm, and in December 1981 he was proud to lay the foundation stone of the Mowmacre Boys' Club (he was its President).

There were many other ways in which he tried to be directly helpful to Leicester. The Minister of Pensions' decision in March 1961 to open a limb-fitting centre in Leicester was the result of a long campaign by Barney, who worked in conjunction with the local branch of the British Limbless Ex-Servicemens's Association. He had raised the matter in the Commons on 20 February 1960 when he pointed out that all fittings for Leicester and county were centralized in Nottingham. He had pressed the War Office to derequisition buildings that were needed for business or other community purposes, and while National Service remained he often raised problems relating to Leicester servicemen and women.

As a city dependent on trade with other parts of Britain and with the world, Leicester very much needed good road and rail connections. In December 1945 Barney was elected Chairman of a Highways Development Committee of the House of Commons. One of the purposes of the Committee was to accelerate the production of a master plan for the framework of Britain's future road system. Not surprisingly, therefore, Barney took a great interest in the building of the M1, the first motorway which was to link London and Yorkshire, taking the strain off the old A1. He pressed successive Transport Ministers relentlessly on this, year after year, stressing how important it was to Leicester. In the early 1960s, when Lord Beeching was cutting back the rail network, Barney insisted that Leicester should not be denuded of its rail facilities.

When Leicester's indutries were in trouble Barney tried to come to their aid. Imports from Hong Kong threatened Leicester's glove industry, and Barney argued in Parliament that it was very important to keep a small industry of this sort alive.

When raising Leicester's problems in the House, he would sometimes quote directly from letters sent to him by constituents, or from articles which appeared in the Leicester newspapers. Just two examples: in 1954 a resident of Barclay Street who wrote to Barney had portions of his letter read out to members of the standing committee of the House on the Housing Repairs and Rents Bill. In 1967, following a campaign in the *Leicester Mercury* about poor compensation being paid by local authorities after houses were compulsorily purchased, Barney showed the *Mercury* material to Bob Melllish, then Parliamentary Secretary to the Ministry of Housing and Local Government; as a result Mellish agreed to look for ways and means of alleviating this hardship.

Whenever he could, given his terribly busy schedule, Barney looked in on the social and other events of his constituency. Apart from the regular May Day rallies, attended by all the Leicester Labour MPs and usually leading Labour politicians — Attlee, Gaitskell, Bevan, Wilson — there were numerous local fairs, shows, dances, socials, garden fêtes.

When we celebrated our golden wedding anniversary in 1977, after Barney had been out of the constituency for some time, we gave a party at Roundfield School. We had set the precedent at our silver wedding, as I've already described.

Barney was continually showing parties from Leicester

around the Palace of Westminster: women's groups, college students, workers and, of course, school-children. There are many letters both from teachers and pupils thanking him for the tour. In 1950 one child wrote:

> On behalf of all the children from Shaftesbury Road School we thank you for the enjoyable day, Tuesday last. I think it was very sporting of you to give up your morning for seventy school children. It must have been a very weary and tiring job to sign all those autographs and I hope I shall never have to sign so many all at once.

Barney enjoyed showing his visitors the statues of some of the former Prime Ministers in the inner lobby and was particularly proud to show them the magnificent full-length bronze figure of Winston Churchill, the work of our good friend the sculptor Oscar Nemon. (One spot on the knee has a shiny gleam where thousands of tourists have touched the likeness of the great man.) Other 'thank you' letters give a good indication of the range of problems Barney dealt with on behalf of his constituents. From the Holy Apostles Vicarage, Fosse Road South, came thanks 'for all you have done for the People of Tristan da Cunha. You certainly got things moving and quickly too.' The parents of a young man Barney helped to get into college wrote: 'We all wish to thank you very much indeed — not only for your successful efforts in putting this matter right — but, what to us is more amazing, all the trouble and kindness you have shown to complete strangers.'

The Leicester Temperance Society and Band of Hope Union wrote thanking Barney for sending a 'Resolution' of theirs to the Minister of Education. He had helped a New Parks Estate resident obtain his Post War Credit: 'May I sincerely thank you, and I am most grateful for bringing my case before the House of Commons, no doubt thousands of others who are in the same boat as myself, benefited from your good deed.' And this, from a non-Labour constituent: 'May I just add that I am not of your political party, but that my wife and I very much appreciate your many efforts on behalf of your constituents.'

It was Mrs Florence Hames, a 71-year old pensioner who addressed Barney in 1968 as 'The man who gets things done'.

She wrote to thank him for protesting to the Chancellor of the Exchequer over plans to reduce the status of the Probate Registry and reminded him:

> I also am the woman who brought a horror comic to you, in an interview in New Walk and you took the book to the House. The firm who printed it was, I believe, heavily fined. Thank you so much for your interest and efforts on our behalf. More power to your elbow.

The people who worked closest with Barney in Leicester during these years were fellow Labour Party workers. They got to know him not only from the intense and often hectic election campaigns, but also from the routine work that constituency workers and their MP have to do all the year round. How did they see him? Colin Grundy told me,

> I think that, forgetting politics and everything else, the thing that most impressed me about Barney, was that he always struck me as being larger than life and that he was a very warm human being with tremendous compassion for people and an understanding of human problems. It was his warmth and humanity which impressed me more than anything else . . . It was a dedication which came from his feeling and his concern for the people. It wasn't the almost academic dedication to the Party; it was a dedication which sprang from a feeling and a concern for humanity.

Janet Setchfield, Chairman of the Leicestershire County Council and daughter of Rowland and Mollie Hill said:

> Once Barney was adopted — after some problems as there always are at adoption meetings — I don't think anyone could have fought more for Barney than my mother and father, particularly mother . . . Barney was part of our family. I always used to say to him, especially after Dad died, that he was my second Dad . . . When I was a child he used to squeeze and hug me so much — in fact I think the last time we met he nearly knocked a tooth out because he squeezed me so much the strain was hurting me. He was

that sort of person to me. He was so warm and friendly and I admired him for his ability and what he'd achieved, but to me it was far more of a personal relationship because I had grown up with him.

George Billington, now Lord Mayor of Leicester, remembers canvassing on the Stadium Estate during one election and finding that there were people who were prepared to vote for Barney though they were normally Tory voters:

I think this explains a great deal of the enormous personal vote he had. This of course was his concern for individuals' problems on an enormous scale. I think that endeared him to so many people. The way youngsters would call after him.

Jack Jacobs, who first met Barney in 1920 at a conference of the Jewish Friendly Societies, and did magnificent work for him in all his elections, tells a similar story: 'There was no limit to Barney's helpfulness. It didn't matter what it was, Barney took it up and would get them satisfied in some way. They still talk about that. They always said that.'

Janet, George and Colin all told me the same thing — that the people of Leicester still feel Barney is alive. I said 'Surely they know he is dead?' 'Yes, they know he's dead, but they still feel he is around. They talk about him constantly. He is a legend.'

When Barney died many Leicestershire people paid tribute to his life and work. The then Lord Mayor, Councillor Archibald Berridge, said:

The people of Leicester owe a great debt of gratitude to Lord Janner for the magnificent way he served them in Parliament for such a long time. We all realize that he loved Leicester . . . there is a tremendous amount of affection and goodwill for him among the people of this City.

A former Lord Mayor, A. T. (Bert) Baker, wrote that Barney was:

A man who was everybody's friend, especially those who

had the pleasure of knowing him for the considerable gentleman he was. It was always a smile and a friendly greeting when one met him and one felt that he was happy to meet friends of many years.

The Lord Lieutenant of Leicestershire, Andrew Martin, also spoke of Barney having

> ... a smile and a friendly word for everyone; he was a great doer of good on an international scale as well as nationally and locally. In his nearly ninety years of life he fought for what he thought to be right and good, not for his own glorification but for what he considered people needed. He was remarkably successful, which now leaves a host of people who mourn a great man.

Barney was not aloof or distant and he was known as a very good dancer — once at a dance-social in the Braunstone Avenue Community Centre Barney was dancing with Janet Setchfield's sister when, because of a faulty floor, he suddenly went flying on to his back! He got up and carried on dancing, and took it all in good part. When Greville first fought the seat everybody said 'If you're as good as your dad you'll be all right', and then one woman said, 'If you dance as good as your father you'll be all right!' In 1970, Greville's first election campaign for the Leicester seat, when Barney had just gone to the Lords and we were in Leicester taking people to the polls, an old lady put her hand on Barney's shoulder and said 'I have always voted for you, Mr Janner, and I always will.' We didn't disillusion her.

And thirteen years later a young assistant of Greville's, canvassing for him in the General Election of June 1983, was quite amazed at the number of people he met on the doorstep who told him 'Oh yes. We knew his father. He used to come here and have a cup of tea with us.' Each one seemed to feel that he was more privileged than anyone else because Barnett Janner had been in his home and had tea.

On 20 June 1972, we celebrated Barney's eightieth birthday with a dinner party at the House of Lords. Michael Comay and

200

Harold Wilson spoke. All our grandchildren were there and two of them, fifteen-year-old Daniel Janner and twelve-year-old Diane Morris proposed the toast to Barney's health. Michael Comay said some wonderful things about Barney and his rôle in the Zionist Movement, but he also spoke of one of Barney's greatest gifts:

> In all his long public life, and at times he has been a very outspoken man — and one takes it for granted that in public life one often makes enemies — Barney had the gift of making friends even of his opponents; and I don't know of any man in public life, certainly not in Jewish life, who was ever as well liked as Barney, who was able to gain affection from everybody.

Harold Wilson made a superb speech, referring in the course of it to the fact that Barney had been his solicitor. About Leicester he said:

> I remember in 1955 chairing a committee set up by the National Executive Committee of the party to look into party organization throughout the country. There was a state of holy war — it wasn't religious, it was very irreligious — about our recommendations for the city Party in Leicester, but in the course of that report we found occasion to note that the organization of this particular constituency was not what it might have been and that a quarter of the work in that 1955 campaign was done by Barney himself, only excelled by the other three-quarters that was done by Elsie herself, together with a few conscripts not from Leicester but from London who were hijacked for this purpose of returning Barney — which they did.

He paid tribute to Barney's Jewish commitment, but especially to his 'all-embracing fight against racialism of any kind throughout the whole of his political life'.

Barney appreciated Harold Wilson's and Michael Comay's words but, as he said in his own speech, 'I am bound to say that I was overpowered by the speeches that were given by my grandson and granddaughter.'

201

To mark his birthday, the *Jewish Chronicle* published a profile by Chaim Bermant:

> No major Jewish occasion is complete without him. Indeed, one searches around for him like some familiar landmark, and there he is at, or near, the centre of the platform, the shoulders heavy, the head slightly thrust forward, the face large, kindly, paternal, one almost says maternal, for there is something about his sense of concern which reminds one of the Jewish matriarch. He is loved by his audience because he loves his audience, and because no adult attending a Jewish meeting can be unaware of his record of public service. He has grown old in service to the community.

In 1974 Barney represented the Board of Deputies of British Jews at the dedication of the million-tree Royal Forest in Israel, the gift of the Jews of Britain and the Commonwealth to mark the silver wedding of Queen Elizabeth II and the Duke of Edinburgh. Zvi Weinberg of the Jewish National Fund in Jerusalem, where the work for the ceremony was done, remembers Barney speaking about the honour he felt at having been allowed to be the spokesman of the Jews of Britain on this occasion. He said that the ceremony expressed a very emotional moment for British Jewry. 'The Queen and her husband, the Duke of Edinburgh, have associated themselves in no uncertain way with Jewish matters.'

Zvi recalls vividly that at the luncheon following the ceremony, which was attended by more than a thousand people, Barney made a special point of:

> standing up and thanking me personally for the tremendous amount of work that had been put in as far as the organization of the ceremony was concerned, as well as to all the other boys and all the other members of staff of the head office of the JNF who had helped to make the ceremony the glorious event it actually was. It seemed to me that Lord Janner loved the Jewish National Fund. He regarded it as an honour to be asked to go on some mission, and I underline the word *mission*, not a 'trip', on behalf of

the JNF, because he loved trees, as I remember, and he loved what he called the wonderful pioneering work that the JNF was doing.

We were both made Freemen of the City of London in 1975 thanks to the nomination of the Chief Commoner, Bernard Morgan. After the ceremony he and Charles Fairweather gave a luncheon for us at the City Livery Club.

On 12 July 1977 we celebrated our golden wedding anniversary. We gave a party at the House of Lords on the evening of 11 July for the family and friends. It was a joy that our four bridesmaids were there — Barney's sister Sally; my sister Edith; my niece Gabrielle Blake; and my cousin Peggy Slotover. On the day itself we entertained in a private room in the Commons a small luncheon party made up of our children, close parliamentary friends, and in particular our doctors. The toast of the day was to those men who had kept both of us alive to see that moment; to my cousin Dr Alfred Rudd, who had looked after us for nearly fifty years; to Mr John Strachan, the surgeon who had given each of us a new hip; and to Dr Walter Somerville, our cardiologist, who had brought me back from the valley of the shadows. In his reply on behalf of his colleagues and himself Dr Somerville said that doctors don't expect any thanks — their satisfaction comes from helping their patients.

Since that day he has continued to be a dear friend and wonderful cardiologist not only to me but until the very last to Barney as well.

Barney filled his life with activity. As Chaim Bermant wrote, 'It is, perhaps, the very fullness of his life which keeps him lively even in the fullness of his years'. It was characteristic of him that at the age of eighty-seven he could join a march of young people from Hyde Park to the Foreign Office protesting against any change in the Government's policy of non-recognition of the PLO; he rode on the float leading the procession as it snaked through Oxford Street, Piccadilly and Trafalgar Square.

Although illness stopped Barney from standing again as Parliamentary candidate for N.W. Leicester in 1970, he was rarely prevented from doing the things he wanted to do during the last twelve years of his life. He kept going at quite an extraordinary pace. He just refused to slow down. An example of this was

when he was well into his eighties. The Industrial Relations Bill
came before the House of Lords. Hundreds of amendments
were not discussed in the Commons because the Tory Government applied the 'guillotine'. (This means there can be no
further discussion on the amendment to the clause under discussion, but a vote must be taken. Then they pass on to the next
clause, and if the guillotine is applied there also, the same
procedure is followed.)

The Labour Opposition decided to try to amend the Bill
during its passage through the House of Lords, where there is
no guillotine. There is an unwritten arrangement that, so as not
to interfere with the principles brought forward by the elected
Chamber, the Opposition in the House of Lords does not
oppose the Second Reading of Government Bills. However,
they do try to alter Bills at the Committee stage, which is taken
on the floor of the House. Amendments carried by the Lords go
back to the Commons for further consideration.

An enormous number of amendments to this Industrial Relations Bill were put on the Lords' Order Paper, and discussions
went on well into the night. The Whips used to press Barney to
go home after midnight, but he refused. He stayed to vote until
the small hours of the morning.

Once they sat all night. At 7.30 am he returned home whistl-
ing as he put his key in the lock. He was as happy as a sandboy
— just like the days in the Commons. He had breakfast, slept
for a few hours; and was back in the House of Lords at 2.30 pm.

Shortly after the dinner in 1975 to mark his fifty years of work
for the Zionist Federation, he had to have a hip replacement,
but he made fine progress and was soon able to return home and
continue his activities. On his eighty-fifth birthday JNF of
America planted a grove of a thousand trees in Israel in his
honour. In the Lords, Lord Hailsham of St Marylebone congratulated him and wished him well on behalf of the House.

In October 1979 Barney attended the opening ceremony in
Leicester of a new block of sheltered flats for the elderly built by
the City Council at Beaumont Leys, and named 'Barnett Janner
House'. He was so delighted and proud.

In January 1980 we holidayed in Barbados, where Barney

gave one of his last interviews. Looking back on his career he said: 'If I had to live my life over I would still choose a political life. I would like to be able to cure the ills of the world.'

When the Board of Deputies of British Jews made us both a presentation for a hundred years of combined service to the Board, Barney was very alert. Like the leader of his people four thousand years earlier, 'His eye was not dimmed.'

He attended the House of Lords in his ninetieth year, in October 1981, but he gradually lost his strength and zest for life. His last public appearance was typical of him. On 15 December 1981, the Board of Deputies celebrated its two hundred and twentieth anniversary with a dinner at the Guildhall at which Margaret Thatcher was the guest of honour. Barney's name was down to propose the toast to the Queen, but he kept saying he was not well enough to go. Then, two days before the dinner, he suddenly said: 'I *must* go.' On the day, he got up and with help put on his dinner jacket suit and went to the Guildhall. He ate his dinner and was then called on by the Toastmaster. He got up, raised his glass and said 'The Queen'.

He was taken into St Stephen's hospital, Fulham, in London, on Thursday 8 April 1982. He was thin and weak, a totally different figure from the one people had known.

His voice had lost its fullness of tone. The nurses and the other people in the ward all adored him, for he still had a wonderful personality and a bright smile. He was cared for with great kindness and devotion.

He was expected to live for some time, but at 7.45 pm on 4 May 1982, he suddenly took a turn for the worse. The hospital telephoned me and I hurried to get there. Alas, at eight o'clock, before I arrived, he took three deep breaths and with two nurses lovingly holding each of his hands, he passed away.

INDEX

Central, 25–6, 27–30; dines with Lloyd George, 28; moves to London, 30–1; becomes company solicitor and secretary, 31; election campaigns, Whitechapel, 32–6, 36–8; member for Whitechapel, 39–60; maiden speech, 39; founds Parliamentary Palestine Committee, 40; trips to Palestine, 42–5, 47; constituency work, Whitechapel, 48; German Jews and, 45, 49–52, 53–4, 55–6, 57, 58–9, 95, 111, 113–15, 146–7, 153–4; ritual slaughter (*shechita*) and, 54, 129–30; to Zionist Congresses, 53, 54, 57–8, 72, 102–3, 185; tours USA, Canada, 55; Parliamentary Palestine Committee and, 58, 65, 72, 94–5; political concerns, 58–60, 93–4, 119–20, 145–6, 149; election defeat, 61–3; Stepney Catholics and, 46; joins Labour Party, 64–5; President of Association of Jewish Friendly Societies, 65–6, 93; selected as candidate for West Leicester, 68; practises as solicitor, 68–9, 71, 140–1; Austrian Jews and, 69–70, 114–15; children evacuated, 72–3; ARP warden, 73; election campaign, 1945, 77, 78–80; New Parks Estate and, 81–2, 195; Aden Jews and, 86–92; Israel and, 95, 166–9, 173, 179–82; election campaign, 1950, 96–9; trips to Israel, 100–3, 111–13, 133, 153, 179–82, 190; election campaign, 1951, 103; Genocide Convention and, 103–13, 192; human rights and, 116–17; tenants' rights and, 118–19; election campaign, 1955, 121–3; becomes President of Board of Deputies, 123–4; as President, 124–33, 156; knighthood, 127; honorary doctorate, 130; Suez crisis and, 133–7; seventieth birthday, 139–40; honoured by Belgium, 140; trees planted in honour of, 140, 204; flick-knives and, 142–5; election campaign, 1959, 145–6; air guns and, 149–50; Highways (Straying Animals) Bill, 150; investiture as knight, 150; election campaign, 1964, 151–2; Parliamentary commitments, 152; Iraqi Jews and, 154–5; USSR Jews and, 156–60, 169, 186; eightieth birthday, 158–9, 200–1; IPU, 160–3; Anglo-Israel Parliamentary Group, 161–2;

honoured by Netherlands, 163–4; election campaign, 1966, 165; B'nai B'rith award, 169; Race Relations Act and, 169–70; speechmaking, 172–3; accepts peerage, 175; tributes to, 175–7; sworn in as peer, 178; made freeman of Leicester, 191; constituency work, Leicester, 192–200; Mowmacre Hill post office, 193–5; tributes to, 198–200; made freeman of City of London, 203; 'Barnett Janner House', 204; death, 205; service of thanksgiving for ix–xi

Kaplansky, S., 33
Kennet, Lord, 182
Keren Hayesod, 102, 165, 190
Khaled al Hassan, 163
Khalid, Leila, 159
Khalil, Mustafa, 184
King, Horace, 177
Klutznick, Barney and Philip, 130

Lansbury, George, 41, 52
Law Society, 141, 150, 170, 176–7, 187
League of Nations, 50, 54, 65, 115
leasehold reform, 28, 60, 94, 164, 189
Lee, W. M., 91
Leftwich, Joseph, 45–6, 48
legal aid, 93, 119–20, 187
Legge-Bourke, Sir Harry, 168
Leicester, 77–8, 96–9, 191–200
Leicester, Bishop of, 177
Leigh, Morris, 23
Lerner, Dr Alec, 181
Lever, Harold, 116, 117
Levi, Rabbi and Mrs Gershon, 75, 138–9, 173–4
Levy, A. B., 48
Lewis, Ted (Kid), 37, 38
Lloyd, Selwyn, 114–15, 176
Lloyd George, David, 8, 11, 15, 26, 27, 28, 30, 31–2, 33, 36, 38, 139
Lloyd George, Gwilym, 142, 143
Lloyd George, Megan, 41, 125
Locker, Berl, 41
London Society of Old Barrians, 53
London Zoo, 127, 189
Longden, Gilbert, 161
Lorch, Natanel, 163, 184
Lougher, Sir Lewis, 27, 30
Lourie, Arthur, 126, 140
Lyons, Edward, 170

M1, 196
Maccabiah, 45
Macdonald, Ramsay, 36, 39, 67
Macdonald-Halifax White Paper, 72
Maclean, Donald, 25, 46
Maclean, Sir Ewen, 25
Macmillan, Harold, 115, 124, 125, 145, 150, 156–7, 177
Mancroft, Lord, 127–8
Marks, Alfred, 47
Martin, Andrew, 200
Mathers, Carol, 165
Maxton, Jimmy, 39

Mayhew, Christopher, 168
Mechanized Transport Corps, 73
Meir, Golda, 138, 177, 180
Mellish, Bob, 175
Mendels, Colonel Morton M., 75
Menzies, Sir Robert, 125, 153
Merry, Cicely, 172–3
Middle East, 179–86 *see also under names of countries*
Mikoyan, Anastas Ivanovich, 157
Mond, Sir Alfred, 8
Mond, Henry, 45
Montagu, Ewen, 136
Morgan, Bernard, 203
Morris, Diane, 201
Morris of Kenwood, Lady, 48, 73, 74, 76, 98, 122, 140, 150
Morris of Kenwood, Lord, 144, 178
Morrison, Herbert, 42, 71, 72
Moses, Miriam, 33
Mosley, Oswald and followers, 37, 39, 60–1, 66, 93, 146, 187
Mowmacre Boys Club, 195
Mowmacre Hill post office 193–5
Murton of Lindisfarne, Lord, 161

Nasser, President Gamal adb-el, 133, 134, 135, 136
Nathansohn, Yehuda, 22
Nathansohn, Henrietta (Yetta), 22
National Front, 186
Nemon, Oscar, 197
Netherlands, Queen of, x, 163–4
Newcastle-upon-Tyne, 22, 23
Nicolson, Harold, 67, 79, 96
Noson, Idl, 22

Ocean Coal Company, 3
O'Shea, Tessie, 19

Palestine: British Mandate, 31, 40, 57, 83–4; Jewish immigration, 32, 57; economic success, 57; Jews in, 52, 83; UN and Partition, 86 *see also following entry*, Balfour Declaration, Israel, Passfield White Paper
Palestine Liberation Organization, 163, 180, 182–3, 185, 203
Palestine National Council, 163
Parliamentary Palestine Committee, 40, 41–2, 55, 65, 72, 94–5
Passfield White Paper, 32, 33, 37, 41, 52
Peake, A. W., 177

209